Grammar and Writing 8

Teacher Packet

Answer Keys and Tests

First Edition

Christie Curtis

Mary Hake

Houghton Mifflin Harcourt Publishers, Inc.

Grammar and Writing 8

First Edition

Teacher Packet

Answer Keys and Tests

ISBN-13: 978-1-4190-9862-8
ISBN-10:   1-4190-9862-4

Houghton Mifflin Harcourt Publishers, Inc.
181 Ballardvale Street
Wilmington, MA 01887

http://saxonhomeschool.com

Printed in the United States of America.

1 2 3 4 5 6 7 8 862 16 15 14 13 12 11 10 09

Writing 8 Table of Contents

To the Teacher

We offer the following suggestions to help you implement the program effectively.

Beginning Class

Notice that each lesson begins with a Dictation or Journal Entry, which students will find in the appendix of their textbooks. To begin their grammar/writing period, students need not wait for teacher instruction, for they will know what to do each day:

Monday:	Copy the dictation to prepare for Friday's test.
Tuesday:	Write on a journal topic.
Wednesday:	Write on a journal topic.
Thursday:	Write on a journal topic.
Friday:	Look over dictation to prepare for dictation test.

Dictations

On the first school day of each week, students copy a dictation to study throughout the week for a test on Friday. To test your students at the end of the week, read the dictation aloud slowly and clearly, allowing time for your students to write the passage with correct spelling and punctuation.

Journal Topics

On Tuesday, Wednesday, and Thursday (non-dictation days), students will spend approximately five minutes writing on a journal topic. We suggest that the student write on these topics in the order they are listed.

Grammar Lessons

Because of the incremental format of this program, lessons should be taught in order. Please do not skip any lessons. After reading a lesson, the students will practice the new concept from that lesson. Guide students through the questions in the Practice section and check their answers before they begin the Review Set. Some lessons have "More Practice," which is optional. Some students may need it; others will not.

Grammar Test and Writing Day

We suggest that you give a grammar test after every five lessons. (Notice that the first test follows Lesson 10.) The short, twenty-question test should allow time for a Writing Lesson, to be completed on test day, although you may prefer to teach the Writing Lessons on days other than on test days. Please remember that Writing Lessons are sequenced and should be taught in order. The program is designed so that you do not have a grammar lesson to teach on test day. In addition, for the following two or more days you may teach Writing Lessons instead of Grammar in order to allow students to complete the writing project they began on test day.

On the next page is a suggested schedule for teaching Grammar Lessons and Writing Lessons. Some students might need to spend more than one day on a difficult lesson, so be flexible.

Eighth Grade Grammar & Writing Schedule

School Day	Grammar Lesson	Writing Lesson	School Day	Grammar Lesson	Writing Lesson	School Day	Grammar Lesson	Writing Lesson
1	1		49	40		96	76	
2	2		50	test 7	10	97	77	
3	3		51	41		98	78	
4	4		52	42		99	79	
5	5		53	43		100	80	
6	6		54	44		101	test 15	22
7	7		55	45		102		23
8	8		56	test 8	11	103		24
9	9		57		12	104	81	
10	10		58	46		105	82	
11	test 1	1	59	47		106	83	
12	11		60	48		107	84	
13	12		61	49		108	85	
14	13		62	50		109	test 16	25
15	14		63	test 9	13	110		26
16	15		64	51		111		27
17	test 2	2	65	52		112	86	
18		3	66	53		113	87	
19		4	67	54		114	88	
20	16		68	55		115	89	
21	17		69	test 10	14	116	90	
22	18		69	56		117	test 17	28
23	19		70	59		118	91	
24	20		71	58		119	92	
25	test 3	5	72	59		120	93	
26	21		73	60		121	94	
27	22		74	test 11	15	122	95	
28	23		75		16	123	test 18	29
29	24		76		17	124	96	
30	25		77	61		125	97	
31	test 4	6	78	62		126	98	
32	26		79	63		127	99	
33	27		80	64		128	100	
34	28		81	65		129	test 19	30
35	29		82	test 12	18	130	101	
36	30		83	66		131	102	
37	test 5	7	84	67		132	103	
38		8	85	68		133	104	
39	31		86	69		134	105	
40	32		87	70		135	test 20	31
41	33		88	test 13	19	136	106	
42	34		89		20	137	107	
43	35		90	71		138	108	
44	test 6	9	91	72		139	109	
45	36		92	73		140	110	
46	37		93	74		141	test 21	32
47	38		94	75		142	111	
48	39		95	test 14	21	143		33

Topical Table of Contents

Capitalization

Punctuation

www.saxonhomeschool.com
©Houghton Mifflin Harcourt Publishers, Inc.

Grammar and Writing 8
Teacher Packet, 9781419098628

Sentence Structure

Eight Parts of Speech

Verbs

Usage

Spelling Rules

Diagramming

Proofreading Symbols

Dictionary Information about a Word

LESSON 1 — Four Types of Sentences • Simple Subjects and Simple Predicates

Practice 1

a. exclamatory

b. declarative

c. imperative

d. interrogative

e. branch <u>Does make</u>

f. branch <u>must explain</u>

g. enforcement <u>comes</u>

h. indirect democracy

i. direct democracy

More Practice 1

See Master Worksheets. (This practice is optional.)

Review Set 1

1. direct

2. declarative

3. interrogative

4. imperative

5. exclamatory

6. subject

7. predicate

8. subject

9. verb

10. verb

11. capital

12. exclamatory

13. interrogative

14. period

15. complete

16. interrogative

17. declarative

18. imperative

19. exclamatory

20. *Johnny Tremain* <u>was awarded</u>

21. (you) <u>describe</u>

22. story <u>comes</u>

23. life <u>was</u>

24. James Otis <u>goes</u>

25. Johnny Tremain <u>is</u>

26. John Adams <u>comes</u>

27. Johnny <u>Does participate</u>

28. Johnny <u>Will fight</u>

29. The apprentices sleep in the attic.

30. Wake up now.

LESSON 2 — Complete Sentences, Sentence Fragments, and Run-on Sentences

Practice 2

a. sentence fragment

b. run-on sentence

c. complete sentence

d. Congress could ask for an army, but it could not make men join.

e. There was a great need for a stronger central government.

f. advert

g. avert

More Practice 2   *Optional*

1. sentence fragment

2. complete sentence

3. run-on

4. sentence fragment

5. complete

6. sentence fragment

www.saxonhomeschool.com
©Houghton Mifflin Harcourt Publishers, Inc.

Grammar and Writing 8
Teacher Packet, 9781419098628

7. run-on sentence

8. run-on sentence

9. complete sentence ("you" understood)

10. sentence fragment

11. sentence fragment

12. complete sentence

Answers may vary for 13-15.

13. The delegates finally agreed to ratify the Constitution.

14. The framers of our Constitution were smart people.

15. Any powers not named in the Constitution belong to the states and people.

16. The Federalists favored strong central government. The Anti-Federalists favored strong state government.

17. Ten states ratified the Constitution, so it was adopted. (*or*) Ten states ratified the Constitution. It was adopted.

18. Many states wanted a "Bill of Rights." These personal liberties were added to the Constitution in 1791.

Review Set 2

1. indirect

2. Advert

3. subject

4. run-on

5. predicate

6. complete

7. connecting

8. verb

9. predicate

10. interrogative

11. A

12. When will Johnny marry?

13. Cilla will be his bride.

14. sentence fragment

15. complete sentence

16. sentence fragment

17. run-on sentence

18. complete sentence

19. you (understood)

20. John Hancock

21. man

22. Johnny

23. holds

24. Keep

25. Can finish

26. hurries

27. Johnny expresses his surprise. Mr. Lapham has fashioned the original sugar and creamer set.

28. Marco is returning from Washington D. C.

30. Marco spent all his money on souvenirs.

| LESSON 3 | **Action Verbs • Diagramming the Simple Subject and Simple Predicate** |

Practice 3

a. protects

b. created, established

c. sips, gulps, slurps, swallows

d. people | elect

e. Members | must be

f. *bell-*

g. bellicose

h. antebellum

More Practice 3

1. must have resided
2. discusses, determines
3. Vote
4. replace
5. serve
6. population | determines
7. you | Have run
8. (you) | Run
9. James Wu | Did win
10. George Washington | was nominated
11. member | represents
12. (you) | Give

Review Set 3

1. indirect
2. Avert
3. Bellicose
4. does
5. verb
6. prepared
7. inherited
8. Did give
9. came

Answers 10-18 may vary

10. walk, stroll, run, hurry, rush, skip, meander, march, etc.
11. whisper, chat, converse, etc.
12. painted, drew, penciled, sketched, etc.
13. Matthew Cheng was describing Johnny's mother.
14. Most of the research was contributed by Lauren Chumen.
15. When Estee entered the classroom, everyone cheered.
16. Johnny's mother gave him a Lyte cup. This proved his relationship to Merchant.
17. The cup had the Lyte motto, which was "Let there be Lyte."
18. Johnny lets Mr. Lapham sleep, but he wakes him after an hour.
19. sentence fragment
20. complete sentence
21. run-on sentence
22. interrogative
23. declarative
24. exclamatory
25. imperative
26. we | Can avert
27. Mr. Lapham | warns
28. punishment | would come
29. (you) | Stop
30. we | Must rest

LESSON 4   **Nouns: Proper, Concrete, Abstract, and Collective**

Practice 4

a. American Revolution, British, Redcoats

b. Boston, Boston Harbor, British

c. dignity—A;
    judge—C;
    verdict—A;
    jury—C;

d. Patriotism—A;
    loyalty—A;
    citizens—C

e. Mr. Gomez—C;
    iguana—C;
    affection—A

f. Senate, committee

g. swarm

h. bunch

i. impeachment

j. bicameral

More Practice 4

1. abstract

2. concrete

3. abstract

4. concrete

5. concrete

6. abstract

7. abstract

8. concrete

9. Ben Franklin—C;
    Alexander Hamilton—C;
    Constitution—C;
    vim—A;
    vigor—A

10. logic—A;
    patience—A,
    representatives—C;
    proposal—A

11. Gouverneur Morris—C;
    New York—C;
    precision—A;
    clarity—A

12. George Washington—C;
    elegance—A

13. Family

14. council, team

15. society, batch, collection

Review Set 4

1. direct

2. advert

3. Antebellum

4. Bicameral

5. noun

6. abstract

7. proper

8. abstract

9. collective

10. concrete

11. Jordan Davis

12. Esther Forbes, Boston

13. Lapham Family, Fish Street

14. Sunday

15. Mrs. Lapham, Gran' Hopper, Johnny's

Answers 16-17 may vary

16. pick, gather, buy, purchase, etc.

17. hold, write, grasp, open, twist, tie, etc.

18. interrogative

19. declarative

20. imperative

21. exclamatory

22. sentence fragment

23. run-on sentence

24. complete sentence

25. The shop owner does not want to lose an illiterate patron. *(Answers may vary)*

26. Johnny enters the butcher shop, but the thought of slaughtering animals sickens him.

27. Johnny daydreams of Cilla. He hopes to accomplish great things for her.

28. bandit | dashed

29. stomach | growls

30. someone | Did put

LESSON 5   Present and Past Tense of Regular Verbs

Practice 5

a. preaches

b. talks

c. boxes

d. tries

e. propped

f. sullied

g. knotted

h. raised

i. amplified

j. braked

k. dripped

l. trotted

m. chewed

n. served

o. affectation

p. affection

Review Set 5

1. direct

2. advert

3. war

4. bicameral

5. Affection

6. cries

7. brags

8. combs

9. studies

10. supplied

11. cupped

12. believed

13. listened

14. relied

15. Johnny Tremain, Mr. Tweedie

16. Fish Street, Dock Square, Long Wharf

17. Sugar Isles, Hancock's Wharf, Monday

18. attracted

19. plays

20. There is only one flaw in Lavinia's marble beauty.

21. Lavinia has black hair and dead white skin. Her features are clear cut.

22. run-on sentence

23. complete sentence

24. sentence fragment

25. interrogative

26. imperative

27. exclamatory

28. (you) | drink

29. Johnny | Does buy

30. secret | lies

Helping Verbs

Practice 6

a. is, am, are, was, were, be, being, been, has, have, had, may, might, must, can, could, do, does, did, shall, will, should, would

b. <u>have</u> begun

c. <u>Shall</u> list

d. <u>might</u> <u>have</u> <u>been</u> hoping

e. <u>must</u> <u>have</u> disappointed

f. appease

g. pacifists

h. *pac-, plac-*

More Practice 6   *See Master Worksheets*

Review Set 6

1. avert

2. *bell-*

3. Impeachment

4. Affectation

5. concrete

6. is, am, are, was, were, be, being, been, has, have, had, may, might, must, can, could, do, does, did, shall, will, should, would

7. <u>has</u> purchased

8. <u>might</u> <u>have</u> broken

9. <u>had</u> <u>been</u> sobbing

10. <u>Does</u> visit

11. <u>Should</u> read

12. Christ's Church, Mr. Lapham, Bible

13. Lapham Family, Christianity

14. run-on sentence

15. complete sentence

16. sentence fragment

17. hurries

18. misses

19. shipped

20. buried

21. abstract

22. concrete

23. abstract

24. concrete

25. cries

26. Johnny is arrested as a thief, and he goes to jail.

27. set

28. interrogative

29. <u>medal | hangs</u>

30. I | <u>might have misunderstood</u>

LESSON
7

Singular, Plural, Compound, and Possessive Nouns • Noun Gender

Practice 7

a. plural

b. singular

c. singular

d. plural

e. birthright, attorneys-at-law, sleepyhead

f. one's

g. Louis's, Geraldine's

h. hosts', hostesses'

i. Congressperson's, President's

j. neuter

k. masculine

l. indefinite

m. feminine

n. writ of habeas corpus

o. pro tempore

Review Set 7

1. avert

2. war

3. bicameral

4. affection

5. *plac-*

6. is, am, are, was, were, be, being, been, has, have, had, may, might, must, can, could, do, does, did, shall, will, should, would

7. juries, impostors, debts

8. egg slicer, afterthought, landmark, rabble rouser

9. Boston's, thieves', mother's

10. Catskill Mountains, Appalachian Mountains, Hudson River

11. indefinite

12. neuter

13. feminine

14. masculine

15. must have chewed

16. May help

17. sentence fragment

18. complete sentence

19. run-on sentence

20. *Example*: Some people like to make interesting sandwiches.

21. Johnny rides a wild horse named Goblin. Soon the horse and the boy become well known around Boston.

22. abstract

23. concrete

24. abstract

25. club, staff, committee, militia

26. exclamatory

27. scratches

28. bullies

29. napped

30. Johnny | Does write

LESSON 8   Future Tense

Practice 8

a. Shall read—future tense

b. passed—past tense

c. amends—present tense

d. needed

e. shall vie

f. examines

g. will

h. shall

i. Shall

j. common

k. mutual

More Practice 8

See "Hysterical Fiction #1" with Master Worksheets. Fun "parts of speech" practice!

Review Set 8

1. advert

2. bellicose

3. impeachment

4. affectation

5. *pac-*

6. shall conquer—future tense

7. carries—present tense

8. loved—past tense

9. will convene

10. sipped

11. enjoys

12. will

13. shall

14. England—singular;
grievances—plural;
colonists—plural;
adjustments—plural

15. stable—singular;
groom—singular;
Miss Lavinia—singular

16. Violet—feminine;
dress—neuter;
prom—neuter

17. stallion—masculine;
rider—indefinite;
scare—neuter

18. boy—masculine;
puppy—indefinite;
meadow—neuter

19. Dr. Warren's, Johnny's

20. warships

21. is, am, are, was, were, be, being, been, has,
have, had, may, might, must, can, could,
do, does, did, shall, will, should, would

22. <u>had</u> <u>been</u> sighted

23. changes

24. sentence fragment

25. We shall board the *Dartmouth*, the *Eleanor*,
and the *Beaver*. Then we shall dump the tea
into the Boston Harbor!

26. opinion—abstract;
Sons of Liberty—concrete

27. colonists—concrete;
tyranny—abstract;
liberty—abstract

28. *Boston Observer*

29. <u>boys</u> | <u>Did dress</u>

30. <u>Dove</u> | <u>scooped</u>

LESSON 9 — Capitalization: Pronoun *I*, Poetry, Titles, Outlines, Quotations

Practice 9

a. I

b. Blue
White
Here
And

c. I. Reasons to travel
    A. See new places
    B. Meet new people

   II. Reasons to stay home
    A. Relax
    B. Enjoy family

d. *Facts About the Presidents*

e. Patrick Henry said, "Something must be
done to preserve your liberty and mine."

f. inhospitable

g. hospice

h. guest

More Practice 9   *See Master Worksheets*

Review Set 9

1. Common

2. pro tempore

3. placate

4. affectation

5. impeachment

6. shall

7. I, And, Twice, Before

8. Ms. Cheung, Notice, Boston, Charles River, Boston Harbor, Fort Point Channel

9. My, Alba, Ode, Ugly, Duckling

10. rummages—present tense

11. encountered—past tense

12. Will appear—future tense

13. wishes

14. shall demand

15. wants

16. Sophia—singular;
plays—plural;
skits—plural

17. flintlocks—plural;
muskets—plural

18. girl—feminine;
Sophia—feminine;
island—neuter;
country—neuter

19. singers—indefinite;
director—indefinite

20. passes

21. tends

22. grandsire

23. God's

24. is, am, are, was, were, be, being, been, has, have, had, may, might, must, can, could, do, does, did, shall, will, should, would

25. <u>had</u> <u>been</u> enjoying

26. Is Johnny unconsciously and unreasonably jealous?

27. jealousy—abstract;
behavior—abstract

28. Give me your attention.

29. <u>Cilla</u> | <u>has changed</u>

30. <u>Rab</u> | <u>Does walk</u>

Practice 10

a. caucus

b. quorum

c. plays

d. senates

e. turnkeys

f. splashes

g. decoys

h. glasses

i. barnacles

j. sentries

k. branches

l. waxes

m. secretaries

n. hoaxes

o. penalties

p. vacancies

q. Barrys

r. Mortys

More Practice 10

1. swatches

2. frays

3. assemblies

4. pinches

5. holidays

6. bellies

7. perches

8. replays

9. democracies

10. boxes

11. birthdays

12. Mandys
13. clutches
14. relays
15. Bettys
16. benches
17. turkeys
18. Alans
19. brasses
20. Tabbys
21. blue jays
22. axes
23. finches
24. pennies
25. Sammys
26. kisses
27. armories
28. suffixes
29. prefixes
30. journeys
31. aviaries
32. shoo flies

Review Set 10

1. *hospes*
2. Mutual
3. pro tempore
4. pacifist
5. affection
6. Will
7. keys
8. Eddys
9. porches
10. pencils
11. spurs, boots, hat

12. faxes
13. sits
14. tripped
15. smashed
16. pried
17. Ortiz's, friend's, friends'
18. sentence fragment
19. I, Edward Lear, There, Was, Old, Man, Beard
20. helped—past tense
21. shall describe—future tense
22. will refuse
23. clapped
24. barracks
25. barn
26. coachman
27. is, am, are, was, were, be, being, been, has, have, had, may, might, must, can, could, do, does, did, shall, will, should, would
28. Johnny discovers the truth. Merchant Lyte is his grand uncle.
29. tenderness
30. Joe | Will be picking

LESSON 11   **Irregular Plural Nouns, Part 2**

Practice 11

a. platefuls
b. fathers-in-law
c. scarves
d. hooves
e. vermin
f. oxen
g. moose

h. geese

i. piccolos

j. torpedoes

k. loaves

l. knives

m. ambivalent

n. ambiguous

More Practice 11

1. cliffs

2. lives

3. elves

4. leaves

5. halves

6. teeth

7. termini

8. mice

9. species

10. women

11. handfuls

12. men

13. children

14. lice

15. geese

16. armfuls

17. calves

18. shelves

19. sopranos

20. mangoes

21. sisters-in-law

22. servicemen

Review Set 11

1. caucus

2. hospice

3. mutual

4. writ of habeas corpus

5. Pacifists

6. leaves

7. attorneys-at-law

8. videos

9. handfuls

10. feminine

11. neuter

12. indefinite

13. emerald, pilgrim, gopher, kitchen

14. screeches

15. fries

16. sipped

17. pacifist's, caucuses', brothers-in-law's, lobby's

18. In, Boston, I, Copp's Hill, Old North Church, Paul Revere

19. drinks

20. shall discover

21. hurried

22. attempted, past tense

23. caught, captured, seized, arrested, jailed, etc.

24. committee, humane society

25. grandsons, pigtail, dog food

26. interrogative

27. <u>has</u> married

28. run-on sentence

29. <u>Cilla</u> | <u>Does like</u>

30. <u>James Otis</u> | <u>might have been defining</u>

Practice 12

a. is

b. had

c. Were

d. was

e. has

f. Does

g. *amare*

h. amicable

i. Amiable

More Practice 12

1. Does

2. has

3. were

4. Do

5. were

6. were

7. was

8. are

9. Were

10. have

11. Does

12. is

Review Set 12

1. Ambiguous

2. quorum

3. guest

4. common

5. writ of habeas corpus

6. sheriffs

7. brothers-in-law

8. studios

9. fistfuls

10. masculine

11. indefinite

12. persistence, pandemonium, democracy

13. are

14. has

15. does

16. worried

17. soldier's, soldiers', uniform's

18. Christina Rossetti, Who, Has, Seen, Wind

19. is

20. will have

21. did

22. shall plant, future tense

23. complain, yell, shout, whisper, etc.

24. Central America, herd, company

25. checklist, sickroom, cash flow

26. declarative

27. is, am, are, was, were, be, being, been, has, have, had, may, might, must, can, could, do, does, did, shall, will, should, would

28. Fully mature adults respect others. They treat people with kindness and compassion.

29. Pumpkin | Does trade

30. British | might have shot

LESSON 13   **Four Principal Parts of Verbs**

Practice 13

a. (is) voting, voted, (has) voted

b. (is) registering, registered, (has) registered

c. (is) impeaching, impeached, (has) impeached

d. (is) qualifying, qualified, (has) qualified

e. (is) rebelling, rebelled, (has) rebelled

f. lobbied

g. census

h. lobby

More Practice 13

1. (is) proceeding, proceeded, (has) proceeded

2. (is) representing, represented, (has) represented

3. (is) constituting, constituted, (has) constituted

4. (is) legislating, legislated, (has) legislated

5. (is) exporting, exported, (has) exported

6. (is) justifying, justified, (has) justified

7. (is) apportioning, apportioned, (has) apportioned

8. (is) appointing, appointed, (has) appointed

9. (is) slandering, slandered, (has) slandered

10. (is) passing, passed, (has) passed

Review Set 13

1. *amare*

2. Ambivalent

3. caucus

4. Inhospitable

5. mutual

6. four

7. (is) averting, averted, (has) averted

8. (is) skipping, skipped, (has) skipped

9. am

10. is

11. are

12. <u>have</u> <u>been</u> lobbying

13. will march

14. dressed

15. grief, abstract;
Johnny, concrete;
Rab, concrete

16. potatoes

17. Martinezes

18. Queens of England

19. geese

20. Aunt Christie, A

21. Next, October, I, New England, Boston's

22. built, designed, constructed, fashioned, etc.

23. I have been renewing a delightful old friendship.

24. woman's, boss's

25. run-on sentence

26. eyewitness, double header

27. countess, feminine;
king, masculine;
parlor, neuter

28. exclamatory

29. Johnny | should have said

30. (You) | hurry

LESSON 14   Prepositions

Practice 14

a. (*See Lesson 14*)

b. In addition to, at, of, for

c. in, because of

d. By means of, into

e. on, after, in, in front of

f. Can

g. May

h. may

i. can

More Practice 14

1. Before, of, with, in

2. Amid, at, of

3. among, inside of, because of

4. to, in

5. on

6. Despite, of, from

7. With, of, of

8. inside, of

9. During, in, on

10. Before, at, with

11. After, without

12. In addition to, for, for, during, to

13. Considering, of, of, regarding, to

14. Apart from, of, since, in front of

15. Throughout, by means of, along with

16. Round about, in, of

17. Without, on, at

18. Besides, for, owing to

Review Set 14

1. lobby

2. love

3. unclear meaning

4. quorum

5. hospice

6. throughout, to, underneath, up, within

7. into, of, on, outside, over

8. across from, along with, aside from,
   because of, down from

9. in front of, in regard to, inside of, on
   account of, on top of

10. run-on sentence

11. (is) slipping, slipped, (has) slipped

12. (a) were
    (b) had
    (c) was
    (d) did

13. tricks

14. mopped

15. will leave

16. tempos

17. shelves

18. bluffs

19. faxes

20. The, *Somerset*, Charles River

21. I. Literature
    A. Poetry
    B. Short stories
    C. Tall tales
    D. Myths

22. freedom, contentment, laziness

23. rebels, indefinite;
    shadows, neuter

24. company, audience, family

25. Bill Dawes dresses like a drunk and smells
    like rum.

26. is, am, are, was, were, be, being, been, has,
    have, had, may, might, must, can, could,
    do, does, did, shall, will, should, would

27. has (stumbled)

28. Along with, onto

29. interrogative

30. Horace P. Corndog | has stumbled

Practice 15

a. has provided, present perfect tense

b. Had desired, past perfect tense

c. shall have studied, future perfect tense

d. contemptible

e. contemptuous

More Practice 15

1. managers | have received

2. President | had pronounced

3. Senators | will have completed

4. We | shall have increased

5. grandfather | Had served

6. Senate | Has approved

Review Set 15

1. Can

2. lobby

3. Amiable

4. conflicting feelings

5. meeting

6. have

7. past

8. had performed, past perfect

9. has gained, present perfect

10. will have hung, future perfect

11. of, to

12. for, of, at

13. According to, of

14.   (a) are
     (b) is
     (c) has
     (d) does

15. sentence fragment

16. Everybody knows something is happening, but no one knows what.

17. (is) giggling, giggled, (has) giggled

18. beliefs

19. egos

20. policies

21. sketches

22. Success, By, To, Requires

23. Lavinia, concrete; discontent, abstract; colonists, concrete

24. pilgrims', Madge's, sluggard's, descendants'

25. has reached, present perfect

26. had desired, past perfect

27. shall have completed

28. salutes

29. Lytes | Have fled

30. Lavinia | must have discovered

LESSON 16   **Verbals: The Gerund as a Subject**

Practice 16

a. Conserving

b. Referring

c. touring

d. Having appointed, perfect tense

e. Executing, present tense

f. appointing, present tense

g. having stood, perfect tense

h. incriminate

i. recrimination

j. *crim-*

k. 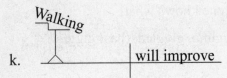 *Walking* | will improve

 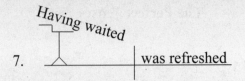

Review Set 16

1. contemptuous
2. May
3. lobby
4. pleasant
5. ambiguous
6. -ing
7. noun
8. shall
9. were
10. Does
11. declarative
12. complete sentence
13. A falcon was sitting on a fence post.
14. strutting
15. act, abstract;
strutting, abstract
spirits, abstract
16. is, am, are, was, were, be, being, been, has, have, had, may, might, must, can, could, do, does, did, shall, will, should, would
17. goodwill, stand-in, check mark, Minute Men
18. Rab's
19. Miss Trang, Your
20. *The Light in the Forest*
21. heroes
22. halves
23. businesses
24. basketfuls
25. (is) pacifying, pacified, (has) pacified

More Practice 16

1. 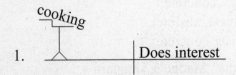 *cooking* | Does interest

2. 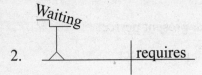 *Waiting* | requires

3. 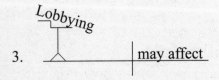 *Lobbying* | may affect

4. 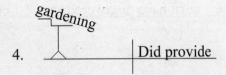 *gardening* | Did provide

5. 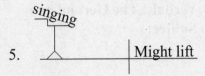 *singing* | Might lift

6. 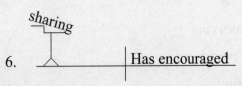 *sharing* | Has encouraged

26. will have wounded, future perfect tense

27. had failed, past perfect tense

28. next to, on, over

29. Rab | has died

30.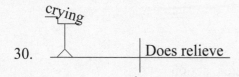
Does relieve

LESSON 17   **The Progressive Verb Forms**

Practice 17

a. was passing, past progressive tense

b. shall be watching, future progressive tense

c. is signing, present progressive

d. had been vetoing, past perfect progressive

e. will have been working, future perfect progressive

f. has been holding, present perfect progressive tense

g. progressive

h. present

i. consul

j. state of the union message

k. Bobby L. | had been lobbying

More Practice 17

1. President | will have been stalling (future perfect progressive tense)

2. Congress | had been hoping (past perfect progressive tense)

3. We | have been waiting (present perfect progressive tense)

4. Dad | Has been reading (present perfect progressive tense)

Review Set 17

1. incriminate

2. contemptible

3. May

4. lobby

5. Amicable

6. gerund

7. perfect

8. progressive

9. have

10. be

11. interrogative

12. sentence fragment

13. In a little frontier town, True Son was born John Butler. He was captured by Indians.

14. Hating

15. tribe, Lenni Lenape

16. Has been adopted

17. father, masculine; Cuyloga, masculine; treaty, neuter; captives, indefinite; people, indefinite

18. son's, lady's, ladies', kidnapper's

19. On, Boston's, Beacon Hill, Acorn Street

20. "The Battle Hymn of the Republic"

21. echoes

22. lives

23. workmen

24. sisters-in-law

25. (is) adverting, adverted, (has) adverted

26. is praying, present progressive tense

27. has been rearing, present perfect progressive tense

28. By means of, of

29.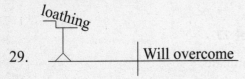

30. Del | Could be laughing

LESSON 18   Linking Verbs

Practice 18

a. (See Lesson 17)

b. appear

c. no linking verb

d. remains

e. sounded

f. seemed

g. no linking verb

h. smelled

i. censure

j. censor

k. censor

l. censure

m. censor

More Practice 18

1. seemed

2. remains

3. feels

4. remain

5. grew

6. stayed

7. became

8. sounded

9. looks

10. is

11. were

12. tastes

13. Has tasted, action

14. tastes, linking

15. sounds, action

16. Does sound, linking

Review Set 18

1. speech

2. recrimination

3. scornful

4. May

5. census

6. noun

7. completed

8. continuing

9. linking

10. linking

11. complete sentence

12. The white prisoners are ungrateful to their rescuers. They want to remain with the Indians.

13. crying

14. rebelliousness

15. is, am, are, was, were, be, being, been, has, have, had, may, might, must, can, could, do, does, did, shall, will, should, would

16. is, am, are, was, were, be, being, been, look, feel, taste, smell, sound, seem, appear, grow, become, remain, stay

17. Tim, On, Pinckney Street, Boston, I, Louisa May Alcott's

19. felt, linking verb

19. Petunia Schnutz, This

20. I. The Light in the Forest
    A. Plot
    B. Characters
    C. Point of view

21. cellos

22. thieves

23. teeth

24. toothbrushes

25. (is) censoring, censored, (has) censored

26. had been scheming, past perfect progressive tense

27. had eaten, past perfect tense

28. over, through, up, by, of

29.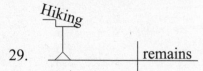
    remains

30. Little Crane | Has been laughing

LESSON 19   The Infinitive as a Subject

Practice 19

a. To recommend, present tense

b. To have overthrown, perfect tense

c. To have censured, perfect tense

d. To fill, present tense

e. probity

f. approbation

g. *prob-*

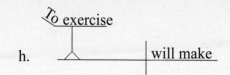
h. | will make

More Practice 19

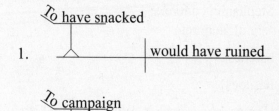
1. | would have ruined

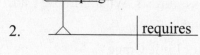
2. | requires

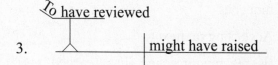
3. | might have raised

4.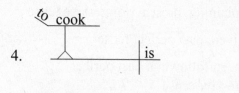
   | is

5. | could reveal

6.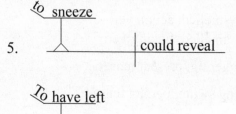
   | would have been

Review Set 19

1. censor

2. President

3. fault

4. despicable

5. able

6. gerund

7. infinitive

8. perfect

9. has

10. Does

11. exclamatory

12. fragment

13. determination, abstract;
    perfection, abstract;
    Stephanie, concrete;
    school, concrete

14. batches

15. fiascoes

16. Homer, Miss Curtis's, What, Mouse, Can,
    Learn, First, Grade

17. On, Fort Pitt, Little Crane

18. munches

19. According to; next to

20. (is) reaching, reached, (has) reached

21. is explaining, present progressive tense

22. had lived, past perfect tense

23. had been following, past perfect
    progressive tense

24. (a) smelled, action verb
    (b) smelled, linking verb

25. Swaggering, present tense

26. Having swum, perfect tense

27. To shake, present tense

28. To have swum, perfect tense

29.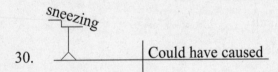

To have sneezed | would have attracted

30. sneezing | Could have caused

Practice 20

a. clause

b. phrase

c. clause

d. phrase

e. Supreme Court | settled

South | had

students | were

f. ex post facto

g. pocket veto

More Practice 20

1. clause

2. phrase

3. clause

4. clause

5. phrase

6. phrase

7. clause

8. phrase

9. clause

10. phrase

Review Set 20

1. *prob-*

2. censure

3. Congress

4. *crim-*

5. contemptible

6. clause

7. abstract

8. progressive

9. Have

10. clause

11. declarative

12. complete sentence

13. appears, linking

14. photos

15. oxen

16. of, next to

17. Graham, Fords, Chevys

18. teaches

19. To have eaten, perfect tense

20. (is) tapping, tapped, (has) tapped

21. will have been excelling, future perfect progressive tense

22. had recognized, past perfect tense

23. looks, present tense

24. Dressing, present tense

25. shall avert

26. are averting

27. True Son | is given

   he | refuses

28. Gordie | understands

   True Son | is

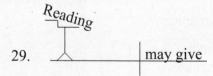

29. Reading / may give

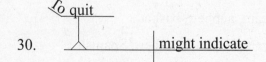

30. To quit / might indicate

Practice 21

a. balance

b. no action verb; no direct object

c. traitors

d. treaties

e. President | May veto | bills

f. S. B. Anthony | led | parade

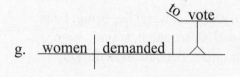

g. women | demanded | to vote

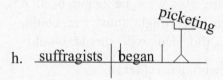

h. suffragists | began | picketing

i. *e.g.*

j. *i.e.*

k. *e.g.*

l. *i.e.*

Review Set 21

1. pocket veto

2. honesty

3. edit

4. consul

5. incriminate

6. completed

7. does

8. Listen to wise words.

9. run-on sentence

10. grace, pacifism, communism

11. *Paul Revere and the World He Lived In*

12. king's, queens', bosses', boss's, James's

13. embargoes

14. proofs

15. knives

16. (is) appeasing, appeased, (has) appeased

17. In front of, about, in

18. detested, past tense

19. had slapped, past perfect tense

20. will have been waiting, future perfect progressive tense

21. is, am, are, was, were, be, being, been, look, feel, taste, smell, sound, seem, appear, grow, become, remain, stay

22. is, am, are, was, were, be, being, been, has, have, had, may, might, must, can, could, do, does, did, shall, will, should, would

23. to have won, perfect tense

24. shopping, present tense

25. clause

26. phrase

27. I | finish

    I | shall read

    I | go

28. I | shall slice | watermelon

29. You | may help | _{to} serve

30. they | Have finished | ^{eating}

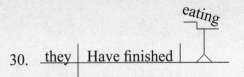

LESSON 22 — **Capitalization: People Titles, Family Words, School Subjects**

Practice 22

a. English, Latin

b. Dad

c. Mary J. Davison, Pastor Hugh Williamson

d. Colonel Lopez

e. jurisdiction

f. judicial

g. judicious

More Practice 22   *See Master Worksheets*

Review Set 22

1. e.g.

2. Ex post facto

3. Approbation

4. blame

5. contemptuous

6. continuing

7. has

8. The Indians rename John Butler.

9. complete sentence

10. doe, feminine;
    eagles, indefinite;
    treetops, neuter

11. stream, nephew, basket

12. My, Next, Uncle Robert, Spanish

13. My, The, Race, South Pole

14. witness's, judge's

15. ratios

16. geese

17. cherries

18. (is) clapping, clapped, (has) clapped

19. In spite of, through, alongside

20. has been brewing, present perfect progressive tense

21. appears, linking verb

22. Does appear, action verb

23. to fly, present tense

24. Having studied, perfect tense

25. clause

26. phrase

27. Len | was

    he | learned

28. Pat | needs / to apologize

29. you | Have tried / surfing

30. (you) | Remember / to smile

LESSON 23 Descriptive Adjectives • Proper Adjectives

Practice 23

a. responsible, comprehensive

b. British, French, American

c. national, absolute

d. Veterans Day

e. impartial, just, cantankerous, etc.

f. trustworthy, political, popular, etc.

g. violet, nation

h. feast, turkey

i. apportion

j. Appellate

k. appropriation

More Practice 23   *See "Hysterical Fiction #2" in Master Worksheets*

Review Set 23

1. law

2. i.e.

3. ex post facto

4. Probity

5. permitted

6. progressive

7. imperative

8. complete sentence

9. Indians, concrete; treaty, abstract; white man, concrete

10. branches

11. attorneys-at-law

12. Mondays

13. Dr. Richard Curtis, Green Street, Pasadena

14. When, I, I, Scottish, Christmas Eve, Grandma, "A Lonely Little Tree, Forest"

15. look, feel, taste, smell, sound

16. (is) dropping, dropped, (has) dropped

17. hungered, past tense

18. had planned, past perfect tense

19. looked, action verb

20. looked, linking verb

21. clause

22. phrase

23. According to, with

24. Danish, strong, black

25. incessant, high, Hong Kong

26. Mediterranean, blue, warm

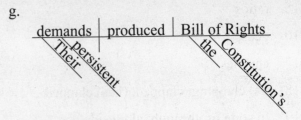

27. Mr. Turkey | Did try | flying

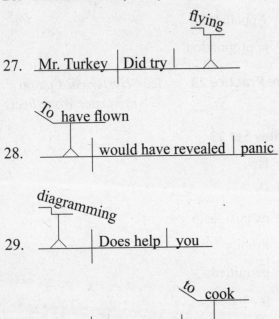

28. To have flown | would have revealed | panic

29. diagramming | Does help | you

30. Harold | Has learned | to cook

LESSON 24   **The Limiting Adjectives •**
Diagramming Adjectives

Practice 24

a. levity

b. alleviate

c. The, Constitution's, the, politicians'

d. His, many

e. those, nine, the

f. These, first, ten, the, our

More Practice 24   *See Master Worksheets*

Review Set 24

1. Appellate

2. Judicial

3. "for example"

4. may

5. count

6. Does

7. imperative

8. complete sentence

9. flock

10. handfuls

11. In, Jon, Japanese, Latin

12. My, General Patton

13. Owing to, for, in, of

14. this

15. Had killed, past perfect tense

16. has been questioning, present perfect progressive tense

17. will sound, action verb

18. sounded, linking

19. phrase

20. clause

21. to have revealed, perfect tense

22. (is) censoring, censored, (has) censored

23. Hester Prynne's, a, scarlet

24. One, this

25. A, the

26. Some

27.

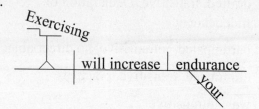

28.

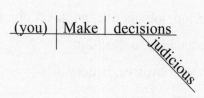

29.

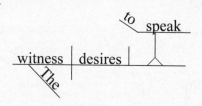

30.

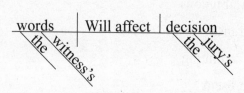

LESSON 25	**Capitalization: Areas, Religions, Greetings • No Capital Letter**

Practice 25

a. The, Southeast, Creole

b. The, Calvinistic, God, Bible

c. The, Smithsonian Institute, East

d. Dear Doctor Franklin,
   You certainly have many talents.
   Fondly,
   Miss Sue

e. In, Father-in-law, Dale

f. The

g. The, Greek

h. The, Chinese

i. Cottonwoods, California, Australian, Brazilian

j. Did, Candice, Juliana

k. suffrage

l. amendment

Review Set 25

1. *lev-*

2. appeal

3. judicial

4. "that is to say"

5. goodwill

6. articles

7. a, an, the

8. reading, present tense

9. "Hester and the Physician"

10. interrogative

11. run-on sentence

12. confession, abstract;
    anguish, abstract;
    Arthur Dimmesdale, concrete

13. (a) logos
    (b) stimuli

14. Matty's, Greek, Hebrew

15. The, Pearl Harbor

16. Hey, Dad, I

17. Would, East, West

18. In addition to, about, of

19. (a) were
    (b) am
    (c) are

20. has fallen, present perfect tense

21. will have been working, future perfect progressive tense

22. appears, linking verb

23. Does appear, action verb

24. phrase

25. clause

26. (is) skipping, skipped, (has) skipped

27. The, arrogant, his, many, a, gracious, merciful

28. Those, evil, vengeful, the, new

29.

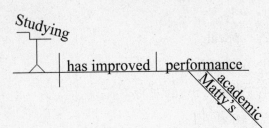

30.

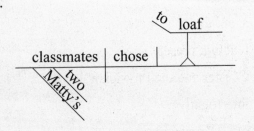

LESSON 26

Transitive and Intransitive Verbs

Practice 26

a. may possess, transitive, guns

b. will be housed, intransitive, no direct object

c. may search, transitive, person

d. Have been reading, intransitive, no direct object

e. delusion

f. allusion

g. illusion

More Practice 26

1. read, intransitive

2. drafted, transitive, Declaration of Independence

3. participated, intransitive, no direct object

4. eliminated, transitive, practices

5. was, intransitive

6. received, transitive, number

7. was elected, intransitive, no direct object

8. faced, transitive, opposition

9. appointed, transitive, nationalists

10. died, intransitive

Review Set 26

1. Amendment

2. lighten

3. apportion

4. Jurisdicion

5. ambiguous

6. transitive

7. continuing

8. present

9. present

10. exclamatory

11. run-on sentence

12. Ashley, feminine; student, indefinite; biology, neuter; census, neuter; fish, indefinite

13. Mortality, pain, childbirth, world, toil, God's, Adam, Eve's, punishment, disobedience

14. (a) wives
    (b) safes
    (c) finches

15. In, Milton's, *Paradise Lost*, Satan's

16. Did, Uncle Bob, Chinese, Tuesday

17. phrase

18. In addition to, of, for

19. sounds, linking

20. writes, action

21. was flattering

22. buzzes

23. (a) have
    (b) have
    (c) has

24. apportion, (is) apportioning, apportioned, (has) apportioned

25. eerie, intelligent, moral

26. the, the

27. English class

28. Having rested, perfect tense

29.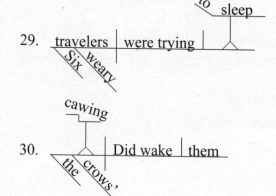

30.

LESSON 27   **Active or Passive Voice**

Practice 27

a. was incarcerated, passive voice

b. had fled, active voice

c. was incriminated, passive voice

d. incriminated, active voice

e. gravitate

f. *grav-*

g. gravid

h. gravity

More Practice 27

1. passive

2. active

3. active

4. passive

5. passive

6. active

7. passive

8. active

Review Set 27

1. delusion

2. changing

3. Alleviate

4. ambivalent

5. quorum

6. intransitive

7. active

8. passive

9. Were hiding, transitive

10. Were hiding, intransitive

11. passive voice

12. active voice

13. to succeed, present tense

14. "I Heard the Bells on Christmas Day"

15. declarative

16. sentence fragment

17. I, Did, Mother

18. A, Primer, Vitamins, *Star News*

19. According to, of

20. have been ingesting, present perfect progressive tense

21. had excreted, past perfect tense

22. promotes, action

23. seems, linking verb

24. clause

25. phrase

26. the, eight, essential, *B*

27. the, *B*, leafy, whole

28. (is) snapping, snapped, (has) snapped

29.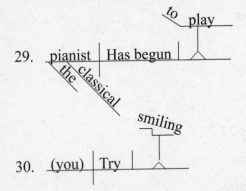

30. (you) | Try

LESSON 28 · Object of the Preposition • The Prepositional Phrase

Practice 28

a. to a speedy *trial;
   by an unbiased *jury;
   in the *state and *district;
   of the *crime

b. in addition to a fair *trial

c. concerning *bails, *fines, and
   *punishments

d. On account of this *amendment

e. hector

f. cicerone

More Practice 28

1. Owing to the *tyranny;
   of *George III;
   from *Britain

2. In the *Declaration of Independence;
   against the *king

3. over the *head;
   of the *tyrant;
   to the English *people

4. In spite of their desperate *petitions;
   by most *people;
   in *Britain

5. After many *attempts;
   at *reconciliation;
   toward *independence

6. between *themselves and *Great Britain;
   by means of a *Declaration

7. On behalf of the American *people;
   with *reliance;
   on Divine *Providence;
   of the *Declaration

8. for *liberty;
   because of a long *history;
   of English *tradition

9. Despite King George's *tyranny;
   over *America;
   in their *country

10. In addition to *John Locke;
    concerning *freedom and *independence

Review Set 28

1. hospice

2. *grav-*

3. illusion

4. amendments

5. peace

6. object

7. speaks, transitive

8. Will speak, intransitive

9. will be taken, passive voice

10. Will take, active voice

11. According to weather *forecasters;
    along the *coast;
    until *noon

12. In spite of the *storm;
    to a *high;
    of *seventy;
    in the *valley

13. Please eat nutritious foods.

14. complete sentence

15. people, concrete;
    health, abstract

16. hero's, heroes', man's, men's

17. (a) alumni
    (b) algae
    (c) larvae

18. (is) crying, cried, (has) cried

19. have discovered, present perfect tense

20. will be taking, future progressive tense

21. to return, present tense

22. having relocated, perfect tense

23. phrase

24. clause

25. Kimberly, feminine;
    vitamins, neuter

26. taxis

27. flies

28. Jonathan | washed

    Lucy | vacuumed

    Nate | fed

29.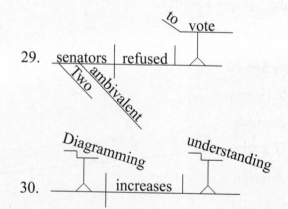

30.

Practice 29

a. "of both houses" modifies "vote";
   "of Congress" modifies "houses"

b. "in regard to women's rights" modifies "work"

c. "from the constraints" modifies "freedom";
   "of the British empire" modifies "constraints"

d. "in their salaries" modifies "increases"

e.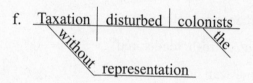
   you | Do know | meaning
                   the of monarchy

f. Taxation | disturbed | colonists
   without representation   the

g. hung jury

h. filibuster

Review Set 29

1. Cicero

2. weighty

3. allusion

4. Suffrage

5. hospice

6. exclamatory

7. sentence fragment

8. (company,) thiamine, pork, grains, beans, nuts, seeds, fish, breads, cereals

9. Mr. VanderLaan's

10. (a) minutemen
    (b) fiascoes
    (c) wrenches

11. In, Plunket University, Riverside County, I

12. I, Grandpa, Uncle Ian's, *A*, *Tale*, *Two*, *Cities*

13. phrase

14. On account of *construction; throughout the *summer

15. owing to dense *fog; at the *airport

16. has prescribed, present perfect tense

17. will provide, future tense

18. cycling, present tense

19. To have promoted, perfect tense

20. remained, action verb

21. remains, linking verb

22. Did land, intransitive verb

23. has been flying, transitive verb

24. Green, adequate

25. Moe's, fresh, tender, red

26. American novelist

27. passive voice

28. active voice

29.

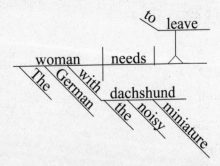

30.

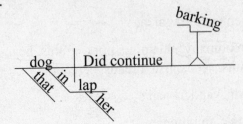

Practice 30

a. faze

b. phased

c. phase

d. John Hancock

e. no indirect object

f. us

g. nation

i.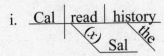

j.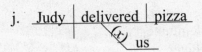

More Practice 30

1. me

2. him

3. us

4. no indirect object

5. Bryon

6. the Schaper Family

7. that careless cyclist

Review Set 30

1. hung jury

2. cicerone

3. Gravid

4. delusion

5. common

6. indirect

7. interrogative

8. complete sentence

9. Central America

10. backdrop

11. (a) ranches
    (b) maids of honor
    (c) Cathys

12. Did, French Revolution, Dad

13. Aunt Emily, My, Dog, Has, Black, Lips

14. clause

15. Lucie and Charles Darnay

16. Besides the *explorers;
    round about the *island;
    for the *treasure

17. has, have, had

18. (a) were
    (b) were
    (c) were

19. will have been sailing, future perfect progressive

20. has sailed, present perfect tense

21. appears, linking

22. exchanges, action

23. Does know, transitive

24. had traveled, intransitive

25. the, a, strict, proper, a, warm, sensitive

26. had been uprooted, passive voice

27. Did uproot, active voice

28.

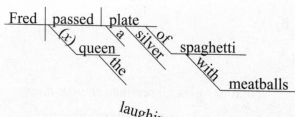

29.

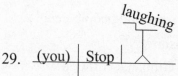

30.

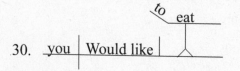

Practice 31

a. I. New Hampshire's ratifying conventions
        A. February, 1788
        B. June, 1788

b. John Langdon adjourned the convention in February to prevent a victory for Antifederalists.

c. Remember these dates.

d. William H. Harrison was born in Virginia.

e. M.A.D.D. stands for "Mothers Against Drunk Driving."

f. The time changes from 11:59 p.m. to 12:00 a.m. at midnight.

g. Dr. Yen received a degree from Harvard University last February.

h. Mr. Baker's dip recipe calls for two teaspoons of chili pepper.

i. In the month of February, it appeared that the Constitution would not be ratified by New Hampshire.

j. New Hampshire lies on the southeast side of Massachusetts and on the east side of New York.

k. M. E. Bradford, Ph.D., wrote the book called *Founding Fathers*.

l. (a) Wed.
    (b) Aug.
    (c) Mr.
    (d) Blvd.

m. nestor

n. hedonism

Review Set 31

1. faze

2. filibuster

3. Hector

4. pregnant

5. inhospitable

6. I. Punctuation marks
   A. Periods
   B. Commas
   C. Quotation marks

7. Mr. Wang arrived at six p.m. for the dinner. His wife came later.

8. Dr. Payne's office building is on the corner of Green Street and Sixth Avenue.

9. declarative, imperative, interrogative, exclamatory

10. run-on sentence

11. ran, walked, sprinted, jogged, raced, limped, sped, etc.

12. Jane Eyre, I

13. Charlotte Bronte, Northern England

14. is living, present progressive tense

15. Jane Eyre, concrete;
    mistreatment, abstract;
    hatred, abstract

16. (a) sopranos
    (b) grandchildren
    (c) potatoes

17. clap, (is) clapping, clapped, (has) clapped

18. Having left, perfect tense

19. phrase

20. the, little, a, princely, heroic

21. Peter

22. alongside of the *boardwalk;
    except for the *bank;
    across from the *post office

23. sounds, linking

24. are elected, passive voice

25. will elect, active voice

26. Does glow, intransitive

27. Will be wearing, transitive

28.

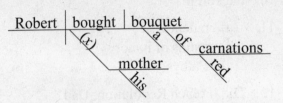

29.

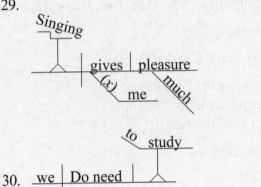

30.

LESSON 32   **Proofreading Symbols, Part 1**

Practice 32

a. ⊙

b. /

c. #

d. ∧

e. ≡

f. /

g. N (or) ∿

h. ⌄

i. ⌐ or —

j.

Nicholas gilman retained the confidence of the small farmers and people people in New Hampshire⊙
People in Mr. Gilman's corner of america found him trustworthy and pleasant.

k. conscious

l. conscientious

m. conscience

n. consciousness

More Practice 32   *See Master Worksheets*

Review Set 32

1. hedonism

2. disturb

3. filibuster

4. number

5. unclear

6. Does

7. Joe and i have been planting Corn since mon day We're tiered.

8. declarative

9. sentence fragment

10. Family

11. (a) scenarios
    (b) photocopies
    (c) birthdays

12. I, Jane Austen's, *Pride, Prejudice, Sense, Sensibility,* I, *Mansfield Park, Persuasion*

13. Hey, Grandma, British, American

14. that

15. will be studying, future perfect progressive

16. had delighted, past perfect

17. is, linking verb

18. is courting, action verb

19. phrase

20. to capture, present tense

21. (is) declining, declined, (has) declined

22. Most

23. Does see, transitive

24. is disliked, passive voice

25. Elizabeth

26. On Thursday, February 3, Mrs. Lopez left for North Africa.

27. passes

28.

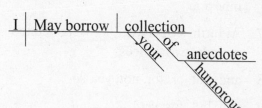

29.

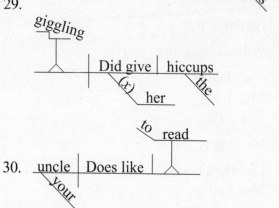

30.

LESSON 33   **Coordinating Conjunctions**

Practice 33

a. and, but, or, nor, for, yet, so

b. and

c. but

d. yet

e. but, for, and

f. or

g. so, and

h. Spartan

i. stentorian

Review Set 33

1. conscience

2. pleasure

3. phase

4. amiable

5. census

6. Mr. Lu will meet us here on Thursday at nine a.m.

7. At birth, Jasper W. Zoot weighted ten pounds, two ounces.

8. and, but, or, for, nor, yet, so

9. and, but, for, yet

10. run-on sentence

11. Will ask, transitive

12. (a) leaves
    (b) lice
    (c) taxes

13. Mr. Darcy, You, I

14. Eight-year-old, Adèle, French, English, Mrs. Fairfax

15. in a *letter;
    to *Elizabeth;
    for his *actions

16. lobby, (is) lobbying, lobbied, (has) lobbied

17. had been harboring, past perfect progressive tense

18. elopes, present tense

19. Young, impetuous

20. Jane and Mr. Bingley become engaged.

21. is proposing, active voice

22. Javier built the snowman.

23. Does seem, linking verb

24. imperative

25. arguing, present tense

26. clause

27. Mr. Bennet

28.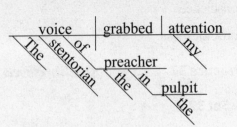

29.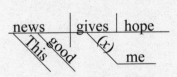

30.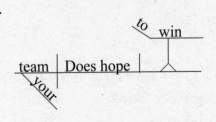

LESSON 34   **Compound Subjects and Predicates • Diagramming Compounds**

Practice 34

a. et al.

b. etc.

c.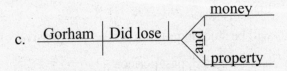

d.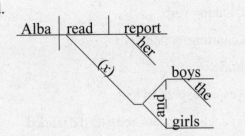

e.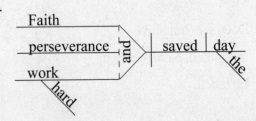

f.

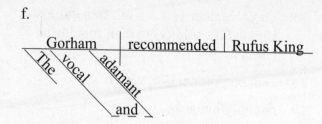

More Practice 34 *See Master Worksheets*

Review Set 34

1. Stentor

2. Consciousness

3. Hedonism

4. phase

5. Can

6. transitive

7. clause

8. remains, linking

9. complete sentence

10. sleepyheads, classroom, daybreak

11. Percival, masculine;
    rooster, masculine:
    mayhem, neuter;
    hens, feminine

12. (a) elk
    (b) sisters-in-law
    (c) busybodies

13. The House of Representatives, Senate,
    President of the United States

14. Molly, Hey, Dad, Boo Radley

15. Was designed, passive voice

16. Because of its *length;
    at the *back;
    of the *magazine

17. "of the book" modifies "back"

18. has aroused, present perfect tense

19. are trying, present progressive tense

20. will have lived

21. have experienced

22. Dr. Zoot asked if Sunday is a day of rest in the state of California.

23. Rhode Island isn't really an island, it's a state bordering massachusetts.

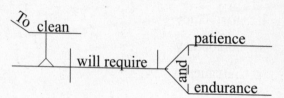

24. (has) hurried

25. and, but, or, for, nor, yet, so

26. for

27.

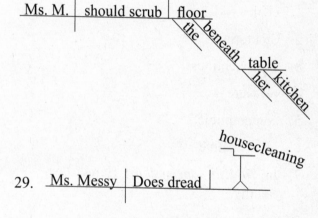

28.

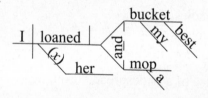

29. Ms. Messy | Does dread | housecleaning

30.

LESSON 35   **Correlative Conjunctions**

Practice 35

a. both/and;
   either/or;
   neither/nor;
   not only/but also

b. either/or

c. neither/nor

d. Both/and

e. Not only/but also

f.
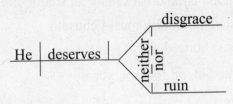

g. plutocrats

h. aristocracy

i. democracy

j. bureaucrats

Review Set 35

1. et al.

2. Stentorian

3. Conscientious

4. pleasure

5. contemptible

6. interrogative

7. In, *To*, *Kill*, *Mockingbird*, Harper Lee, South

8. disease, prejudice

9. (a) ladies
   (b) delays
   (c) editors in chief

10. Because of a widespread *drought;
    in *Kenya;
    during the *summer;
    of *2004

11. (a) was
    (b) were
    (c) were

12. are threatening, action verb

13. has been improving, intransitive

14. The, unkempt, ignorant, the, prejudiced, gentle

15. On December 1, at 8 a.m., General Josh Lim led his soldiers to their remodeled barracks.

16. and, but, or, nor, for, yet, so

17. not only/but also

18. had dressed, past perfect tense

19. fishing, present tense

20. to surf, present tense

21. phrase

22. (is) hurrying

23. declares, active voice

24. Equality, prejudice

25. Mrs. Yu sees steam rising out of the manhole covers in Manhatten, New york.

26. either/or;
    neither/nor;
    both/and;
    not only/but also

27. Ann

28.
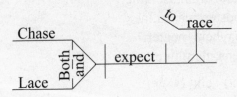

29.
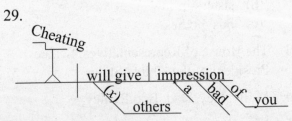

30.

Practice 36

a. stoic

b. stoic

c. sybaritic

d.

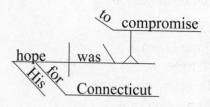

e.

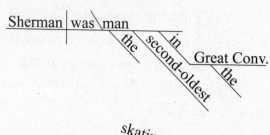

f.

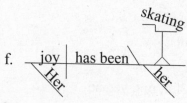

g.

She | became \ representative
a
trustworthy

Review Set 36

1. power

2. etc.

3. loud

4. Conscious

5. recriminations

6. declarative

7. party

8. (a) Wendys
   (b) keys
   (c) ditches

9. Earnest Hemingway, The, Old, Man, Sea

10. Myrtle wilson wsa hit bya yellow care
    ad killed

11. trap, (is) trapping, trapped, (has) trapped

12. phrase

13. Because of the car's *description

14. had struck, transitive

15. (a) Have
    (b) Does

16. sought, past tense

17. distraught, the, unaware

18. I. *The Great Gatsby*
    A. Genre
    B. Setting
    C. Principal characters

19. On Friday, Dr. and Mrs. Paziouros will move to 259 West Atara Street, Monrovia, California 91010.

20. was mourned, passive voice

21. and, but, or, nor, for, yet, so

22. or, and

23. neither/nor;
    not only/but also;
    either/or;
    both/and

24. Neither/nor

25. either/or

26. Does smell, linking

27. chieftain

28. To have secured, perfect tense

29.

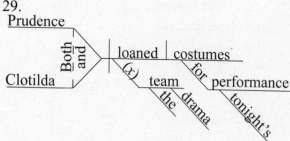

30.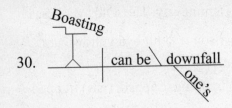

LESSON 37   **Noun Case**

Practice 37

a. nominative case, subject

b. nominative case, predicate nominative

c. possessive case

d. nominative case, subject

e. object of a preposition

f. indirect object

g. direct object

h. nominative case

i. objective case

j. possessive case

k. felicitous

l. fortuitous

Review Set 37

1. Stoics

2. *krat-*

3. people

4. Spartans

5. official

6. Christie's, possessive;
   stack, nominative;
   novels, objective;
   floor, objective;
   thud, objective

7. clause

8. believes, action

9. is tempted, passive voice

10. Do vanish, intransitive

11. To usurp, present tense

12. has been plotting, present perfect progressive tense

13. pop, (is) popping, popped, (has) popped

14. According to *plan;
    with *drink;
    on the *guards

15. *The Taming of the Shrew*

16. I. *Macbeth*
    A. Type of work
    B. Setting
    C. Principal characters
    D. Story overview

17. Everybody but Banquo believes that King duncan's sons mudered there father. (corrections: *their*, *r*)

18. Col. Robert Andrews resides at 456 Doolittle Street, Arcadia, Texas.

19. poet, dramatist

20. (a) attorneys
    (b) glassfuls
    (c) flies

21. and, but, or, for, nor, yet, so

22. either/or;
    neither/nor;
    not only/but also;
    both/and

23. Elle, Belle

24. exclamatory

25. run-on sentence

26. (is) spinning

27.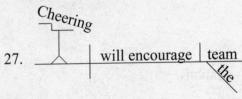

28.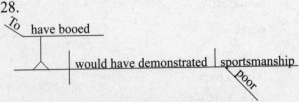

29.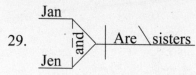

30.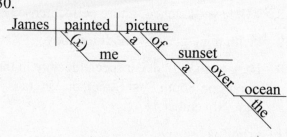

LESSON 38   Diagramming Predicate Adjectives

Practice 38

a. position | was \ difficult

b. states | remained \ timid / and / obstinate

c. speech | proved \ effective

d. voice | Did sound \ confident

e. advent

f. intervene

Review Set 38

1. felicitous

2. Stoic

3. Demos

4. things

5. censor

6. predicate

7. subject

8. fry/fries, (is) frying, fried, (has) fried

9. Does seem, linking verb

10. phrase

11. imperative

12. run-on

13. (a) justices of the peace
    (b) bibliographies
    (c) lives

14. Meg, Jo, Beth, Amy, Civil War, Christmas

15. "of the March girls" modifies "oldest"

16. will become

17. had demonstrated

18. will be marrying, future progressive tense

19. One of ~~of~~ the girls becomes ~~it is~~ it beth?

20. takes, transitive verb

21. everyone

22. The, lonely, an, older, German, a, genteel

23. I. Themes of *Little Women*
    A. Joys of youth
    B. Deep love of family

24. and, but, or, for, nor, yet, so

25. novel

26. was written, passive voice

27.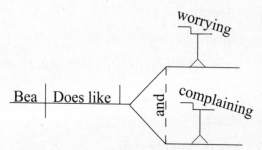

28. friend | is becoming \ anxious (My)

29. this | Is \ cause / a / for \ worry

30. 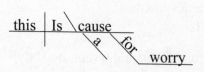 To worry | would be \ foolish

Practice 39

a. wiser, comparative

b. trimmest, superlative

c. vigorous, positive

d. most valuable, superlative

e. healthier, comparative

f. snowy, positive

g. ruder, rudest

h. more ambiguous, most ambiguous

i. explicit

j. implicit

Review Set 39

1. venire

2. Felicitous

3. stoic

4. people

5. integrity

6. objective case

7. trim, (is) trimming, trimmed, (has) trimmed

8. declarative

9. clause

10. proves, linking verb

11. wanders, intransitive

12. (a) altos
    (b) tablespoonfuls
    (c) Henrys

13. piggy wants law and Order, but Ralph prefers freedom.

14. symbolizes, active voice

15. stronger

16. most intelligent

17. either/or;
    neither/nor;
    not only/but also;
    both/and

18. will have sketched, future perfect tense

19. "with thick glasses" modifies "boy"

20. Dr. Cough will give a special lecture in the library on South First Street, on Veterans Day, November 11.

21. primitive, savage

22. leader

23. nominative

24. case

25. nominative

26. barking, present; howling, present

27. to burn, present tense

28.

29.

30.

Practice 40

a. much

b. many

c. best

d. more

e. little

f. better

g. susceptible

h. perceptible

i. capere

More Practice 40

1. less

2. better

3. worst

4. better

5. more reliable

6. more

7. most conniving

8. smarter

9. farther

10. fewer

11. fewer

12. less

Review Set 40

1. Implicit

2. come

3. Fortuitous

4. Sybaris

5. people

6. taller

7. run-on sentence

8. clause

9. (a) banjos
   (b) tariffs
   (c) ponies

10. Natalie, Florence, Italy

11. In addition to *Simon;
    at the *hands;
    of Jack's *mob

12. steals, transitive

13. Does feel, linking verb

14. has murdered, present perfect tense

15. Ralph

16. Ⓐ white-uniformed, naval, (the), filthy, stick-wielding

17. plot/plots, (is) plotting, plotted, (has) plotted

18. objective case

19. On Friday morning, Dr. Corndog parked too close to a fire hydrant on East Bay Avenue.

20. Brittney

21. object of a preposition

22. Having studied, perfect tense

23. to pass, present tense

24. sillier, silliest

25. applies, active voice

26. Emiko smile^s at at everyones she meets⊙

27. declarative sentence

28.

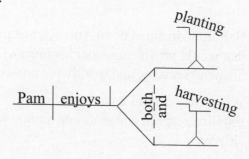

29.

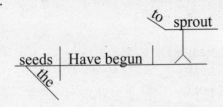

30.

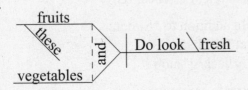

LESSON 41   **The Comma, Part 1: Dates, Addresses, Series**

Practice 41

a. Altogether

b. already

c. all ready

d. all together

e. all right

f. Hamilton's speech on June 18, 1787, lasted for five hours!

g. On July 10, 1787, the other delegates from New York left the Constitutional Convention in disgust.

h. Thanksgiving fell on Thursday, November 28, in the year 2002.

i. The Constitutional Convention took place in Philadelphia, Pennsylvania, in 1787.

j. Anchorage, Alaska, has beautiful scenery.

k. Will you visit Dublin, Ireland, UK, next summer?

l. Hamilton dreamed of an American empire that would provide national happiness, financial security, and worldwide power.

m. Will strong central government create stability, respect, and ambition among its citizens?

n. January, March, May, July, August, October, and December have thirty-one days.

More Practice 41   *See Master Worksheets*

Review Set 41

1. *capere*

2. Implicit

3. appropriate

4. hedonism

5. Aristocracy

6. fewer

7. abstract

8. younger

9. many

10. subject

11. linking

12. Miss Eltoe called from Mount Baldy to apologize for being late to her nine a.m. interview at the Holiday Craft Company.

13. (a) deer
    (b) stereos
    (c) watches

14. *A Connecticut Yankee in King Arthur's Court*

15. George Washington was actually born on February 11, 1732.

16. On his *quest;
    round about the *countryside

17. is trying, present progressive

18. have been oppressed, passive voice

19. The, virtuous, a, kingly, a, righteous

20. clever, inventive

21. creates, transitive

22. wheeze(s), (is) wheezing, wheezed, (has) wheezed

23. objective case

24. clause

25. Will Margaret proofread and edit this manuscript?

26. run-on sentence

27.
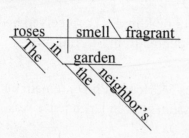

28.
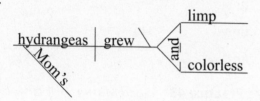

29.
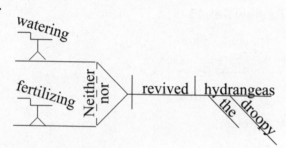

30.
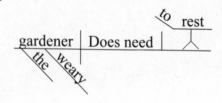

LESSON 42   **Appositives**

Practice 42

a. agenda

b. agitated

c. *ag-*

d. William Livingston

e. a vigorous Whig

f.
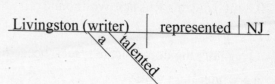

g. Antifederalists, opponents of Federalists, believed that the Constitution gave too much power to the central government and too little to states.

h. James Madison wrote some of the Federalist papers, essays explaining that the new government would respect the rights of states and individuals.

Review Set 42

1. already

2. seize

3. implied

4. advent

5. integrity

6. hungriest

7. fewer

8. Have been waiting, intransitive

9. pack, huskies, Curley, dog, ship

10. shipmate's, shipmates', husky's, huskies'

11. sentence fragment

12. (a) radii or radiuses
    (b) portfolios
    (c) wishes

13. Aunt Bea, Uncle Jake, "The Emperor's New Clothes"

14. Deb bathed the dog, brushed the llama, and fed the cats.

15. Was written, action verb

16. sells

17. will learn

18. In addition to many other *lessons; against a *man; with a *club

19. a, sly-eyed, powerful, lead

20. my cousin's Russian Wolfhound

21. Over#time, the domesticated Buck becaem a ~~a~~ wilder ness wolf

22. On the first Tuesday in September, Mr. Levi B. Green will be here at two p.m. to discuss the advantages of Richfoods, Inc.

23. either/or;
both/and;
not only/but also;
neither/nor

24. wolf

25. possessive case

26. objective case

27. phrase

28. to survive, present tense

29.

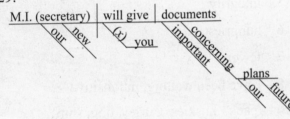

30.

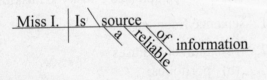

LESSON 43 — The Comma, Part 2: Direct Address, Appositives, Academic Degrees

Practice 43

a. Delegates, please find your seats so that we can begin business promptly.

b. Did you realize, Professor Cameron, that Jonathan Dayton was the youngest delegate at the Constitutional Convention?

c. Jonathan Dayton, a faithful follower of William Paterson, was concerned with the rights of the small states.

d. Elias Boudinot, an associate of Jonathan Dayton, speculated in western lands.

e. Benjamin Franklin, Ph.D., received his honorary degree from St. Andrews University.

f. Did James McHenry, Ph.D., remain in his profession after independence was achieved?

g. finale

h. finite

i. *fin-*

More Practice 43 *See Master Worksheets*

Review Set 43

1. *ven-*

2. all ready

3. Perceptible

4. clear

5. intervene

6. planned

7. are

8. superlative

9. comparative

10. positive

11. complete sentence

12. clause

13. (Amanda), poetry, (filly,) (Mercedes)

14. (a) stitches
(b) bays
(c) liabilities

15. One Time, Buck save^d John thornton's li^f e.

16. across from *Trung;
down the *street;

from the vegetable *stand;
alongside the *river

17. Had been refusing, past perfect progressive tense

18. were piling up, past progressive tense

19. grows, linking verb

20. (a) lower, lowest
    (b) more ambivalent, most ambivalent
    (c) subtler, subtlest

21. intervene(s), (is) intervening, intervened, (has) intervened

22. Buck's prey, a bull moose, was six feet tall and a formidable quarry.

23. and, but, or, for, nor, yet, so

24. Mr. Yio arrived on Tuesday, October 25, 2004.

25. nominative case

26. Fighting, present tense

27. My father, Ivan Kutz, volunteers at a hospital in Denver, Colorado.

28.
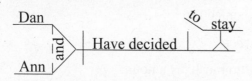

29.
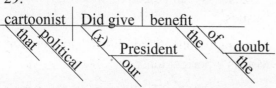

30.
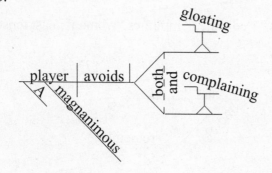

Practice 44

a. tedious, monotonous, dull, tiresome, lengthy, interminable, wearying, humdrum, long-winded

b. helpful, informative, knowledgeable

c. pleasant, exciting, enjoyable, relaxing

d. pungent, penetrating, offensive, foul

e. That sort of job does not appeal to me.

f. Lucita brought both of them to the meeting.

g. anyway

h. any way

i. any way

j. anyway

More Practice 44   *See "Hysterical Fiction #3" in Master Worksheets*

Review Set 44

1. end

2. do

3. all right

4. Susceptible

5. intervene

6. fewer

7. phrase

8. are talking, intransitive

9. (Loneliness,) Buck, (times)

10. (a) tomatoes
    (b) hobbies
    (c) runners-up

11. I. Themes of the story
    A. Survival of the fittest
    B. Love for animals

12. Except for his occasional *return; to John Mornton's *camp;

like a wild *animal;
in the *forest

13. run-on sentence

14. (a) had
    (b) has
    (c) have

15. led, past tense

16. became, linking

17. The, sinister, a, brutish

18. both/and;
    either/or;
    neither/nor;
    not only/but also

19. the

20. At two p.m., Mr. J. B. Cruz, Jr., will be here to discuss career opportunities at Minnie's Catering Co. in New York City.

21. Aunt Ella, please send my mail to 1200 Dermit Drive, Iowa City, Iowa.

22. possessive case

23. Faust, a scholar-alchemist, expresses his indescribable discontent.

24. Was attempting, active voice

25.

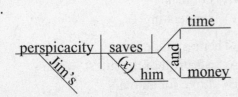

The poodle bark**ed** growled, and ran about the house.

26.

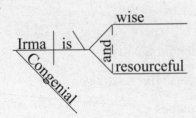

27.

28.

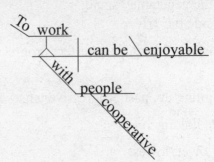

29.

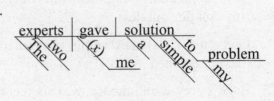

30.

you | Did hear | singing

LESSON 45

Verbals as Adjectives; Infinitives and Participles

Practice 45

a. trajectory

b. conjecture

c. *ject-*

d. "to blush" is a noun

e. "to discuss," an adjective, modifies "issues."

f. "Having belonged" modifies "Gouverneur Morris"; perfect tense

g. "practicing" modifies "lawyer"; present tense

h. "educated" modifies "woman"; past tense

i.

j.

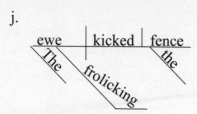

More Practice 45

1.

We | need | chance
a
to improve

2.

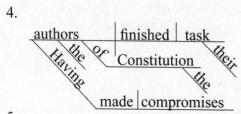
man | was \ Son of Liberty
The a
fighting

3.

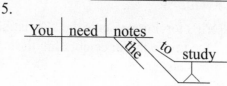
Peace | was \ cause
with a
British lost
the

4.

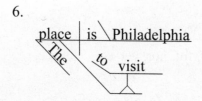
authors | finished | task
the of Constitution their
Having the
made | compromises

5.

You | need | notes
the
to study

6.

place | is \ Philadelphia
The
to visit

Review Set 45

1. Anyway

2. last

3. agenda

4. altogether

5. President

6. exclamatory

7. intransitive

8. appositive

9. taller

10. Faust finally divines that Mephisto is the Devil. The two of them banter back and forth.

11. (a) Sundays
    (b) biographies
    (c) halves

12. The, *Faust*, German

13. clause

14. was saved, passive voice

15. (a) were
    (b) was
    (c) were

16. remains, linking verb

17. will have received, future perfect tense

18. agitate(s), (is) agitating, agitated, (has) agitated

19. English

20. compassionate, knowledgeable

21. Both/and

22. On Saturday, June 2, Mrs. Sanchez will hire plumbers, roofers, and electricians to fix up her house at 207 Brick Road, Edmond, Oklahoma.

23. poodle, nobleman, slave

24. objective case

25. the Devil

26. Though faust had sinned, he still struggled towrads growth and knowledge.

27.

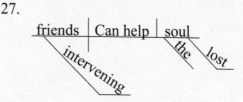
friends | Can help | soul
intervening the lost

28.

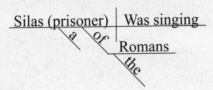

29.

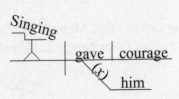

30.

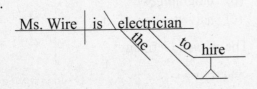

LESSON 46   Pronouns and Antecedents

Practice 46

a. they/Americans; their/Americans

b. he/George Clymer

c. He/Charles Townshend

d. While Addy and Gaby were singing, Addy hit a wrong note.

e. Gaby thought Abby had misread the music.

f. comprises

g. compose

Review Set 46

1. *ject-*

2. anyway

3. finale

4. agitate

5. all together

6. transitive

7. demonstrative

8. possessive

9. focuses

10. flap(s), (is) flapping, flapped, (has) flapped

11. Ghost, Christmas, ⟨flashbacks,⟩ Scrooge's, childhood

12. Tonight, Uncle Joe, *A Christmas Carol*, "The First, Three, Spirits"

13. Scrooge's nephew invites Mr. scrooge too him house for diner.

14. (a) people
    (b) knives
    (c) foxes

15. clause

16. On account of an *F; from the boarding *school

17. shall be examining, future tense

18. hotter

19. most hospitable

20. Was blaming, active voice

21. On Wednesday, September 5, 2003, Sean-Carlos informed Dr. Van Spronsen of his intention to attend the university.

22. sentence fragment

23. objective case

24. feels, linking verb

25. The Spirit's torch represents the "Christmas Spirit," the joy found in celebrating the Christmas season.

26. a

27. Miss Informed

28. and, but, or, for, nor, yet, so

29.

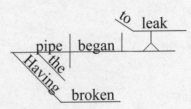

30.

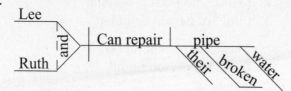

LESSON 47

The Comma, Part 3: Greetings and Closings, Last Name First, Introductory and Interrupting Elements, Afterthoughts, Clarity

Practice 47

a. Dear Thomas,
Congratulations on your promotion to brigadier general.
Love,
Adele

b. Use the index of your history book to find the writings of "Hamilton, Alexander."

c. John Locke's *Two Treatises of Government*, I believe, talks about people's natural rights.

d. Governments, said Thomas Jefferson, get their power from the consent of the governed.

e. No, the Articles of Confederation did not provide for a bicameral legislature.

f. They failed to create effective leadership, I have heard.

g. Ever since, he has studied harder.

h. Thanks to Kevin, Jordan has transportation to school.

i. retraction

j. intractable

k. *tract-*

More Practice 47   *See Master Worksheets*

Review Set 47

1. Comprise

2. conjecture

3. any way

4. Finite

5. i.e.

6. louder

7. does

8. complete sentence

9. phrase

10. Does grieve, intransitive

11. Is, linking verb

12. are discussing, active voice

13. (a) Randys
    (b) peaches
    (c) senators-elect

14. interrogative

15. Scrooge refuse two reveel thee identity of the coprse.

16. Grief, compassion, sympathy, anger, shock, and disbelief normally accompany the death of a loved one.

17. Without *exception;
    of *London;
    about Scrooge's *death

18. lobby (is) lobbying, lobbied, (has) lobbied

19. Scrooge's, a, poor, more, their

20. greedy, grouchy, stingy, disgruntled, selfish, unkind, merciless, etc.

21. both/and;
    either/or;
    neither/nor;
    not only/but also

22. Now Scrooge, a new man, promises to honor Christmas in his heart.

23. he, Scrooge;
    their, Christmas Spirits;
    his, Scrooge

24. man

25. objective case

26. Bob Cratchit

27. shocked, modifies Fred

28. to celebrate, modifies opportunity

29.

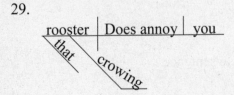

30.

LESSON 48   **Personal Pronouns**

Practice 48

a. Every one

b. everyone

c. Any one

d. anyone

e. me, first person

f. she, third person

g. you, second person

h. us, plural

i. me, singular

j. indirect object

k. direct object

l. possession

m. subject

More Practice 48

1. (*answers*)
   we, first person plural;
   you, second person singular

2. they, 3rd person plural

3. (You), 2nd person singular;
   him, 3rd person singular

4. They, 3rd person plural;
   their, 3rd person plural

5. you, 2nd person singular or plural

6. her, 3rd person singular

7. (You), 2nd person singular;
   your, 2nd person singular

8. I, 1st person singular;
   them, 3rd person plural

9. They, 3rd person plural;
   my, 1st person singular

10. She, 3rd person singular;
    us, 1st person plural

11. (*answered*)
    we, subject; you, object

12. they, subject;

13. (you), subject; him, object

14. They, subject; their, possession

15. you, subject

16. her, object

17. (You), subject; your, possession

18. I, subject; them, object

19. They, subject; my, possession

20. She, subject; us, object

Review Set 48

1. *tract-*

2. include

3. guess

4. Any way

5. seriousness

6. has

7. antecedent

8. before

9. go

10. before

11. pronoun

12. run-on sentence

13. clause

14. nestor's, nestors', James's

15. spent, action verb

16. (a) dairies
    (b) waltzes
    (c) days

17. imperative

18. *The Maltese Falcon*, San Francisco, California

19. The Main charcater is ~~is~~ s̲am Spade, a young d̲etective.

20. Near the enemy *encampment;
    with *arrow;
    on *string;
    at either *end;
    of the *pass

21. hurry or hurries, (is) hurrying, hurried, (has) hurried

22. The, beautiful, intelligent, some, clever

23. On Monday, October 10, 2005, Jacqueline auditioned for the part of Miss Wonderly.

24. not only/but also

25. Miles Archer, Spade's older partner, is to tail Thursby.

26. were questioning; active voice

27.

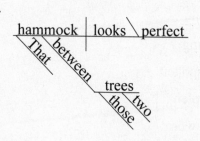

28. They | love

29.

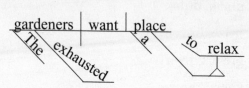

30.

LESSON 49   **Irregular Verbs, Part 2**

Practice 49

a. *ducere*

b. deduction

c. conducive

d. deduction

e. drunk

f. sang

g. rung

h. swore

i. wore

j. thrown

k. broke

l. tore

m. stolen

n. blown

o. frozen

More Practice 49

1. bore, borne

2. began, begun

3. blew, blown

4. chose, chosen

5. drank, drunk

6. froze, frozen

7. grew, grown

8. knew, known

9. rang, rung

10. sang, sung

11. spoke, spoken

12. stole, stolen

13. swore, sworn

14. tore, torn

15. threw, thrown

16. wore, worn

Review Set 49

1. Any one

2. retraction

3. Compose

4. Anyways

5. Judicious

6. have

7. superlative

8. predicate nominative

9. indirect

10. second

11. plural

12. third, singular

13. Does give, transitive

14. agency, truth

15. On, Wednesday, Aunt Jenny, Have, *A Tale*, *Two Cities*

16. in *The Maltese Falcon*, modifies "character"

17. efficient

18. complete sentence

19. phrase

20. (a) turkeys
    (b) stories
    (c) dishes

21. know(s), (is) knowing, knew, (has) known

22. bore, borne

23.
   Dear miss Informed,
   you said you would meet me at one p.m.
   what happened?
   yours turly,
   aunt Lilly

24. Miss Wonderly hires Sam Spade to find a missing person, her seventeen-year-old sister.

25. killing

26. On April 3, 2002, Mr. and Mrs. Steu gave birth to a six pound daughter and named her Calla Mary.

27. she, Christina;
    his, Tom;
    her, Christina

28. closed, door

29.
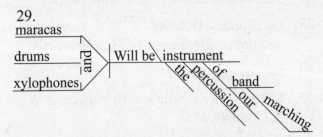

30.
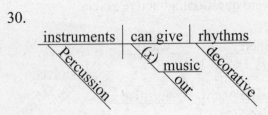

Practice 50

a. sing. 1st I; 2nd you; 3rd he/she/it.
   pl. 1st we; 2nd you; 3rd they

b. They called for the independence of America.

c. The Loyalist in the red vest was he.

d. She and I will march in the parade.

e. I, she, they, he, we

f. she

g. they

h. he

i. I

j. envelop

k. envelope

l. envelope

m. envelop

Review Set 50

1. *ducere*

2. anyone

3. withdrawal

4. make up

5. parts

6. most

7. first

8. second

9. wore

10. stolen

11. (a) juries
    (b) sheep
    (c) wolves

12. Had searched, past perfect tense

13. clause

14. sentence fragment

15. identifies, action verb

16. "Uncle Wiggily and the Crawly Snake"

17. began

18. more conscientious, most conscientious

19. Dear Aunt Lilly,
    I lost my watch. Please forgive me.
    Regretfully,
    Miss Informed

20. pleading (modifies "eyes")

21. flashed, intransitive

22. objective case

23. him, Douglas MacArthur;
    he, Douglas MacArthur

24. sing(s), (is) singing, sang, (has) sung

25. (a) threw, thrown
    (b) tore, torn

26. dancing, present

27. Was worn, passive voice

28. and, but, or, for, nor, yet, so

29.

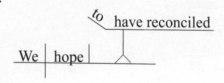

30.

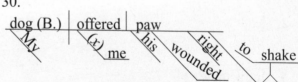

Practice 51

a. sing. 1st . . . . me
       2nd . . . you
       3rd . . . him
            her
            it
    pl.   1st . . . us
       2nd . . . you
       3rd . . . them

b. King George aggravated the Patriots and us.

c. A docent told them the history.

d. Liza canned apricots with him and me.

e. Aunt Sukey winked at my cousin and me.

f. me, him, them, her, us

g. me

h. her

i. them

j. sequence

k. consequential

l. follow

Review Set 51

1. Envelop

2. lead

3. Every one

4. Intractable

5. appropriation

6. third

7. case

8. knew

9. grown

10. torn

11. rung

12. better

13. phrase

14. (a) factories
     (b) chimneys
     (c) loaves

15. sang, action

16.
deer/Katrina,

please thank grandma for Making those squash pies, they ~~was~~ were delicous.

grate fully,
Leling

17. (a) chose, (has) chosen
     (b) broke, (has) broken

18. more susceptible, most susceptible

19. objective

20. nominative

21. My neighbor planted that fir tree.

22. Georges Bizet, a French composer, wrote the opera *Carmen*.

23. possessive case

24. his, Napoleon

25. Crackling

26. The, good, many, diverse

27. Both/and

28.
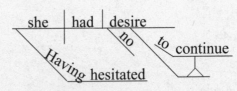

29.
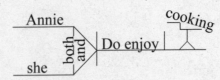

30.
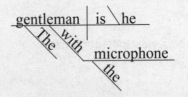

Practice 52

a. objective case

b. nominative case

c. possessive case

d. direct object

e. possession

f. subject

g. indirect object

h. object of a preposition

i. predicate nominative

j. We

k. me

l. disinterested

m. uninterested

Review Set 52

1. sequi

2. Envelope

3. Conducive

4. Everyone

5. lighten

6. clause

7. (a) inches
   (b) feet
   (c) yardsticks

8. wrote, transitive

9. Poe used dark surroundings and ghostly symbols to create a sense of fear.

10. swear, (is) swearing, swore, (has) sworn

11. less, least

12.

Voltaire, a french Writer and philsopher, was was born in paris on november 21, 1694.

13. Of course, Mom, I shall help you weed the garden, dump the trash, and feed the dog.

14. and, but, or, nor, for, yet, so

15. Did seem, linking

16. will be introducing, future progressive tense

17. Roderick Usher wrote his one personal friend, the Narrator, and requested his presence at the ancestral Usher home.

18. his, Narrator; he, Narrator

19. phrase

20. sing. 1st I
    2nd . . . you
    3rd . . . he
    she
    it
    pl. 1st . . . we
    2nd . . . you
    3rd . . . they

21. aristocracy's, nestor's, nestors'

22. The emcee is she.

23. (a) blew, (has) blown
    (b) shrank, (has) shrunk

24. A

25. terrifying

26. fishing, reading

27.

28.

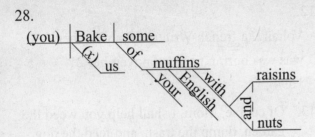

29.

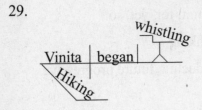

30.

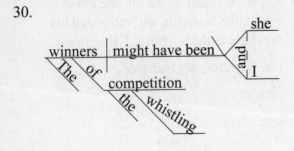

LESSON 53

Possessive Pronouns and Possessive Adjectives • Diagramming Pronouns

Practice 53

a.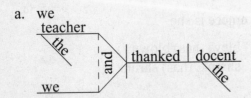

b.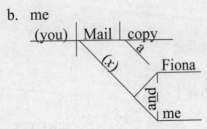

c.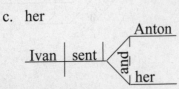

d. its, its

e. theirs

f. your

g. They're

h. It's

i. apollonian

j. bacchanalian

k. gods

More Practice 53

1. their

2. their, they're

3. its

4. ours

5. hers

6. yours

7. your

8. they're, there

9. its, it's

10. You're, your

Review Set 53

1. impartial

2. follow

3. envelop

4. encourage

5. Levity

6. her

7. yours

8. pronoun

9. (a) cities
   (b) men
   (c) rules of thumb

10. The hoodlum's intractable behavior annoyed everyone in the crowd.

11. grow(s), (is) growing, grew, (has) grown

12. crazier, craziest

13. Mr. usher had a a sistre her name was Alfie.

14. "The Making of an Explorer"

15. attacked, action verb

16. both/and, not only/but also, either/or, neither/nor

17. will flee, future tense

18. The Russian artist Marc Chagall painted *I and the Village*, an abstract painting that looks like something from a dream.

19. it, mansion

20. phrase

21. sing. 1st . . . . me
       2nd . . . you
       3rd . . . him
            her
            it
  pl. 1st . . . us
       2nd . . . you
       3rd . . . them

22. B

23. to read, adjective

24. (a) spoke, (has) spoken
   (b) stole, (has) stolen

25. lying

26. Having won, perfect

27. jury

28.
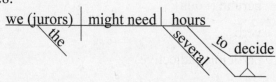

29.
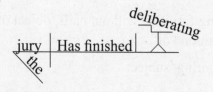

30.
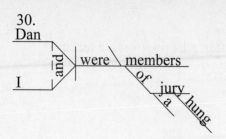

LESSON 54   Dependent and Independent Clauses • Subordinating Conjunctions

Practice 54

a. dependent

b. independent

c. independent

d. dependent

e. Because

f. even though

g. Until

h. biennial

i. biannual

j. twice

k. other

More Practice 54   *See Master Worksheets*

Review Set 54

1. Apollonian

2. indifferent

3. Consequential

4. vote

5. illusion

6. yours

7. its

8. He

9. Your

10. faster

11. sung

12. was listening, past progressive tense

13. sing. 1st I
    2nd . . . you
    3rd . . . he
            she
            it
    pl. 1st . . . we
    2nd . . . you
    3rd . . . they

14. (Poverty) (life,) Family

15.
Mom warned, "oh, what a tangled web we weave when first we practice too deceive" this was a quote form sir Walter Scott's poem "marmion."

16. clause

17. good: captivating, moving, articulate, motivating, delightful, magnificent, powerful, effective, charming, pleasant, eloquent, impressive, etc.

18. know, (is) knowing, knew, (has) known

19. (These,) joyous, the, Britain's

20. "to develop" is an adjective modifying "contrast"

21. must have glistened, intransitive

22. objective

23. antecedent

24. nominative

25. seems, linking

26. (a) sons-in-law
    (b) mouthfuls

27. Edward Tudor invites Tom Canty into the palace.

28. Mark Twain, a social and political satirist, wrote *The Prince and the Pauper*.

29.

30.

LESSON 55 **Gerunds Vs. Participles and Verbs • Gerund Phrases**

Practice 55

a. Dionysian

b. Delphic

c. Dionysian

d. "protecting the interests of the smaller states" is the direct object

e. "Our wearing red, white, and blue on Wednesdays" is the subject

f. "holding any political positions" is the object of the preposition "before"

g. "reading mystery stories" is the predicate nominative

h. his

i. Your

j. my

k. gerund (noun)

l. verb

m. participle (adjective)

More Practice 55

1. building furniture without nails, object of preposition "of"

2. Her snoring, subject

3. telling the truth, object of preposition "for"

4. spying on the British, direct object

5. Spying on them, subject

6. living simply, object of preposition "on"

7. collecting antique spoons, predicate nominative

8. his pestering her, direct object

Review Set 55

1. Biannual

2. Bacchanalian

3. disinterested

4. resultant

5. bully

6. your

7. theirs

8. many

9. stole

10. she

11. run-on sentence

12. phrase

13. Miss Ogaz said, "On Saturday, November 16, 2003, I practiced my Spanish dance steps, watched a British movie, and mopped the kitchen floor."

14. dependent

15. case

16. objective

17. (a) participle
    (b) gerund
    (c) verb

18. rescues, transitive

19. will have been singing, future perfect progressive tense

20. and, but, or, for, nor, yet, so

21. Did assume, action

22. (a) eyelashes
    (b) boxes
    (c) lilies

23. wear(s), (is) wearing, wore, (has) worn

24. (While) Edward Tudor lives as a beggar

25. B

26. Shall we recommend Dudley and her?

27.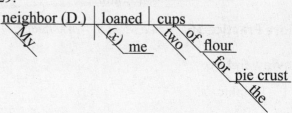

28. Robert vacuumed the living room.

29.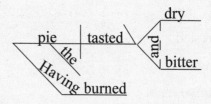

30.

LESSON 56 **Participle Phrases • Diagramming Participle and Gerund Phrases**

Practice 56

a. flare

b. flair

c. flare

d. Homophones

e. "sitting in the back row" modifies "Antony"

f. "Participating little in the Revolution" modifies "Jacob Broom"

g. "torn by the fierce hurricane" modifies "flag"

h. "built by Jacob Bloom" modifies "mill"

i.

Building | cotton mill
a
required | ingenuity

j.

workers | look \ weary
The
harvesting | cotton

More Practice 56   *See Master Worksheets*

Review Set 56

1. Delphic

2. Biennial

3. calm

4. uninterested

5. delaying

6. nominative

7. worn

8. yours

9. gerund

10. him

11. more

12. (a) Abbys
    (b) caddies
    (c) grants-in-aid

13. young, handsome

14. was returning, past progressive tense

15. both/and, either/or, neither/nor, not only/ but also

16. Lieutenant Rinaldi met a British nurse.

17. phrase

18. affected, transitive

19. became, linking

20. drink(s), (is) drinking, drank, (has) drunk

21. Dear Professor Droner,
    On Thursday, November 13, 2003, you gave a lecture titled "The Social and Cultural History of the Ancient World." I do not remember the last half of it.
    Regretfully,
    Ms. Snoozer

22. The Nile, the longest river in the world, flows north through Egypt and empties into the Mediterranean Sea.

23. them

24. she, Malia; her, Malia

25. Frederic desserts the <u>italian</u> army and tr<del>y</del>^{ie}s t<del>w</del>o find Catherine⊙

26. false

27. (As) the police chased Frederic

28.

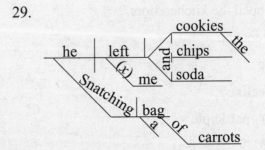

29.

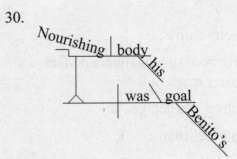

30.

Nourishing | body
his
was \ goal
Benito's

Practice 57

a. I

b. himself

c. You

d. themselves

e. <u>Martin (himself)</u> | defended | captain
                                          the

f. mercurial

g. jovial

h. jovial

i. mercurial

More Practice 57

1. himself

2. themselves

3. themselves

4. I

5. me

6. themselves

7. he

8. himself

9. themselves

10. she

Review Set 57

1. homophones

2. Dionysian

3. introduce

4. nestor

5. conscience

6. first

7. second

8. he

9. hers

10. (a) lice
    (b) Nancys
    (c) trenches

11. My aunt and I sailed on a junk down the Yangtze River in China last Friday, the seventh of October.

12. The ancient Egyptians built those reservoirs.

13. and, but, or, for, nor, yet, so

14. is wandering, action

15. imperative, declarative

16. Dr. Payne did my foot surgery, did he do your's also?

17. hers, possessive case

18. flows, intransitive

19. phrase

20. (Even though) Fidel Castro is the communist national leader of Cuba

21. B

22. sentence fragment

23. your, his, its, their

24. Grandpa's

25. most jovial

26. ring(s), (is) ringing, rang, (has) rung

27. The Volga River, the longest in Europe, begins north of Moscow, Russia, and flows into the Caspian Sea.

28.

cousin (Dale) | bought | house
My   (x)   a   run-down   to repair
            himself

29.

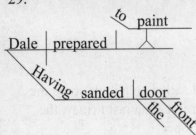

30.

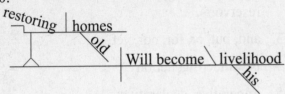

LESSON 58 — The Comma, Part 4: Descriptive Adjectives, Dependent Clauses

Practice 58

a. The preoccupied, near-sighted Luther Martin bumped into a cow, tipped his hat, and apologized.

b. A disgusted, disillusioned delegate left the convention early.

c. no comma

d. Because Luther Martin supported Samuel Chase, some scholars believe he opposed the Constitution for financial reasons.

e. Even though this seems reasonable, other scholars believe otherwise.

f. While some people doubted his motives, he actually had good intentions.

g. libel

h. slander

More Practice 58   *See Master Worksheets*

Review Set 58

1. Jovial

2. Flair

3. unclear

4. frenzied

5. unconcerned

6. me

7. himself

8. third

9. him

10. theirs, ours

11. (a) itineraries
    (b) letters of credit
    (c) placebos

12. Dear Uncle William,
    Officer Green's salad, I believe, calls for one pound of chopped spinach, one teaspoon of crushed garlic, and three California peppers. I hope you enjoy it.
    Love,
    Sal

13. According to the *encyclopedia,
    along the *bank,
    of a *river,
    in *Australia

14. himself

15. imperative

16. a

17. He, nominative case; his, possessive case

18. Does speak, intransitive

19.
    Young Manolin ~~brang~~ brought food an **d** ~~an~~ bait to ~~to~~ Santiago's shack⊙

20. ⟨whenever⟩ he falls asleep

21. A baritone sang the closing hymn.

22. run-on sentence

23. towing the boat

24. Tom's

25. sillier

26. wrapped

27. Flowing into the Indian Ocean, the Ganges River widens into a delta, a broad fan-shaped deposit of mud and sand.

28.

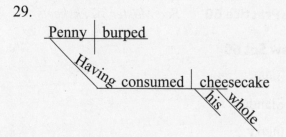

29.

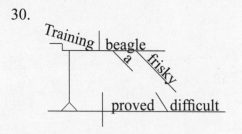

30.

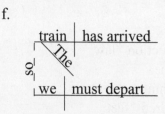

LESSON 59

Compound Sentences • Coordinating Conjunctions

Practice 59

a. simple

b. compound, yet

c. compound, so

d. compound, but

e. simple

f.

train | has arrived
The
so
we | must depart

g. *ambi-*

h. ambient

i. ambidextrous

j. ambivalent

Review Set 59

1. Libel

2. Mercurial

3. flare

4. unrestrained

5. Spartan

6. I

7. themselves

8. first

9. her

10. yours, ours

11. simple sentence

12. (a) platypuses or platypi
    (b) zeros or zeroes
    (c) mousetraps

13. After she had shaken hands with a hundred people at the reception, Ms. Li wanted to get out of her Sunday suit, toe-pinching high-heels, and heavy clip-on earrings.

14. himself

15. the

16. his, possessive case

17. Are devouring, transitive

18. the next morning, the othre fisher men finded the skeleton off the marlino

19. When the smoke alarm went off

20. Dudley baked that pizza with the crispy crust.

21. sentence fragment

22. to catch the big marlin

23. coated with pitch

24. dreaming about lions

25. most peaceful

26. envelop(s), (is) enveloping, enveloped, (has) enveloped

27. Tchaikovsky, a Russian composer, wrote a famous ballet called *The Nutcracker*.

28. book, ⟨themes,⟩ ⟨courage,⟩ ⟨endurance,⟩ ⟨suffering⟩

29.

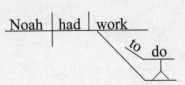

30.

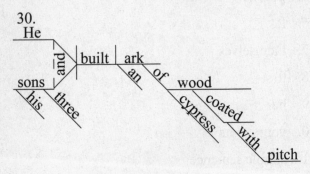

Confederation as a threat to state sovereignty."

   i. tortuous

   j. torturous

   k. tortuous

   l. torturous

More Practice 60   *See Master Worksheets.*

Review Set 60

1. *ambi-*

2. Slander

3. merry

4. flare

5. et al.

6. themselves

7. me

8. she

9. false

10. stole

11. their

12. (a) pianos
    (b) bookshelves
    (c) shoeboxes

13. Aunt Emma and Uncle Fred took an Alaskan vacation. They paddled in a kayak around a lake, viewed glaciers from a helicopter, and fished for salmon in a stream.

14. phrase

15. were, linking

16. According to election *law,
    for public *office,
    from *campaigning,
    within one hundred *feet,
    of a polling *place

17. run-on sentence

18. he, nominative case, Hank Aaron

LESSON
60

**The Comma, Part 5:
Compound Sentences, Direct
Quotations**

Practice 60

1. and, but, or, nor, for, yet, so

b. for

c. yet

d. and

e. Passionate Federalists lived in Maryland, but there were ardent Antifederalists as well.

f. Samuel Chase spoke against the Constitution, so Daniel Carroll replied to him in the article, "A Friend to the Constitution."

g. "John Francis Mercer," writes M. E. Bradford, "was an ardent Antifederalist connected with the Samuel Chase faction in Maryland."

h. Mr. VanLeeuwen said, "John Francis Mercer even viewed the Articles of

19. Please remind ms. Flake that posessive pronouns donot have apos trophie's.

20. (Although) many actors have portrayed Tarzan

21. The Amazon, the world's second longest river, starts in the Andes Mountains in Peru and flows through the rain forest in Brazil.

22. Having lost his car keys, perfect tense

23. singing the railroad song

24. simple sentence

25. more tortuous

26. choose, (is) choosing, chose, (has) chosen

27. and, or, and

28. Roger swept the floor and washed the windows.

29.

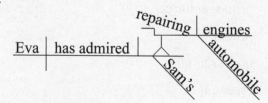

30.

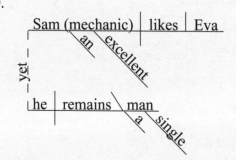

LESSON 61

Relative Pronouns • Diagramming the Dependent Clause

Practice 61

a. who

b. whom

c. whomever

d. that

e. whom

f.

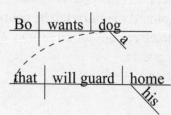

g. epidermis

h. *ep-* or *epi-*

i. ephemeral

More Practice 61

1. who

2. who

3. whom

4. whom

5. whom

6. who

7. who

Review Set 61

1. Tortuous

2. Ambivalent

3. Slander

4. unpredictable

5. bureaucrat

6. himself

7. were, themselves

8. they

9. yours

10. grown

11. begun

12. their

13. coordinating

14. Grandpa said, "If you help me, we can tie up this intruder so that he doesn't escape."

15. Dear Grandma and Grandpa,
    Since you captured the intruder, he cannot bother anyone else. I am proud of you, for you are courageous.
    With admiration,
    Jaime

16. active voice

17. your or yours

18. begins, intransitive

19. The architect from ~~pasadena~~ showed me ~~me~~ the building plan ~~o~~ i like it.

20. (a) oases
    (b) calves
    (c) theories

21. ⟨when⟩ Jesus lived in Judea

22. William Shakespeare used interesting metaphors, figures of speech, in his writing.

23. Infuriated by Messala's prideful attitude, Judah Ben-Hur

24. herself

25. most jovial

26. tear, (is) tearing, tore, (has) torn

27. compound sentence, for

28. simple sentence

29.

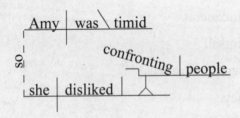

30.

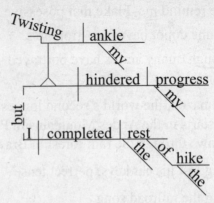

LESSON 62

The Comma, Part 6: Nonessential Parts • *That* or *Which*

Practice 62

a. primal

b. primogeniture

c. primal

d. nonessential

e. essential

f. nonessential

g. which

h. which

i. that

j. that

Review Set 62

1. outer

2. Torturous

3. Ambidextrous

4. Libel

5. avert

6. I

7. they

8. who

9. known

10. his

11. Did Ben-Hur drive the Romans out of Judah?

12. dependent

13. Latin, which was the language spoken in ancient Rome, influenced the development of other languages.

14. French, Spanish, Italian, and Portuguese are called Romance languages, for they developed out of Latin.

15. complete sentence

16. we

17. (a) has been feeling, linking
    (b) has been feeling, action

18. he, nominative case; his, possessive case

19. (a) Jameses
    (b) Lopezes
    (c) Jerrys

20. (While) Ben-Hur is on the way to Nazareth

21. had saved, past perfect tense

22. In the year 44 B.C., Julius Caesar, a Roman dictator, was assassinated on the Ides of March.

23. adopting him as his own son, present tense

24. Having trained as a Roman soldier, modifies "servant"

25. more bellicose

26. freeze, (is) freezing, froze, (has) frozen

27. compound sentence, and

28. simple sentence

29.

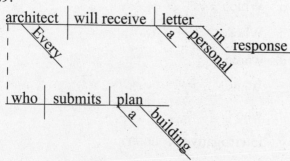

30.

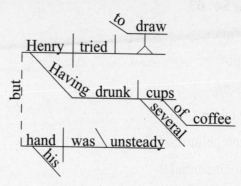

LESSON 63   **Pronoun Usage: Appositions and Comparisons**

Practice 63

a. We

b. us

c. us

d. I

e. we

f. supine

g. supine

h. prone

i. prone

More Practice 63

1. he

2. We

3. us

4. she

5. him

6. she

7. he

8. they

9. We

10. us

Review Set 63

1. primus

2. epi-

3. turns

4. Ambient

5. antebellum

6. nonessential

7. he

8. whom

9. she ("is" omitted)

10. We

11. who

12. Whom

13. my

14. nominative

15. Redheaded Eric, a fierce Viking, sailed west past Iceland and discovered Greenland.

16. On Tuesday, November fourth, in Hampton, Virginia, Col. Peterson will present a documentary on the adventurous explorer Leif Ericson.

17. their

18. hires, transitive

19. Because of the *disarray, in my *garage, in spite of the large *conglomeration, or *tools and *gadgets, round about the work *area

20. (a) fireflies
    (b) lunches
    (c) dairies

21. (As soon as) he escapes

22. My bird book is vary old, the brids may have evolved since it was ~~wrote~~ written.

23. Ben-Hur slays the soldier abusing a Jewish man.

24. "abusing a Jewish man," modifies "soldier"

25. best

26. drop, (is) dropping, dropped, (has) dropped

27. essential (I must have more than one Dinah.)

28.

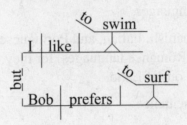

29.

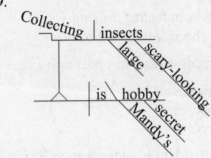

30.

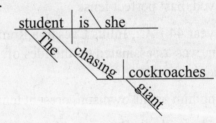

LESSON 64   **Interrogative Pronouns**

Practice 64

a. who

b. Which

c. Whose

d. whom

e. Whose

f. who

g. interrogative pronoun

h. adjective

i. modus vivendi

j. modus operandi

More Practice 64

1. Who's

2. Whose

3. Who

4. whom

5. Whom

6. Who's

7. Whose

8. whom

9. Who

10. Whom

Review Set 64

1. supine

2. first

3. Ephemeral

4. pain

5. bellicose

6. I ("did" omitted)

7. me

8. whom

9. We

10. Whose

11. she

12. which

13. his

14. objective

15. Dear Professor Droner,
Unfortunately, I slept through your lecture on world history, so I failed the exam on Friday.
If you will give me a second chance, I will do better next time.

Your student,
Ima Snoozer

16. Dr. Droner, my history teacher, lectured for three hours and twenty minutes last Tuesday.

17. me

18. nonessential (we have only these two dogs and no others.)

19. Does train, action verb

20. (a) tragedies
(b) Commanders in Chief
(c) Tonys

21. When Ben-Hur hears; that the King of the Jews has arrived in Jerusalem

22. Jesus looks calm and kind, he looks like a king.

23. phrase

24. Friends' compliments encourage Casper.

25. worse

26. were looking, past progressive tense

27. "Having healed Ben-Hur's mother and sister of leprosy," modifies "Jesus"

28.

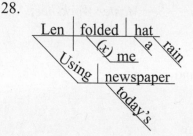

29.

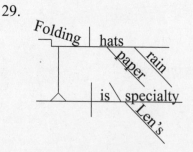

30.

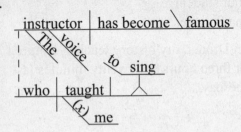

LESSON 65   Quotation Marks, Part 1

Practice 65

a. none

b. none

c. "The powers of the government relate to external objects," said Madison, "and are but few."

d. "Of all the dispositions and habits which lead to political prosperity," said George Washington, "Religion and Morality are indispensable supports."

e. loathe

f. loath

More Practice 65   *See Master Worksheets*

Review Set 65

1. modus operandi

2. downward

3. Primogeniture

4. Epidermis

5. bicameral

6. we ("have" is omitted)

7. we

8. clumsiest

9. us

10. yours

11. his

12. whom

13. that

14. Lew wallace's *Ben-Hur* are a mixture of history an intrigue

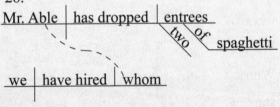

15. In his Inaugural Address, on January 20, 1961, President John F. Kennedy proclaimed, "The rights of man come not from the generosity of the state but from the hand of God."

16. The reader expected fewer details.

17. your or yours

18. will be celebrating, future progressive tense

19. becomes linking

20. While *Ben-Hur* chronicles a man's rise out of slavery

21. (a) yourselves
    (b) pocketfuls
    (c) analyses

22. nonessential (I have only one father)

23. clause

24. best

25. shop, (is) shopping, shopped, (has) shopped

26. Apologizing for our mistakes

27. Leaping like a kangaroo, modifies "Ieling"

28.

```
Mr. Able | has dropped | entrees
                              two  of  spaghetti

we | have hired | whom
```

29.

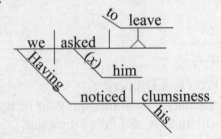

30.

we | Should have given | chance
(x) him — another — to improve

LESSON 66   Quotation Marks, Part 2

Practice 66

a. Ad hominem

b. ad hoc

c. ad hominem

d. ad hoc

e. Jody ran into the kitchen. "We got a letter!" he cried.
His mother looked up from a pan of beans. "Who has?"
"Father has. I saw it in his hand."
Carl strode into the kitchen then, and Jody's mother asked, "Who's the letter from, Carl?"

f. "The Used Car Lot" is a chapter from John Steinbeck's *The Grapes of Wrath*.

g. Have you ever heard the song "Winter Wonderland"?

h. James Thurber wrote an essay entitled "The American Literary Scene."

More Practice 66   *See Master Worksheets*

Review Set 66

1. Loath

2. modus vivendi

3. upward

4. eldest

5. affectation

6. I ("do" omitted)

7. I

8. more

9. us

10. ours

11. that

12. which

13. my

14. which (nonessential clause)

15. who

16. Dear Ms. Snoozer,
Grades have closed, so I cannot give you a second chance on the exam. Fortunately, you will have another opportunity to hear my lecture this Thursday, February 2, at the public library on Maple Avenue.
Sincerely,
Dr. Droner

17. I

18. Galileo, a modest and enthusiastic professor, performed the bulk of his scientific work at the University of Padua.

19. Had frozen, intransitive

20. even though the Pope condemned Galileo's findings

21. (a) donkeys
(b) ladies
(c) hypotheses

22. nonessential ("which" and commas are clues)

23. phrase

24. Lucy kept on humming the song "Take Me Out to the Ball Game."

25. worst

26.
Dear mrs. Chesterfield,
My base ball broke your stained glass window. i'm sorry. how much do i oew you?
sincerely,
Frankie Howard

27. "Devastated by his wife's death and his own blindness," modifies "Galileo"

28.

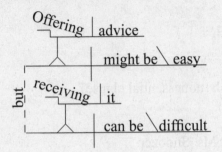

29.

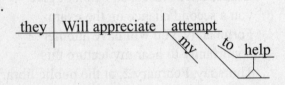

30.

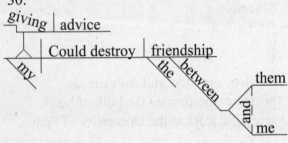

LESSON 67   Demonstrative Pronouns

Practice 67

a. grizzly

b. grisly

c. grizzly

d. This

e. Those

f. This

g. These

h. This

i. pointing

Review Set 67

1. Ad hoc

2. Loathe

3. prone

4. affection

5. appease

6. I

7. I ("did" omitted)

8. That, theirs, ours

9. deeper

10. This, us

11. who

12. that (essential clause, no commas)

13. Is trying, present progressive tense

14.
Victor Frankenstein became obsessed with the idea of creating life itself.

15. B

16. Dear Professor Droner,
By Friday, December 19, 2003, I will no longer be enrolled at this university. I plan to transfer to the University of Southern California, so I will not be able to attend your lecture.
Regretfully,
Ima Snoozer

17. they

18. Frankenstein, Victor's creation, now demands a mate.

19. sounds, linking verb

20. (after) he kills Victor's bride

21. (a) brothers-in-law
    (b) step-sisters
    (c) crises

22. Victor told the story to Robert Walton.

23. clause

24. "I think," said Amanda, "that John Paul Jones named his ship in honor of Benjamin Franklin, author of *Poor Richard's Almanac*."

25. most courageous

26. hurry (or hurries), (is) hurrying, hurried, (has) hurried

27. standing over Victor's body, modifies "monster"

28.

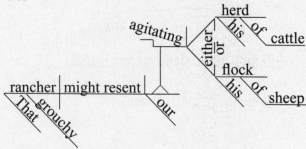

29.

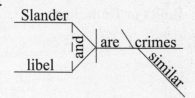

30.

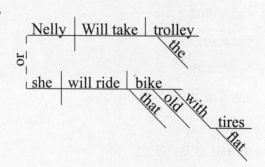

LESSON 68   Indefinite Pronouns

Practice 68

a. all, plural

b. Nothing, singular

c. agree

d. Do

e. speaks

f. share, their

g. is, its

h. wants, his/her

i. vorare

j. carnivorous

k. herbivorous

More Practice 68

1. E
2. P
3. S
4. S
5. S
6. E
7. S
8. P
9. S
10. P
11. S
12. P
13. S
14. S
15. P
16. E
17. S
18. P
19. E
20. E

Review Set 68

1. Grisly
2. Ad hominem
3. adjective
4. appease
5. peace
6. me
7. he ("does" omitted)
8. Whose

9. that

10. we

11. my

12. himself

13. Those, themselves

14. appreciates

15. Mary Shelly, the author of *Frankenstein*, liked to exchange scary stories with friends.

16. Have finished, present perfect tense

17. them

18. *Frankenstein* spawned two new literary genres, science fiction and horror.

19. essential ("that"/no commas)

20. (Since) Mary Shelly was vacationing with some of England's greatest writers

21. portrayed, action verb

22. H. G. Wells wrote *The Time Machine*.

23. An inquistive scientist beleives in ~~in~~ travel through ~~threw~~ time.

24. clause

25. noisier

26. steal, (is) stealing, stole, (has) stolen

27. "Engulfed by the fear of losing contact with his own age," modifies "Time Traveler"

28.
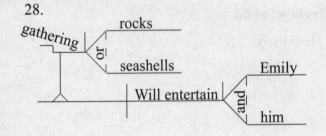

29.
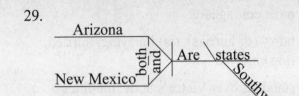

30.
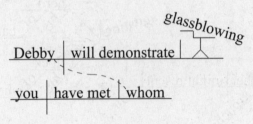

LESSON 69   **Italics or Underline**

Practice 69

a. lightning

b. lightening

c. lightning

d. lightening

e. The Purple Mountain Muse

f. huh

g. mimus polyglottos

h. bonjour

i. Nina

More Practice 69   *See Master Worksheets*

Review Set 69

1. vorare

2. Grizzly

3. verb

4. for a little while

5. mutual

6. he, themselves

7. I ("do" omitted)

8. washes, his or her

9. which (nonessential clause, commas)

10. us

11. His

12. those

13. remembers

14. "Unfortunately," said Ernie, "I missed the bus on Elm Street, so I took a taxi instead."

15. (a) parentheses
    (b) armloads
    (c) virtuosos

16.

Henry James ~~writed~~ wrote *The turn Of the Screw*, a_n_ early pyschological thriller⊙ I read it last year.

17. we

18. Manatees are nonaggressive herbivores, plant-eating animals.

19. nonessential (Notice the "which" and commas)

20. (While) the mystery surrounding the prior governess's death causes some alarm

21. were jumping, intransitive

22. either, singular

23. herself

24. complete sentence

25. better

26. The children's secrecy puzzles the governess.

27. "Having learned about Mr. Quint and Miss Jessel," modifies "governess"

28. Nihao

29.

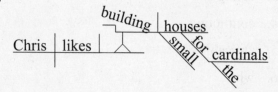

30.

cousins | sound \ immature
Those / quarreling

Practice 70

a. caught, (has) caught

b. fought, (has) fought

c. ate, (has) eaten

d. felt, (has) felt

e. beat, (has) beaten

f. drove, (has) driven

g. flowed, (has) flowed

h. fell, (has) fallen

i. built

j. bought

k. cost

l. come

m. drag

n. eaten

o. credence

p. *credere*

q. credulity

More Practice 70   *See Master Worksheets*

Review Set 70

1. Lightning

2. eat

3. Grisly

4. inhospitable

5. caucus

6. her

7. himself, we ("did" omitted)

8. plural

9. that (essential clause, no commas)

10. us

11. his

12. theirs

13. matches

14. My dad read me a chapter titled "Turning on the Light," but I didn't understand it, for it was too technical.

15. "Yes," said Ms. Wong, "We shall review the history of France next Monday."

16. relies

17. us

18. Shall squeeze, future tense

19. nonessential (Notice the commas and "which")

20. as soon as I finish this homework assignment

21. The ending surprised the governess.

22. several, plural

23. Andrew listens to his conscience he is is not afraid to stand alone.

24. phrase

25. most conducive

26. bring, (is) bringing, brought, (has) brought

27. to sit

28. Iliad

29.
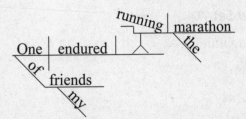

30.
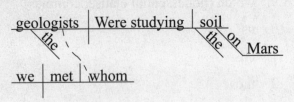

LESSON 71 **Irregular Verbs, Part 4**

Practice 71

a. made, (has) made

b. raised, (has) raised

c. lost, (has) lost

d. hid, (has) hidden

e. held, (has) held

f. laid, (has) laid

g. rode, (has) ridden

h. rose, (has) risen

i. lent, (has) lent

j. led

k. went

l. put

m. run

n. noisy

o. noisome

More Practice 71   *See Master Worksheets*

Review Set 71

1. *credere*

2. Lightening

3. eating

4. conflicting

5. amicable

6. who

7. whom

8. appreciates, his or her

9. which

10. We

11. our

12. this

13. whom

14. brought

15. This novel is about a young man whose soul sells his ~~sole~~ for worldly vanity.

16. Henry Wotton tempts Dorian Gray.

17. our

18. everybody, singular

19. nonessential (Notice commas and "which")

20. (that) today was a holiday

21. might have been snoring, intransitive

22. all none, any, some, most

23. Having mastered the irregular verbs, perfect tense

24. sentence fragment

25. (a) trunkfuls
    (b) Justices of the Peace
    (c) calamities

26. build, (is) building, built, (has) built

27. Albrecht Dürer, a German artist who lived over five hundred years ago, painted a realistic, lifelike picture called *Young Hare*.

28. The Snail

29.

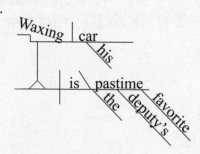

30.

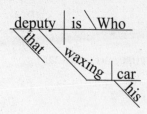

LESSON 72   Irregular Verbs, Part 5

Practice 72

a. shut, (has) shut

b. shone, (has) shined

c. shined, (has) shined

d. shook, (has) shaken

e. strove, (has) striven/strived

f. woke/waked, (has) waked/woken

g. taught

h. wrote

i. told

j. strove

k. swum

l. swung

m. figuratively

n. literally

o. figuratively

p. literally

More Practice   *See Master Worksheets*

Review Set 72

1. noisy

2. believe

3. Lightening

4. eating

5. census

6. whom

7. whom

8. needs, his/her

9. that (essential clause, no commas)

10. We

11. my

12. Those

13. hers

14. dove

15. Banishing the procrastinators, the sluggards, and the hoodlums, the queen keeps only the punctual, the diligent, and the conscientious in her palace.

16. "Next Tuesday," said Tina, "I shall fly from Denver, Colorado, to Dallas, Texas."

17. his

18. Much, singular

19. nonessential clause (Notice commas and "which")

20. herself

21. to expose, adjective (modifies "phony")

22. "Pontificating loudly from the balcony" modifies "Lord Chesnut"

23. Dorian gray will give his soul to stay yung

24. he, Lord Chesnut

25. less

26. eat, (is) eating, ate, (has) eaten

27. Does the artist Basil Hallward destroy the portrait of Dorian Gray?

28. *Homarus americanus*

29.

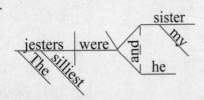

30.

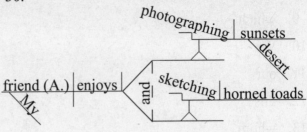

LESSON 73 — **The Exclamation Mark • The Question Mark • The Dash**

Practice 73

a. Impressive! Look . . . accomplished!

b. Do . . . Virginia militia?

c. Was it James McClurg?

d. Good deduction! You're right!

e. Volume One of the journal was dedicated to—let's see—James McClurg.

f. James McClurg deplored the leaders of his state—George Mason, John Blair, and Edmund Randolph.

g. Gus said, "Don't bump into the—" as Oscar hit the wall.

h. fiduciary

i. *fides*

j. affidavit

k. fiduciary

More Practice   *See "Hysterical Fiction #4" in Master Worksheets*

Review Set 73

1. Literally

2. Noisome

3. belief

4. Can

5. contemptuous

6. waves, who

7. whomever

8. wants, her

9. which (nonessential clause, notice commas)

10. us

11. Rex's

12. Those, ours, yours

13. saw, that

14. bitten

15. If you will pay attention, I shall read you a chapter titled "Forgiveness Brings Healing."

16. Lord Henry leads Dorian Gray down the path off level.

17. her, hers

18. (a) Has proved, action
    (b) Did prove, linking

19. essential (no commas, "that")

20. clause

21. evaluating your essays

22. complete sentence

23. had come

24. (whenever) I talk about baking rhubarb pies

25. (a) theses
    (b) Curtises
    (c) editors in chief

26. fall, (is) falling, fell, (has) fallen

27. Dorian Gray pursued a life of wild joys.

28. Merrimac, Monitor

29.

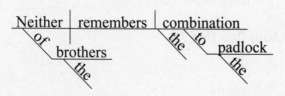

30.

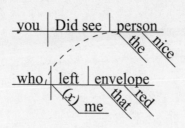

LESSON 74 — Subject-Verb Agreement, Part 1

Practice 74

a. suggests

b. listen

c. displease

d. signs

e. explains

f. absorb

g. concurrent

h. *currere*

i. cursory

More Practice 74

1. taste

2. sounds

3. live

4. grow

5. are

6. love

7. was

8. were

9. was

10. have

Review Set 74

1. *fides*

2. Figuratively

3. unrelated

4. Credence

5. incriminate

6. who

7. her

8. has, its

9. that

10. We

11. Rob's

12. Those, were

13. Their, already

14. taken

15. "Hey!" yelled Rob. "Where are my socks?"

16. Basil Hallwood beged Dorian Gray two repent of his sins.

17. your, yours

18. saved, transitive

19. nonessential clause

20. his, Dorian Gray

21. to solve, adjective

22. most exuberant

23. Some, singular

24. (before) he throws away the old ones

25. tell, (is) telling, told, (has) told

26. Lord Henry, the devil's advocate, had poisoned Dorian's soul.

27. (a) elves
    (b) latches
    (c) secretaries

28. The Horse and His Boy

29.

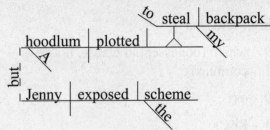

30.

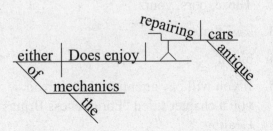

LESSON 75 — Subject-Verb Agreement, Part 2

Practice 75

a.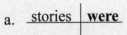
stories | were

b.
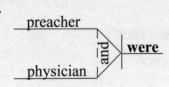
preacher
and > were
physician

c. list | reads

d.
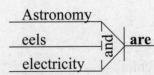
Astronomy
eels
and > are
electricity

e. limp

f. limpid

g. limp

h. limp

More Practice 75

1. sits

2. smells

3. is

4. come

5. are

6. reminds

7. makes

8. is

9. live

10. flies

Review Set 75

1. *currere*

2. faith

3. figurative

4. consul

5. censure

6. whomever

7. she

8. washes, his or her

9. which

10. us

11. our

12. tastes

13. hers

14. mistaken

15. The theme of "Our Town," by Thornton wilder, is the magic of the ~~the~~ mundane.

16. Dear Mr. Wilder,
    Your play helps people to treasure everyday life.
    Your fan,
    Sophia

17. and, but, or, for, nor, yet, so

18. Did appear, linking

19. essential clause

20. phrase

21. to bring, noun

22. nominative, objective, and possessive cases

23. each, singular

24. (that) represents vanity and ostentation

25. go, (is) going, went, (has) gone

26. "Using the simplest scenery and props," modifies "Stage Manager"

27. Did a haze obscure the stars last night?

28. <u>Mud Valley Herald</u>

29.

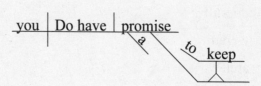

30.

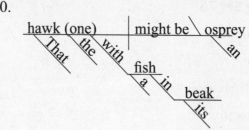

LESSON 76	Subject-Verb Agreement, Part 3

Practice 76

a. isn't

b. help

c. weren't

d. There are

e. speaks

f. *flectere*

g. genuflect

h. flexor

More Practice 76

1. allow

2. were

3. isn't

4. complains

5. wants

6. expects

7. works

8. plans

9. sleeps

10. hopes

11. leaves

12. doesn't

13. weren't

14. aren't

Review Set 76

1. Limpid

2. run

3. affidavit

4. literally

5. commendation

6. Who

7. me

8. wants, her

9. who

10. we

11. his

12. stand

13. They're, their

14. has, ridden

15.
   during the Great Depression, which lasted from 1929 to 1939, millions of americans lost thier jobs, their homes, and their financial security.

16. "Furthermore," said Uncle Sid, "I lived in Iowa during the 1930s. Food and other supplies were rationed, so it was a difficult time for everyone."

17. playing chess

18. has been sneezing, present perfect progressive tense

19. nonessential clause

20. run-on sentence

21. worse

22. us

23. some, plural

24. she, April

25. give, (is) giving, gave, (has) given

26. In Samuel Taylor Coleridge's poem, "Rime of the Ancient Mariner," the Mariner kills an albatross, a web-footed sea bird, which is later tied around his neck.

27. (a) birches
    (b) bays
    (c) selves

28. In *Moby Dick*, Ishmael clings to a shipmate's coffin floating in the ocean.

29.

30.

LESSON 77   **Subject-Verb Agreement, Part 4**

Practice 77

a. remains

b. keeps

c. provides

d. examines

e. park

f. has

g. is

h. denotes

i. connotes

j. denotes

k. connotes

Review Set 77

1. *flectere*

2. Limp

3. Cursory

4. fiduciary

5. Constitution

6. Has

7. was

8. whoever

9. he, their

10. passes, his, or her

11. your

12. sleeps

13. hers

14. there, gone

15. Dr. Pain says that my ambiguous statements confuze her.

16. Dear Mr. Van Winkle,
    Why did you sleep twenty years? Were you tired?
    Sincerely,
    Mr. Longfellow

17. either/or, neither/nor, not only/but also, both/and

18. Did follow, transitive

19. nonessential clause

20. phrase

21. "to unravel," adjective

22. nominative, objective, possessive

23. any, singular

24. Since I know that wise people take advice, I shall consider what you say.

25. strive, (is) striving, strove, (has) striven/strived

26. "grumbling about high prices" modifies "Jo."

27. passive voice

28. Belshazzar's Feast

29.
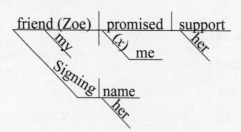

30.
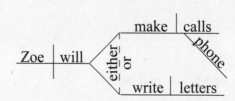

LESSON 78   **Negatives • Double Negatives**

Practice 78

a. ever

b. could

c. anything

d. ever

e. any

f. posthumous

g. posterior

h. post

i. posterior

More Practice 78

1. an
2. anything
3. anywhere
4. anything
5. any
6. any
7. ever
8. any
9. anyone
10. either

Review Set 78

1. mean
2. bend
3. limp
4. Concurrent
5. *i.e.*
6. whom
7. He and I, you and her
8. is, his or her
9. which
10. We
11. our
12. wants
13. doesn't, yours
14. swum
15. have
16. "All right," replied Rawlin, "I will feed the chickens, collect the eggs, and clean the coop while you, Caleb, are surfing at Newport Beach."
17. thinking about other people's needs
18. had been producing, past perfect progressive

19. essential clause
20. (after) the squirrel chewed it
21. more generous
22. they
23. much, singular
24. she, Mrs. Curtis
25. sleep, (is) sleeping, slept, (has) slept
26. In teñ poem "Casey at Bat," five thousand fanˢ saw casey strike out.
27.   (a) Sherrys
      (b) bagfuls
      (c) sons-in-law
28. C, Coopers, Changs
29.

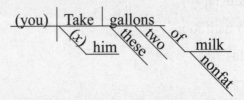

30.

LESSON 79   **The Hyphen: Compound Nouns, Numbers**

Practice 79

a. flaunt
b. flout
c. flaunt
d. flout
e. send-off
f. twenty-five, forty-eight
g. ninety-year-old

More Practice 79

1. thirty-one
2. forty-six
3. seventy-two
4. eighty-nine
5. 1-0
6. sign-in
7. cover-up
8. up-and-down
9. great-grandfather, father-in-law's
10. free-for-all

Review Set 79

1. *post-*
2. suggest
3. flexor
4. clear
5. gravitate
6. participle
7. She and I, you and him
8. has, his or her
9. any
10. I
11. my
12. accomplishes
13. Weren't
14. woven
15. In *The Divine Comedy*, Dante ridiculed Plato and other "pagan" philosophers.
16. Last Tuesday, March 3, I found several pizza coupons that had expired on December 31, 1998.
17. to scream, noun
18. had earned, past perfect tense
19. nonessential clause
20. (even though) I wanted to scream with frustration; (as) other students were doing
21. both/and, either/or, neither/nor, not only/ but also
22. it
23. most, singular
24. in addition to *sleuthing
25. run, (is) running, ran, (has) run
26. Does look, linking
27. sentence fragment
28. S̶o̶ Paul was inspired to write, "for now we see t̶h̶r̶e̶w̶ through a glass darkly . . . ."
29.

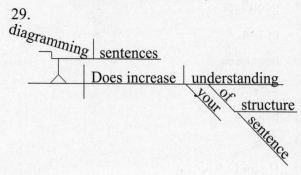

30.

LESSON 80   Adverbs that Tell "How"

Practice 80

a. "Publicly" and "wholeheartedly" modify "fought."
b. "Viciously" and "methodically" modify "criticized"
c. "Sincerely" modifies "believed"
d. adjective, modifies "Charles Pinckney"
e. adverbs, modify the verb "sought"

f. adjective, modifies "Constitutional Convention"

g. adverb, modifies "opposed"

h. *Odyssey*

i. Penelope

j. odyssey

k. odyssey

Review Set 80

1. flaunt

2. after

3. denote

4. genuflect

5. power

6. negatives

7. they

8. has, its

9. ever

10. He and I, she

11. us

12. is

13. Is

14. saw

15. I

16. "One-third of my class has already read the first fifty-two chapters of the Spanish novel," said Ms. Flores, the department head.

17. "Having completed her essay" modifies "Blanca"

18. is memorizing, present progressive tense

19. essential

20. (even though) she had a sore throat

21. (a) basketfuls
    (b) cliffs
    (c) axes

22. him

23. most, singular

24. hungriest

25. lose, (is) losing, lost, (has) lost

26. Are complaining, intransitive

27. complete sentence

28. <u>Les Miserables</u>

29.

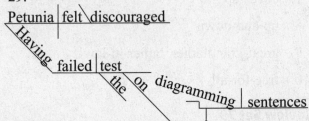

30.

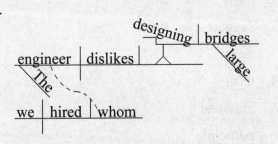

LESSON 81   **Using the Adverb *Well***

Practice 81

a. well

b. good

c. well

d. good

e. well

f. constituents

g. Gerrymandering

h. Constituents

More Practice 81

1. good

2. well

3. well

4. good

5. good

6. well

7. well

8. good

9. well

10. good

Review Set 81

1. Odysseus

2. flout

3. back

4. connote

5. sensible

6. adverbs

7. She and I, he

8. our

9. themselves

10. Aren't

11. hers, doesn't, theirs

12. whom

13. that

14. eaten

15. meaner

16. The Monday before last, Dr. Baker spent twenty-five minutes reading us a short story by Hans Christian Andersen. Its title was "The Princess and the Pea."

17. (a) gerund
    (b) participle
    (c) verb

18. The librarian read several captivating stories by Dr. Seuss to all fifty children.

19. nonessential

20. so that the prince will never see Cinderella

21. and, but, or, for, nor, yet, so

22. he

23. (a) adverb
    (b) adjective

24. he, Kurt

25. catch, (is) catching, caught, (has) caught

26. phrase

27. In spite of the *darkness; throughout the *night; for the escaped *cougar; from the local *zoo

28. run-on sentence

29.

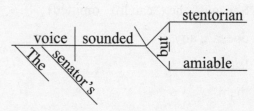

30.

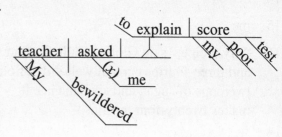

LESSON 82   **The Hyphen: Compound Adjectives**

Practice 82

a. G-rated

b. re-search

c. self-nominated

d. none

e. ten-foot

f. latter

g. later

h. latter

i. later

Review Set 82

1. Gerrymandering

2. odyssey

3. defy

4. after

5. appropriation

6. could

7. is

8. has

9. We

10. She and I, he ("can lift" omitted)

11. doesn't, any

12. leaves, its

13. them

14. driven

15. me

16. "My recipe," said Gloria, "calls for four and three-fourths cups of well-sifted flour, two cups of sugar, and six bananas. It makes twenty-four muffins."

17. (a) gerund
    (b) participle
    (c) verb

18. has lost, present perfect tense

19. (as soon as) the audit is complete

20. nonessential clause

21. (a) Krises
    (b) sheaves
    (c) editors-in-chief

22. she

23. (a) adverb
    (b) adjective

24. Aunt Helen often repeats her favorite old saying, "A stitch in time saves nine."

25. cost, (is) costing, cost, (has) cost

26. tastier

27. Alice had a curious dream you can read about it in *Alice in Wonderland.*

28. Los Angeles Times

29.

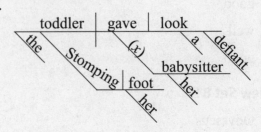

30.

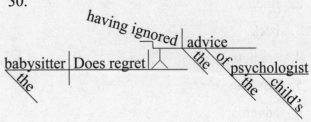

LESSON 83   **Adverbs that Tell "Where"**

Practice 83

a. "out" modifies stands

b. "up" modifies has come

c. "around" modifies were following

d. "nowhere" modifies has traveled

e.

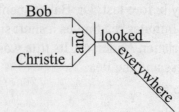

f.

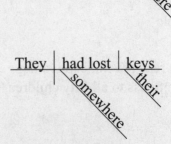

g. enacting clause

h. eminent domain

Review Set 83

1. Later

2. redrawing

3. journey

4. giddiness

5. suffrage

6. good

7. she and I, him

8. doesn't, my

9. I

10. isn't

11. doesn't, yours, hers

12. who

13. which

14. ridden

15. most

16. "Pardon me, Mrs. Curtis, but isn't this a one-way street?" asked Fernando.

17. (a) participle
    (b) verb
    (c) gerund

18. Have studied, present perfect tense

19. essential

20. (wherever) she went

21. Most, plural

22. you

23. (a) adverb
    (b) adjective
    (c) adjective

24. phrase

25. feel, (is) feeling, felt, (has) felt

26. My parents admonished me not to climb the tree during a thunderstorm again.

27. to write, adjective

28. Mr. Abernathy says that his aunt might have been acquainted with the Queen of Scotland.

29.

30.

LESSON 84   Word Division

Practice 84

a. none

b. emi-nent

c. odor-ous

d. none

e. none

f. sixty-four

g. Proteus

h. Procrustes

i. protean

j. procrustean

More Practice 84

1. none

2. none

3. con-note

4. none

5. Pro-crus-tes

6. posthumous

7. none

8. con-stitu-ent

9. affi-davit

10. photo-copy

11. cre-dence

12. cur-sory

13. con-cur-rent

14. hepta-gon

15. step-mother

16. oxy-gen

17. as is

18. herbi-vor-ous

19. hemi-sphere

20. light-ning

Review Set 84

1. Eminent domain

2. later

3. constituent

4. Penelope

5. allusion

6. doesn't, a

7. is

8. was

9. us

10. they

11. she, sing

12. has, his or her

13. Those

14. they

15. blew

16. "Yes," Tom admitted, "I served time in prison for a terrible crime."

17. (a) participle
    (b) verb
    (c) gerund

18. have been picking, present perfect progressive tense

19. true

20. (When) Rose of Sharon's baby arrived

21. Steinbeck's *The Grapes of Wrath*, a masterpiece, portrays a family's optimism despite a harsh struggle against death and greed.

22. your

23. (a) adverb
    (b) adjective

24. clause

25. set, (is) setting, set, (has) set

26. most destructive

27. (a) categories
    (b) geniuses
    (c) testimonies

28. The Saturday Evening Post

29.

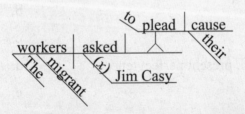

30.

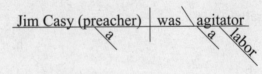

LESSON 85   Adverbs that Tell "When"

Practice 85

a. "Earlier" modifies "had favored"

b. "eventually" modifies "became"

c. "daily" modifies "cautioned"

d. "tomorrow" modifies "will resolve"

e. Mom | quotes | Ben Franklin
   daily

f. He | loathed | laziness
   always

g. ascent

h. assent

i. assent

Review Set 85

1. Procrustes

2. eminent domain

3. Latter

4. legislative

5. hector

6. well

7. he, her and me

8. my

9. me

10. aren't

11. doesn't, yours

12. whom

13. that

14. flew

15. less

16. Dear Mr. Steinbeck,
    The Grapes of Wrath is an unforgettable story. Thank you for encouraging us to be more responsible and compassionate.
    With appreciation,
    Stacy

17. (a) verb
    (b) gerund
    (c) participle

18. have been scrutinizing, present perfect progressive tense

19. who is running for the senate, nonessential; that he opposed yesterday, essential

20. ⟨although⟩ we know it as *Mona Lisa*

21. either, singular

22. my

23. (a) How? (answered)
    (b) When?
    (c) Where?

24. and, but, or, for, nor, yet, so, either/or, neither/nor, not only/but also, both/and

25. stand, (is) standing, stood, (has) stood

26. Last Week end Annie read a book
    by Rudyard Kipling, she she doesn't
    remember its title.

27. (a) no hyphen
    (b) as is
    (c) tooth-brushes

28. Smithsonian

29.

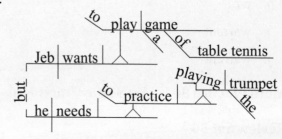

30.

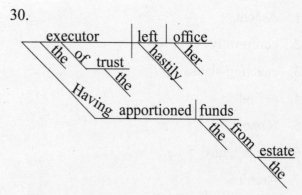

Practice 86

a. "extremely" modifies the adjective "incisive"

b. "rather" modifies the adverb "poignantly"

c. "absolutely" modifies the predicate adjective "certain"

d. "very" modifies the predicate adjective "appreciative"

e. "n't" modifies "did receive"

f.

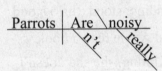

g.

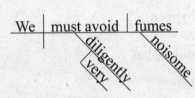

h. writ

i. warrant

j. warrant

More Practice 86   *See Master Worksheets*

Review Set 86

1. Ascent

2. conformity

3. enacting clause

4. period

5. Nestor

6. doesn't, any

7. Aren't

8. makes

9. We

10. he, we ("speak" omitted)

11. know, their (swimmers can be counted)

12. saw, those

13. drew

14. me

15. declarative

16. On July 17, 2004, a team of twenty-six swimmers met in Ocean Grove, New Jersey, for a relaxing, refreshing, revitalizing weekend.

17. (a) participle
    (b) verb
    (c) gerund

18. Spunk seemed rude and uneducated because of his poor table manners; did you notice?

19. "which leaves no room for creativity," nonessential clause

20. Unfortunately, my dog Spunk consumed the whole pumpkin pie.

21. more protean

22. our

23. (a) restful, restfully
    (b) careful, carefully

24. compound

25. sit, (is) sitting, sat, (has) sat

26. Peter Ilych Tchaikovsky, a great Russian musician, composed a famous ballet called *The Nutcracker*.

27. (a) oxen
    (b) pocketfuls
    (c) calves

28. The Peaceable Kingdom

29.

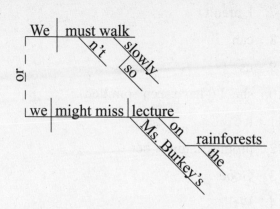

30.

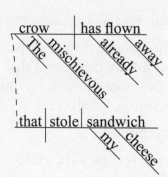

LESSON 87 — Comparison Adverbs

Practice 87

a. highest

b. more vehemently

c. better

d. most skillfully

e. worse, worst

f. bootleg

g. prohibition

More Practice 87

1. most faithfully

2. less

3. hardest

4. better

5. longer

6. worse

7. best

8. faster

9. less

10. most

Review Set 87

1. warrant

2. Assent

3. Procrustean

4. aware

5. few

6. well

7. they

8. well prepared

9. well-prepared

10. our

11. doesn't, aren't, ours

12. who, any

13. which

14. beaten

15. loudest

16. "Wait!" shouted Inspector Sniff. "I am not finished. I shall inspect the sewer, test the gas line, and examine the soil after lunch."

17. "Having ruled out our compost pile" modifies "Inspector Sniff"

18. dreamed, past tense, intransitive

19. simple

20. sentence fragment

21. who

22. us

23. (a) joyful, joyfully
    (b) truthful, truthfully

24. to exaggerate, noun

25. write, (is) writing, wrote, (has) written

26. everyone, singular

27. fifty-five, up-to-the-minute

28. In 1757, Jonathan Edwards accepted the presidency of the College of New jersey, Which latter became Princeton University.

29.

30.

LESSON 88   **The Semicolon**

Practice 88

a. The list . . . first; . . . second; and

b. Briefs . . . scandalous matter; they are limited to fifty pages.

c. The Congresswoman's speech . . . re-election; therefore, it was labeled "bunk."

d. premiere

e. premier

f. premier

More Practice 88   *See Master Worksheets*

Review Set 88

1. Prohibition

2. authorization

3. upward

4. Proteus

5. *etc.*

6. feeds

7. I, aren't

8. can

9. us

10. she, I ("have seen" omitted)

11. led

12. promises, his or her

13. Good

14. Well

15. to prove, adjective; to protect, adjective

16. "No," said Amelia to the sleepy camper, "You might fall asleep; therefore, I shall guard the campsite tonight." (or) . . . might fall asleep. Therefore, I shall . . .

17. guarding the campsite

18. is thinking, present progressive tense, action verb

19. where he finds a job on a whaling ship

20. clause

21. essential part

22. and, but, or, for, nor, yet, so

23. better

24. Ishmael and Queequeg board the *Pequod*, a whaling ship in the wind-swept Atlantic.

25. swing, (is) swinging, swung, (has) swung

26. The crew spots Moby Dick, a larger-than-usual sperm whale with a white forehead and a malicious temper.

27. A fierce typhoon descends upon the *Pequod*, and raging winds rip the sails still Captain Ahab urges the vessel forward to hunt down Moby Dick.

28. good, nice

29.

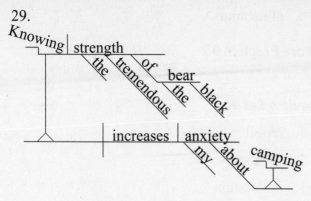

30.

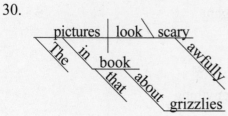

LESSON 89   **Descriptive Adverbs • Adverb Usage**

Practice 89

a. repeal

b. appeal

c. appeal

d. accurately, falsely, confidently

e. politely, loudly, often, softly, uncontrollably

f. surely

g. really

h. really

i. badly

j. real

k. bad

More Practice 89

1. surely

2. really

3. certainly

4. really

5. really

6. badly

7. bad

8. badly

9. badly

10. bad

Review Set 89

1. premier

2. restricted

3. writ

4. plutocrat

5. Sybaritic

6. she, themselves

7. ever, ridden, them

8. more

9. out-of-town

10. out of town

11. my

12. doesn't, isn't, ours

13. whom

14. well

15. flown

16. "Stop!" screamed Doris to the rooster. "Do you realize that vicious animals live beyond the fence? They might harm you, but I shall protect you."

17. One-legged Captian Ahab has sworn death for ~~for~~ the gigantic white whale that cripled him.

18. Will crow, future tense, intransitive

19. (so that) I can sleep

20. (a) gerund
    (b) participle
    (b) verb

21. nonessential

22. we

23. best

24. compound sentence

25. teach, (is) teaching, taught, (has) taught

26. nevertheless

27. Samara brought my three favorite ice cream flavors—fresh strawberry, French vanilla, and chocolate chip.

28. Ishmael, a simple seaman, narrates the story of *Moby Dick*.

29.

30.

LESSON 90   **The Colon**

Practice 90

a. . . . 9:00 a.m. daily.

b. Hebrews 12:14-15 offers . . .

c. . . . the following amenities: one hundred eighty forested acres, . . .

d. Dear President Lincoln:
Thank you . . .

e. . . . about Henry Clay: "I don't like . . . ."

f. assonance

g. consonance

h. alliteration

More Practice 90   *See "Hysterical Fiction #5" in Master Worksheets*

Review Set 90

1. repeal

2. Premier

3. prohibition

4. extravagant

5. lucky

6. weren't, ever

7. Those, anything

8. Does

9. we

10. they, I

11. adverb

12. really, well

13. has, his or her

14. striven

15. me

16. infinitive

17. gerund

18. "Come back here, you silly rooster!" yelled Doris. "You do not belong to me; nevertheless, I feel responsible for you since you are my guest." (or) ". . . belong to me. Nevertheless, I feel . . ."

19. phrase

20. enters, present tense, action verb

21. (as) he ends his sermon about Jonah and the whale

22. either, singular

23. more carefully

24. think, (is) thinking, thought, (has) thought

25. run-on

26. on the other hand

27. (a) shouldn't
    (b) north-eastern

28. Jen brought lettuce, tomatoes, and cheese; and Rob brought chips, salsa, and tortillas.

29.
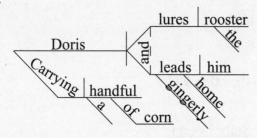

30.

1.
This was my aunts sugarcoated plea. My dearest niece, will you please feed my gila monster while Im away?" "Oh, anything but that!" I replied, for those monsters gila really frighten me.

m. malodorous

n. malevolent

More Practice 91   *See Master Worksheets*

Review Set 91

1. consonance
2. repealed
3. premiere
4. fortuitous
5. come
6. Does
7. she, really, well
8. grown
9. began, were
10. Your, there
11. his
12. who
13. more
14. Moby Dick bit off Ahab's leg.
15.

"Only Ishmael lives too tell the tail tale of Moby Dick, Ahab, and the *Pequod*," said Mr. Vega.

16. "Having taken part of Heaven with him" modifies "Moby Dick."

17. "If you search deeply," commented Mrs. Pencall, "you will see that Herman Melville's novel reveals the struggle between good and evil."

LESSON 91   **Proofreading Symbols, Part 2**

Practice 91

a. ⌄⌄
b. ⊙
c. ⌄
d. ⌃;
e. ¶
f. ⌃
g. ⌃
h. =
i.
j. (tr)
k. ⌇

18. Herman Melville recognized the power of both God and the devil.

19. *Moby Dick* has captured the interest of many people: young readers, naturalists, historians, and literary scholars.

20. looked, past tense, linking verb.

21. (that) the ship and its crew will eventually meet catastrophe

22. essential

23. she

24. snap, (is) snapping, snapped, (has) snapped

25. run-on sentence

26. compound sentence

27. however

28. mal-o-dor-ous

29.

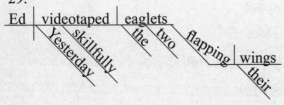

30.

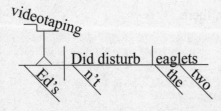

LESSON 92   The Prepositional Phrase as an Adverb • Diagramming

Practice 92

a. "like a gentleman" modifies "behaved"

b. "as a brigadier general" modifies "served"

c. "over the troops" modifies "watchful"

d. "in public opinion" modifies "high"

e.

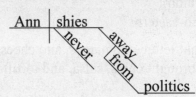

f.

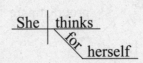

g. as

h. as

i. like

j. Like

More Practice 92

1.

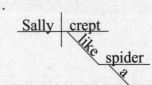

2.

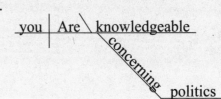

3.

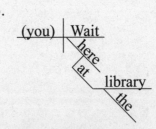

4. as the *"Little Giant"

5. In *1854; of *protest; from the Northern *opposition

Review Set 92

1. mal-

2. Consonance

3. revoke

4. arrival

5. Explicit

6. ever, eaten

7. he, really

8. conscience-stricken

9. conscience stricken

10. my

11. doesn't, its

12. Whom

13. hardest

14. slain

15. Aeschylus wrote *Prometheus Bound*, a classical tragic drama.

16. "to avoid" is an adjective

17. <u>sopa con frijoles</u>

18. Dear Zeus,
    I cannot support your edict to destroy all mankind, for it seems too violent.
    Your subject,
    Prometheus

19. Does Zeus usurp the throne from the old Titan King Chronus?

20. hopes, present tense, transitive

21. (Even though) mankind appears flawed

22. essential

23. him

24. buy, (is) buying, bought, (has) bought

25. Prometheus gived people fire and teached them how to use it.

26. in addition

27. obe-dient

28. Ian purchased these camping supplies: lanterns, tarps, propane, and marshmallows.

29.

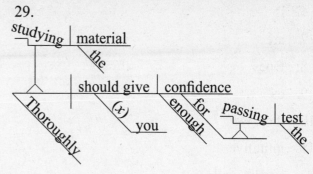

30.

LESSON 93   Preposition or Adverb? •
                 Preposition Usage

Practice 93

a. adverb

b. preposition

c. preposition

d. adverb

e. besides

f. into

g. among

h. catacombs

i. catapult

j. cataclysm

k. down or against

Review Set 93

1. as

2. bad

3. Assonance

4. blaze of light

5. noticeable

6. is

7. are

8. Does

9. us

10. they, we

11. infinitive

12. surely, well

13. keeps

14. sung

15. which

16. (a) Chrises
    (b) Dannys
    (c) beaches

17. <u>Sus scrofa</u>

18.
In Greek mythology, Prometheus, a Titan god, bestows upon humanity the gift of fire this angers Zeus.

19. Wilhelm Konrad Roentgen, a great German physicist, discovered X rays in 1895.

20. Zeus demands revenge for Prometheus's treasonous crimes.

21. where an eagle preys on him

22. essential

23. most carefully

24. sell, (is) selling, sold, (has) sold

25. one, singular

26. at the same time

27. A man with red hair and a mustache—I don't remember his eye color—tip-toed past the security guard and into the museum after hours.

28. The museum has been robbed; several ancient artifacts have disappeared.

29.

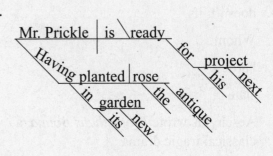

30.

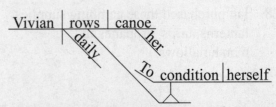

LESSON 94

The Infinitive as an Adverb • The Infinitive Phrase • Diagramming

Practice 94

a. *cub-*

b. incumbent

c. succumb

d. incumbent

e. recumbent

f. noun

g. adverb

h. adjective

i. to hike Mt. Whitney, enough

j. to join the hikers, hopeful

k. To reach the summit tomorrow, must start

l.

Vivian | rows | canoe
(diagram: her, daily, To condition | herself)

More Practice 94

1.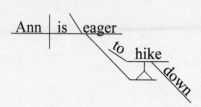

2.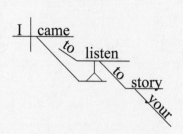

3.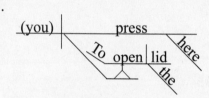

4.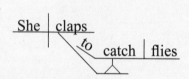

5.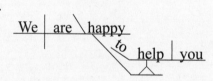

6.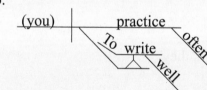

Review Set 94

1. cata-

2. as

3. Malodorous

4. vulnerable

5. Altogether

6. her, really

7. doesn't, anybody

8. fast-moving

9. fast moving

10. our

11. There are, hers

12. who

13. surely, well

14. risen

15. flown, farther

16. into, among

17. not, quite, very, rather, somewhat, too

18.
   Oceanus says to Prometheus, "Please ask forgiveness from Zeus."
   "No," answers Prometheus, "I would rather suffre."

19. (a) rose bushes
    (b) truckloads
    (c) geese

20. will have been married, future perfect progressive tense, action verb

21. compound sentence

22. and, but, or, for, nor, yet, so

23. them

24. make, (is) making, made, (has) made

25. asso-nance

26. for this reason

27. Merrimac, Monitor

28. I have memorized the eight parts of speech: nouns, pronouns, verbs, adjectives, adverbs, conjunctions, prepositions, and interjections.

29.

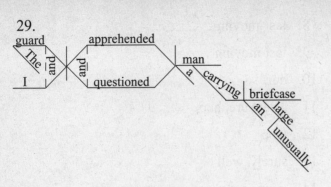

30.

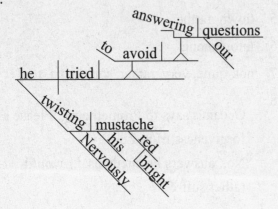

LESSON 95   The Apostrophe: Possessives

Practice 95

a. prototype

b. proto-

c. protocol

d. protoplasm

e. sisters-in-law's

f. James's

g. mice's

h. ex-Presidents'

i. deer's

j. Ross's

More Practice 95

1. gallery's

2. chief's

3. bus's

4. slave's

5. prototype's

6. boss's

7. puppy's

8. baboon's

9. trout's

10. flies'

11. Democrats'

12. nuclei's

13. societies'

14. men's

15. cattle's

16. radii's

Review Set 95

1. *cub-*

2. cataclysm

3. as

4. all together

5. stir

6. anything

7. is

8. Isn't

9. We

10. we, laugh, they

11. adverb

12. surely

13. remains

14. lay, well

15. that, its

16. One day prometheus would be freed from bondage, an Zeus would be defeated.

17. here, still, almost, now, quite

18. Dear Io,

　　　I am so sorry that Zeus turned you into a cow. Someday you will be restored to your true form.

　　　With compassion,
　　　Prometheus

19. to drive a car—adjective

20. Have been ripping—present perfect progressive tense, transitive, active voice

21. (whatever) you want; (if) you'll help me to clean up the feathers

22. essential clause

23. anyone—singular

24. hold, (is) holding, held, (has) held

25. more gently

26. consequently

27. Miss Beagle, Buttercup, and Fluffy had littered the floor with their toys—catnip-filled balls, rawhide bones, and stuffed animals.

28.
The drama *Prometheus Bound* seized Elle's imagination; moreover, it caused her to reflect on some philosophical ideas.

29.
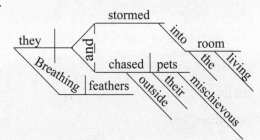

30.
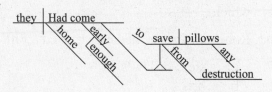

Practice 96

a. haven't, studyin'

b. Wasn't, livin', '46

c. She's, it's

d. c.o.d.'s

e. hadn't

f. we're

g. ade

h. aid

i. aide

j. aid

More Practice 96　　*See Master Worksheets*

Review Set 96

1. *proto-*

2. Incumbent

3. catapult

4. do

5. boundaries

6. he, really

7. adverb

8. full-time

9. full time

10. our

11. ours, theirs, anywhere

12. whom, doesn't

13. Badly

14. flew

15. more

16. besides, between

17. a. The Rivases'
    b. Larry's
    c. brother-in-law's

18. "The Blue Socks, a women's softball team from Azusa City, have had bad luck," said Lorna. "They haven't won a single game."

19. Bob replied, "They'd do better if they practiced the essential skills—batting, throwing, catching, and running."

20. In 1719, Daniel Defoe, an English novelist and journalist, wrote *The Life and Adventures of Robinson Crusoe*, a tale about a shipwrecked sailor marooned on an island.

21. compound sentence

22. If you cut Samson's hair; (while) he is sleeping; (when) he awakes

23. she

24. Robinson Crusoe

25. clause

26. mal-odorous

27. nevertheless

28. Robinson Crusoe domesticated goats for their milk, butter, and meat.

29.

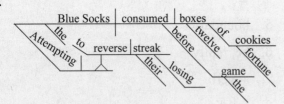

30.

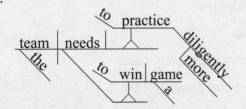

Practice 97

a. rectus

b. rectify

c. rectitude

d. noun clause (sentence subject)

e. adjective clause

f. noun clause (direct object)

g. adverb clause

h. noun clause (predicate noun)

Review Set 97

1. Aid

2. prototype

3. Incumbent

4. *fin-*

5. anyway

6. any

7. believes

8. those, their

9. Is

10. We, they ("have had" omitted)

11. transitive

12. really

13. promises, her

14. striven

15. which

16. Robinson Crusoe had constructed a raft.

17. a. sisters-in-law's
    b. Chris's
    c. The Cruzes'

18. "Phooey!" yelled the coach after another dismal loss. "My team lost again;

nevertheless, we shall not give up." (or) "... again. Nevertheless..."

19. Do~es~ everyone Ɖrown ~accept~ except
Robinson#Crusoe?

20. most loudly

21. No one-singular

22. (Since) all other crewmen perish; (where) no one else lives

23. and, but, or, for, nor, yet, so

24. wake, (is) waking, woke or waked, (has waked

25. "putting on her batting gloves" modifies woman

26. proto-plasm

27. hence

28. Had been keeping- past perfect progressive tense; action verb

29.

Tamara | ran | bases
(diagram with: the, gleefully, Having hit | ball, a, high, fly, to, field, center)

30.

fielder | Does have | reputation
(diagram with: the, center, a, for, catching | balls, high, fly)

LESSON 98   **Diagramming the Noun Clause**

Practice 98

  a. euthanasia

  b. eu-

c. eulogy

d. euphoria

e.
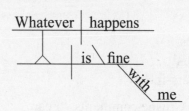

f.
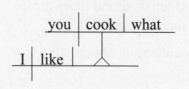

g.
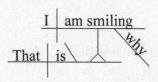

h.
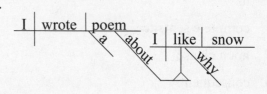

Review Set 98

1. rectus

2. aide

3. Protocol

4. any way

5. trajectory

6. noun

7. clause

8. long-lost

9. me, your

10. Brian's

11. who

12. doesn't, any

13. worse

14. worst

15. A hurricane and an earthquake damage Robinson Crusoe's supplies.

16. Crusoe begins too read the bible and seke forgiveness.

17.
    a. foxes'
    b. ladies'
    c. fathers-in-law's

18. Robinson Crusoe comments, "Fear of danger is ten thousand times more terrifying than danger itself."

19. either/or, neither/nor, not only/but also, both/and

20. most malevolently

21. essential

22. (when) I arrive in Palm Beach; (if) the phones are working

23. us

24. complete sentence

25. noun clause

26. consequently

27. Wally's Whaler II

28. Will feel- future tense, linking verb

29.

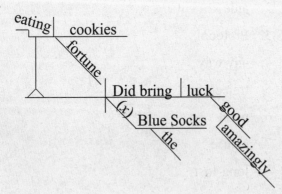

30.

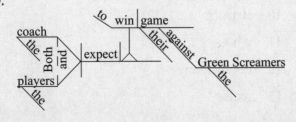

LESSON 99

The Complex Sentence • The Compound-complex Sentence • Diagramming the Adverb Clause

Practice 99

a. simple

b. complex

c. compound-complex

d.

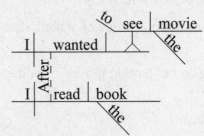

e. dyslexia

f. dys-

g. dysfunction

h. dysfunctional

i. dyspepsia

j. dyspeptic

More Practice 99

1. complex

2. compound

3. simple

4. compound-complex

5. complex

6.

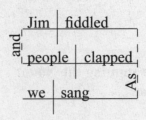

Additional Diagramming Practice
See Master Worksheets

Review Set 99

1. *eu-*
2. rectify
3. lemonade
4. throw
5. compose
6. she
7. really well
8. sixty-ton
9. exclamatory
10. your
11. a, themselves
12. that
13. who, doesn't
14. shone
15. better
16. between
17. (a) Ms. Cox's
    (b) pilgrims'
    (c) Jonathan Edwards's
18. Friday and Robinson Crusoe rescued two
    man from a boiling pot.
19. Allison's gentle words ameliorate strained
    relations; moreover, her magnanimous acts
    of kindness bring peace.
20. more loudly
21. nonessential
22. (that) his island is near Trinidad
23. I
24. simple
25. adverb clause
26. exempli gratia
27. for example

28. Having been managing—present perfect
    progressive tense; transitive

29.

30.

LESSON 100   **Parallel Structure**

Practice 100

a. B
b. A
c. B
d. At . . . a leopard, an elephant, and a
   python. (or) a leopard, elephant, and
   python.
e. On . . . against hunger, against thirst, and
   against fear. (or) . . . against hunger, thirst,
   and fear.
f. bona fide
g. caveat emptor
h. carpe diem

More Practice 100

1. Maribel placed . . . around her room, inside
   her wallet, and on her refrigerator.
2. I will leave the key *either* outside the door
   or inside the house.
3. Hans has *neither* the time *nor* the money to
   take a vacation.

4. Mia <u>studied</u> her Mandarin, <u>called</u> her friend, and <u>walked</u> her dog.

5. This . . . <u>organizing</u>, <u>cleaning</u>, and <u>packing</u> for the trip.

6. Rawlin has <u>the strength of</u> an ox, <u>the speed of</u> a cheetah, and <u>the wisdom of</u> an owl.

7. . . . the desire, energy, and conviction . . . (or) . . . <u>the</u> desire, <u>the</u> energy, and <u>the</u> conviction . . .

8. . . . <u>without</u> . . . computer games, <u>without</u> . . . restaurants, and <u>without</u> her television set. (or, use the preposition with only the first part.)

9. . . . Mario likes <u>to read</u> historical novels, <u>to play</u> chess, and <u>to work</u> jigsaw puzzles.

10. <u>Mr. Li grows</u> *not only* delicious plums, *but also* large, juicy apricots.

Review Set 100

1. *dys-*

2. right

3. good

4. comprises

5. stubborn

6. doesn't, any

7. returns

8. were

9. those

10. us

11. intransitive

12. surely

13. has, his

14. shone

15. that

16. comes

17. (a) people's
    (b) seamstress's
    (c) matron of honor's

18. Dear Mr. Canty,
    I've wonderful news for you. Your son Tom has switched places with the Prince of Wales.
    Truly,
    Miles Hendon

19. Will Tom Canty find a monk named Father Andrew at the monastery?

20. dys-function

21. his—Tom Canty

22. eat, (is) eating, ate, (has) eaten

23. either/or, neither/nor, both/and, not only/but also

24. complex

25. adjective clause

26. "Wearing the Prince's clothes" modifies Tom.

27. moreover

28. has observed—present perfect tense; action verb

29.

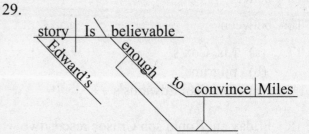

30.

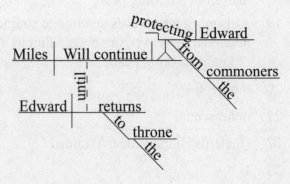

Practice 101

a. Combine the sugar, flour, and spices

b. Should we vote to reelect him for President?

c. We shall study anthropology for a month.

d. Your writing style is unique.

e. The rancher from Iowa had never seen the ocean.

f. The monument in Colorado marks the continental divide.

g. We have been reading Longfellow's poetry.

h. Hepsy listened attentively.

i. *Rogare*

j. interrogate

k. abrogate

l. arrogate

Review Set 101

1. Bona fide

2. bad

3. Euthanasia

4. draw

4. Any one

6. he

7. surely, well

8. complex

9. subordinate

10. doesn't, anything

11. our

12. whom

13. coordinating conjunction

14. faster

15. shined

16. among

17.   (a)   stallions'
      (b)   apprentices'
      (c)   men's

18. "Molly, if you wish to avoid Dad's displeasure," warned Kurt, "You will wash the dirty plates, cups, and spoons."

19. Johnny's employer, Mrs. Lapham, gives Madge, Dorcas, and Cilla permission to marry Mr. Tweedie; however, the three girls have their own preferences. (or) . . . Mr. Tweedie. However, . . .

20.   (a)   calamities
      (b)   Ashleys
      (c)   Maxes

21. nonessential

22. most notoriously

23. me

24. simple

25. as soon as the engine parts arrive; adverb

26. To Kill a Mockingbird

27. consequently

28. While on vacation, Kalvin plans to stay in a luxurious hotel, eat delicious food, and swim in a heated pool.

29.

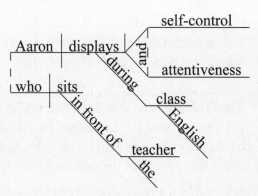

30.

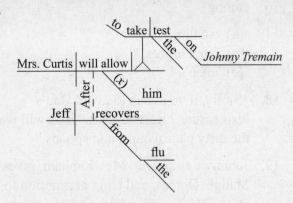

LESSON 102   Dangling or Misplaced Modifiers

Practice 102

a. B

b. A

c. B

d. B

e. acquisitive

f. requisition

g. *quaerere*

h. inquisition

More Practice 102

1. (1) Dangling modifier—Sounds like my fork is eating dinner. (2) While I was eating dinner, my fork flipped off the table.

2. (1) Misplaced participle phrase—Sounds like France has been written and revised. (2) The terms of the Louisiana Purchase having been written and revised, France was ready to accept the document.

3. (1) Misplaced prepositional phrase—Sounds like an orangutan was on its way to school! (2) On the way to school, Yin saw an orangutan.

4. (1) Dangling modifier—Was France doubling its size? (2) France agreed to sell the Louisiana Territory to the U.S., doubling its size.

5. (1) Dangling modifier—Sounds like the bus was tying the writer's shoe. (2) While I was tying my shoe, the bus left without me.

6. (1) Dangling modifier—Were the seats leaving the chamber? (2) As we were leaving the Old Senate Chamber, the seats were empty.

7. (1) Misplaced modifier—Was the loophole examining the Constitution? (2) Examining the Constitution, Thomas Jefferson found a loophole.

8. (1) Dangling modifier—Was the law attempting to act quickly? (2) Attempting to act quickly, Congress passed the law.

9. (1) Misplaced modifier—Sounds like Mom is cold and windy. (2) Mom recommended we come inside since it was cold and windy.

10. (1) Misplaced prepositional phrase, "after class." Does it tell when Tui wanted to know, or when the teacher said something? (2) Place "after class" either at the beginning or end of the sentence.

11. (1) Dangling modifier—Sounds like a fly was boiling potatoes! (2) While I was boiling potatoes, a fly landed in the pot.

12. (1) Misplaced modifier—Sounds like the writer was blocking traffic. (2) I could hardly wait till the road construction was finished because it was blocking traffic.

Review Set 102

1. *rogare*

2. *Caveat emptor*

3. impaired

4. every one

5. Everyone

6. aren't, any

7. enjoys, his or her

8. hand-drawn

9. she ("has" omitted)

10. We

11. compound-complex

12. really

13. attend

14. risen

15. which

16. The kittens were meowing softly.

17. (a) Andy's
    (b) The Yans'
    (c) Mr. Kruis's

18. Dr. Breanna Walker, I hope, will perform Mrs. Buxton's kidney transplant scheduled for Thursday, October 26, at 9 a.m.

19. "Where is your assignment?" asked Professor Chen.
     "It is finished," whispered Jon, "but I left it at home."

20. teach, (is) teaching, taught, (has) taught

21. Louisa May Alcott, a nurse during the American Civil War, wrote classic novels such as *Little Women* and *Little Men*, which depict a deep sense of family loyalty and intimacy.

22. proto-type

23. his—Denver; it—grammar book

24. compound sentence

25. (that) we postpone the math test—adjective

26. passive voice

27. moreover

28. Ashley's chores include washing the dishes, mopping the floor, and feeding the dog.

29.

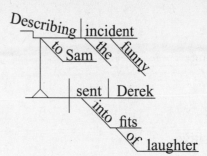

30.

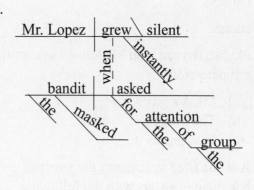

LESSON 103   **Parentheses • Brackets**

Practice 103

a. [Thurgood Marshall]

b. (205)

c. (disruptive people in Congress)

d. (wow!)

e. complement

f. *ple-*

g. deplete

h. replete

Review Set 103

1. *quis*

2. ask

3. Carpe diem

4. deduction

5. envelope

6. she

7. really, well

8. active

9. passive

10. anything

11. our

12. who

13. intransitive

14. hardest

15. shone

16. Skylar, Brycen, and Madeline have written a superb story.

17. (a) Ms. Vargas's
    (b) The Vargases'
    (c) Wednesday's

18. Adelina tried to reassure the worried Nicaraguan sisters with the following words: <u>Para Dios no hay nada imposible</u>.

19. "I cycle every day to keep in shape, and I haven't had a flat tire yet.," declared Mr. Sousa.

20. (a) Rufuses
    (b) gratuities
    (c) ladies-in-waiting

21. B

22. more (or less) succinctly

23. our

24. complex sentence

25. (as) Samantha guided the Shetland pony through the market place—adverb clause

26. active voice

27. on the other hand

28. Sam says he bought a bike, a helmet, and a tire pump.

29.

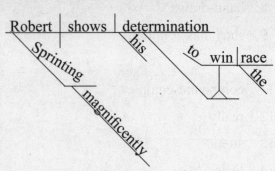

30.

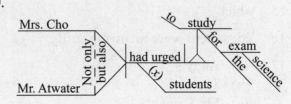

LESSON 104   Interjections

Practice 104

a. Ah

b. Goodness!

c. Well

d. Cool!

e.

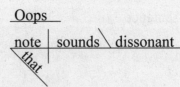

f.

Oops

note | sounds \ dissonant
that

g. dissonant

h. *Son-*

i. sonata

j. sonorous

Review Set 104

1. fill

2. obtain

3. interrogate

4. conclusion

5. sequence

6. isn't, anyone

7. leaves, his

8. I ("have" omitted)

9. chocolate covered

10. us

11. surely, well

12. dangling modifier

13. has

14. that

15. Using scraps of wood, Maggie made a unique birdhouse.

16. has been bringing—present perfect progressive tense

17. (a) island's
    (b) Laertes's
    (c) philosophers'

18. Reading the <u>Global Review</u>, Mrs. Sykes discovered that tickets for balcony seats cost two hundred fifty dollars ($250) each, but she and Lauren are still going to see <u>The Tempest</u>.

19. "I think," said Mrs. Sykes to her daughter, "that experiencing a live play will change your opinion of William Shakespeare."

20. Prospero, the rightful Duke of Milan, is the main character in *The Tempest*.

21. B

22. essential—no commas (I have more than one friend)

23. drive, (is) driving, drove, (has) driven

24. simple sentence

25. (that) Prospero treats him kindly—noun clause

26. Prospero calls up a storm.

27. Prospero gives his governmental power to Antonio; however, Prospero does not approve of Antonio's seizure of the throne.

28. Antonio takes the reins of government, captures Prospero and Miranda, and sets them adrift at sea.

29.

30.

LESSON 105   **Directory Information about a Word**

Practice 105

a. 1. to pay little attention to. 2. lack of attention

b. noun

c. effluvia, effluviums

d. ef·fer·ves·cent

e. ef˘·i·ka´·sh□s

f. Latin

g. Anatomy

h. erratic

i. *errare*

j. aberrant

k. erroneous

Review Set 105

1. son

2. complement

3. interrogation

4. order

5. neutral

6. isn't, anyone

7. phrase

8. surely

9. he

10. Besides

11. any

12. your

13. whom

14. transitive

15. lesser

16. I slept well last night because I had finished all my homework.

17. Has cast—present perfect tense, transitive

18. (a) Gonzalo and Sylvius's
    (b) play's
    (c) costumes'

19.
    "Sebastian and antonio's plot to kill Alonso Was downright wicked," said Mrs. Curtis

20. My favorite characters from *The Tempest* are these: Prospero, Miranda, Ariel, Caliban, and Gonzalo.

21. (a) Marquezes
    (b) Emilys
    (c) theses

22. B

23. most (or least) awkwardly

24. their

25. compound-complex

26. (as) he mourns his father—adverb clause

27. Prospero gave Ferdinand menial work.

28.
Prospero rejoices at the devotion between Miranda and Ferdinand; (nevertheless,) Prospero demands proof of Ferdinand's devotion.

29. Jesse prepared for the test by memorizing the prepositions, studying the vocabulary, and practicing sentence diagrams.

30.

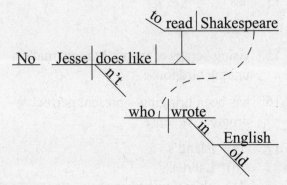

LESSON 106   **The Subjunctive Mood**

Practice 106

a. were

b. were

c. stay

d. were

e. call

f. recession

g. *cedere*

h. procession

i. precedent

Review Set 106

1. *errare*

2. sound

3. completes

4. Bacchus

5. Apollo

6. she ("has" omitted)

7. us

8. dangling modifier

9. phrase

10. Eppie's

11. any

12. which (nonessential)

13. transitive verb

14. worse

15. loan

16. were

17. (a) lady's
    (b) Silas's
    (c) friends'

18. A witness said, "The shop owner [Hargus Bigg] threw a jar of pickles at the masked bandit."

19.

    "Did the jar of pi^ckles actually hit the masked bandit?" asked the ~~the~~ reporter. ¶ "No," replied Mr. Bigg.

20. Silas Marner, once a respected elder in a small fundamental sect, is now a lonely, bitter man.

21. A

22. essential

23. sell, (is) selling, sold, (has) sold

24. simple sentence

25. (that) his life was growing more and more empty—noun clause

26. Squire Cass threw the nightly parties in Raveloe.

27. Silas Marner acknowledged his obsession with money; (nevertheless,) he continued to accumulate gold and caress his coins.

28. Rita raised her grades by doing her homework, by watching less TV, and *by* asking for help with difficult concepts.

29.

30.

LESSON 107

Spelling Rules: Silent Letters *k, g, w, t, d,* and *c*

Practice 107

a. wres(t)le

b. (w)ho

c. (g)nu

d. (k)now

e. (k)nit

f. (k)nelt

g. (G)nostic

h. (w)rangler

i. *verbum*

j. verbose

k. verbatim

l. verbiage

Review Set 107

1. Cedere

2. Aberrant

3. music

4. Delphic

4. natural talent

6. we

7. surely

8. clause

9. Besides

10. were

11. Thurvis's

12. who

13. any, between

14. more

15. Through the fog, the stop sign was barely visible.

16. Had been hiding—past perfect progressive tense, transitive

17. (a) Eppie and Cass's
    (b) squires'
    (c) citizens'

18.

"If Jasper ~~was~~ were malevolent, I wouldn't trust him," said Ann. ¶ "What makes you think he's trustworthy?" asked Kim.

19. Some significant characters in *Silas Marner* have uncommon names: Silas, Godfrey, Dunstan, and Eppie.

20. (a) Marquezes
    (b) Godfreys
    (c) analyses

21. A

22. most serenely

23. her

24. compound sentence

25. even though Godfrey is her father— adverb clause

26. Eppie rejects Godfrey

27.

Mr. Blab's speeches are usually verbose; on the other hand, his written reports are succinct.

28. Godfrey is thankful for his wife, *his* life, and his daughter.

29. B

30.

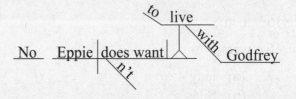

LESSON 108   **Spelling Rules: Silent Letters** *p*, *b*, *l*, *u*, *h*, *n*, and *gh*

Practice 108

a. g**u**illotine

b. thorou**gh**

c. **h**arisma

d. **h**hinoceros

e. so**l**der

f. **gh**ost

g. cou**l**d

h. cha**l**k

i. de**b**t

j. **p**neumatic

k. bom**b**

l. yo**l**k

m. *ped-*

n. pedicure

o. centipede

p. pedometer

q. impede

Review Set 108

1. Verbiage

2. procession

3. aberrant

4. Replete

5. sequence

6. intransitive verb

7. has, his

8. they

9. self-conscious

10. We

11. phrase

12. well

13. after

14. between

15. Richard (also called Doc, Monty, and Orthocratus) straightens people's teeth beautifully.

16. (a) wh(a)ck
    (b) he(d)ge
    (c) (k)nowle(d)ge

17. (a) mistress's
    (b) Shinji and the master's
    (c) shadows'

18. In November, 2004, <u>Zoological Digest</u> magazine featured an article titled "The Heavy Elephant."

19. "What's the title of that modern <u>japanese</u> novel by Yukio Mishima?" asked Phil. ¶ "I don't remember," replied Jenny.

20. Yukio Mishima, a Japanese novelist, wrote during the 1950s and '60s about the dichotomy between traditional Japanese values and the spiritual barrenness of the contemporary life.

21. B

22. essential part (I have other friends besides Mildred. —no commas)

23. slay, (is) slaying, slew, (has) slain

24. complex

25. (where) we were going—noun clause

26. Scot drove Sybil and Lilibet to the airport.

27. *The Sound of Waves* portrays the triumph of good over evil; in addition, it gives us a simple picture of island life.

28. In *Their Eyes Were Watching God*, Zora Neale writes to relieve her frustrations, to strike out for equality, and to find her identity.

29. A

30.

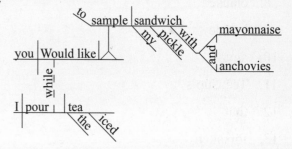

LESSON 109   **Spelling Rules: Suffixes, Part 1**

Practice 109

a. shameless

b. drowsily

c. weariness

d. steadiest

e. forceful

f. slaving

g. lately

h. tamer

i. famous

j. skating

k. plentiful

l. *dole-*

m. condolence

n. dolorous

o. doleful

Review Set 109

1. *verbum*

2. *ped-*

3. erroneous

4. *son-*

5. complement

6. me

7. she, really

8. clause

9. beside

10. any

11. Tea Cup's

12. that

13. forsaken

14. I think anchovies taste terrible.

15. Tea Cup spent more than fifty dollars ($50) on a party for his railroad friends.

16. (a) lam(b)
    (b) (g)nome
    (c) (p)syc(h)e

17. (a) refugees'
    (b) lice's
    (c) chicken's

18. C'est la vie, a French phrase meaning "that's life," sums up my attitude after my flight to Europe was cancelled.

19.
"I'm sorry," said the doctor, "but Tea Cup has con tracted rabies from the ~~the~~ dog bite."

20. (a) groomsmen
    (b) alumni
    (c) rallies

21. B

22. more hastily

23. their

24. compound-complex

25. (As) we watched the sad movie together— adverb clause

26. Tornadoes and dust storms impeded our journey across the country.

27. We should break for lunch because it's after one o'clock; (besides), I'm hungry.

28. Because of his eye injury, Reuven remains in the hospital, receives visitors, and listens to the radio.

29. B

30.

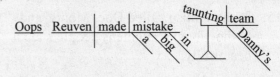

LESSON 110

Spelling Rules: Suffixes, Part 2

Practice 110

a. chipped

b. flopping

c. badly

d. eyeful

e. sadness

f. retro-

g. retrograde

h. retrospect

i. retrograde

j. retrogress

Review Set 110

1. *dole-*

2. hinder

3. verbatim

4. precedent

5. stray

6. anyone

7. promises, his/her

8. she

9. fast-moving

10. us

11. brackets

12. well

13. really

14. between

15. (a) lecturing
    (b) blameless
    (c) rectified

16. (a) knickers
    (b) neighbor
    (c) patch

17. (a) Mr. Saunders's
    (b) The Adamses'
    (c) Danny's

18. <u>Procyon lotor</u> is the scientific name for raccoon, a black-masked mammal that lives in trees in North and Central America.

19.

My brothers left ~~there~~ their muddy socks on the porch. They should toss them into the washing machine.

20. Reuven and Danny, Jewish teenagers, play on opposing baseball teams.

21. A

22. nonessential part

23. All the painted walls look fresh and clean.

24. simple sentence

25. that inched across my burrito—adjective clause

26. The screeching brakes frightened Hatteras Pinochle.

27.

John has backed up his computer files and installed new software; in addition, he has scanned the computer for viruses.

28. Cats generally don't like swimming for recreation, riding in cars, or sharing their food.

29. B

30.

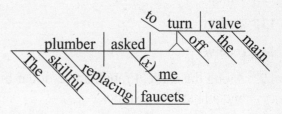

LESSON 111   **Spelling Rules: *ie* or *ei***

Practice 111

a. niece

b. seize (exception)

c. reprieve

d. receipt

e. weight

f. sleigh

g. *loqu-*

h. colloquy

i. loquacious

j. soliloquy

Review Set 111

1. walks

2. retrograde

3. doleful

4. speak

5. unusual

6. them

7. they, really

8. phrase

9. fast thinking

10. were

11. those

12. which

13. striven

14. receive

15. Along the shore, I found a five-dollar bill and a heart-shaped rock.

16. (a) guardian
    (b) plumber
    (c) folk

17. (a) Chris's
    (b) dogs'
    (c) sheep's

18. Harper Lee's most famous novel, <u>To Kill a Mockingbird</u>, illustrates the maturing of a young girl named Scout.

19.
The meadowlark is a ~~very~~ unique North <u>american</u> songbird that sings aⁿ exuberant, flute-like, bubbling song from a ~~a~~ conspicuous perch.

20. (a) prefixes
    (b) oxeye daisies
    (c) Thomases

21. (a) hopping
    (b) gladly
    (c) plotted

22. most succinctly

23. them

24. compound sentence

25. (that) he is lost in Africa—noun clause

26. Dale and his brothers-in-law built this three-story mansion.

27. false

28. B

29. Like my uncle, I always enjoy catching crawdads.

30.

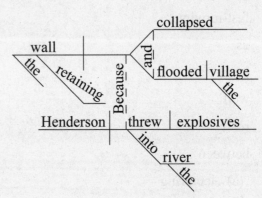

Writing Lessons Answer Key

Lesson 1   During a thunderstorm, Manny found a wet, shivering cocker spaniel on his porch. First Manny checked the dog's license and found the owner's phone number. Then he notified the owner, a Mrs. Perez, and gave her his address. After the heavy rain ceased, Mrs. Perez picked up her lost dog and handed Manny a freshly-baked loaf of bread to thank him.

---

a.   While she sleeps, Margaret dreams about chess tournaments. Upon waking she begins thinking about how she can convince her friends to play games of chess with her. Throughout the day, she ponders new strategies for winning the game. There is nothing she would rather do than play chess. <u>Margaret is a chess enthusiast.</u>

---

b.   <u>Opossums are a benefit to any area they inhabit.</u> They eat cockroaches and garden pests such as slugs and snails. They also eat the overripe fruit that litters the ground. Resistant to disease, these friendly creatures seldom carry rabies. Constantly grooming themselves, they are almost always clean. Best of all, they are not aggressive and will not attack humans.

---

c.   Quan has been studying geology, botany, and zoology. He reads every book he can find on these subjects, and he watches many nature documentaries on television. <u>Quan is preparing to become a forest ranger.</u> Whenever he has an opportunity, he goes hiking and camping in the wilderness, where he feels at home, and where he can identify every plant, animal, and insect he sees.

---

d.   Melissa wanted to write a report on her favorite music composer. First she searched her uncle's vast book cases but found nothing about this composer. She didn't find any helpful books on the shelves of the school library either. ~~Washing dishes is more fun than doing homework.~~ Even the large municipal library had no books about a composer named Hieden. When the search engine on her computer also produced nothing, Melissa felt like screaming with frustration. Finally, her teacher pointed out that she had misspelled the composer's name, which is Haydn instead of Hieden.

---

e.   I am running out of patience with my bicycle tires. They were flat yesterday morning, so I had to pump them, which made me late for school. Later, I spent all my allowance on new bicycle tires. ~~Besides that, I flunked my spelling test.~~ And now, after riding along the horse trail for less than a mile, I have found more than a dozen puncture weeds in each of my new tires. Surely they cannot hold air; they are full of holes! What am I going to do?

Lesson 2   1. The ability to communicate clearly and effectively in writing connects us with people and enhances our prospects for future success in school and in the workplace.

2. Learning to write well is one of the most important skills we need to master.

3. In the first place, writing well allows us to communicate with other people.

4. In the first place...

5. In conclusion...

Lesson 14   I. Essay types
  A. Persuasive
  B. Expository
  C. Narrative
  D. Descriptive

II. Poetry types
  A. Sonnet
  B. Limerick
  C. Haiku
  D. Free Verse   (Topics and subtopics may be in any order.)

I. American Presidents
  A. George Washington
    1. Father of our country
    2. Chopped down a cherry tree
  B. Abraham Lincoln
    1. Gettysburg Address
    2. Freed the slaves
  C. George W. Bush
    1. Former governor of Texas
    2. Twenty-first century President

          (Topics and subtopics may be in any order.)

Lesson 33   a.   Some birds that live in New Jersey migrate south for the winter. (footnote, **no footnote**)

b.   Chase Blackbeard decided to follow the birds that were flying south. (**footnote**, no footnote)

c.   Many species of birds spend the winter in Central America. (footnote, **no footnote**)

d.   With his digital camera, Chase Blackbeard wants to photograph the American redstart and the rose-breasted grosbeak. (**footnote**, no footnote)

e.   Birds are the most colorful during mating season. (footnote, **no footnote**)

Give after Lesson 10

For 1–4, write whether the sentence is declarative, interrogative, exclamatory, or imperative.

1. I'm reading *Johnny Tremain* by Esther Forbes. ___declarative___
(1)

2. Have you read any other Newbery Honor books? ___interrogative___
(1)

3. Memorize the Preamble of the Constitution of the United States of America. ___imperative___
(1)

4. You did it! ___exclamatory___
(1)

5. Circle each letter that should be capitalized in the following sentence: On (m)onday, (u)(s) citizens
(4) will celebrate (i)ndependence (d)ay.

In the space to the right, diagram the simple subject and simple predicate of sentences 6 and 7.

6. Have you heard of the Sons of Liberty?   you | Have heard
(1, 3)

7. Johnny burned his hand.   Johnny | burned
(1, 3)

For 8–15, circle the best word to complete each sentence.

8. The United States has a(n) (indirect, direct, belligerent) democracy.
(1, 3)

9. A pitbull with a(n) (antebellum, indirect, bellicose) disposition frightened Shant's German
(1, 3) shepherd.

10. The thief's (impeachment, affection, affectation) of innocence didn't fool me.
(4, 5)

11. (Advert, Avert, Appease) means "to turn away" or "to prevent."
(2)

12. A (bicameral, bellicose, direct) legislature has two branches.
(4)

13. (Affectation, Affection, Belligerence) is tender feeling, or fondness.
(5)

14. To "refer to" is to (advert, avert, appease).
(2)

15. To (advert, avert, impeach) is to bring formal charges against a public official.
(4)

For 16–18, write whether the word group is a sentence fragment, run-on sentence, or complete sentence.

16. Indians kidnap a four-year-old boy he acts like an Indian after eleven years. ___run-on sentence___
(2)

17. The stairway terrifies John Butler. ___complete sentence___
(2)

18. Feeling a dreaded sickness coming on. _sentence fragment_
(2)

Make complete sentences from fragments 19 and 20. Answers will vary.

19. The pain in his forehead. _The pain in his forehead eventually went away._
(2)

20. Floating down the river. _The explorers were floating down the river on a raft._
(2)

21. Add a period and capital letter to correct the following run-on sentence: True Son had stayed in
(2) the insidious company of white people too long. Their milkwarm water had gotten into his blood.

22. Circle each action verb in the following sentence: White men (shot) and (scalped) Little Crane, True
(3) Son's friend.

For 23 and 24, replace the blank with the singular present tense form of the italicized verb.

23. Most students usually _remember_ their assignments, but Andrew always ___remembers___ his
(5) assignments.

24. Justin and Trevor _study_ their vocabulary. Jared ___studies___ his vocabulary.
(5)

25. Circle the correct verb form for this sentence: My dog dug a hole and (buries, (buried)) his bone.
(5)

1. In the sentence below, circle each noun and label it *S* for singular or *P* for plural.
(7)
                    P   P   S
The skillful (players) dribbled and tossed (basketballs) up and down the (court).

2. In the sentence below, circle each noun and label it *F* for feminine, *M* for masculine, *I* for
(7) indefinite, or *N* for neuter.
                    I   M   F   N
In his new (family), True Son has (sisters) with dark (eyes).

3. Circle the compound noun in the following sentence: The boys remained hidden during the
(7) (daytime).

4. Circle the possessive noun in the following sentence: (Uncle Wilse's) scalp will always bear the
(7) marks of the (boys') tomahawks.

5. Circle the correct verb form for the following sentence: The boys discussed their mission and
(5) then (steal, (stole)) a canoe.

6. In the sentence below, circle the verb phrase and label it past, present, or future.
(5, 8)
    True Son and Half Arrow (will find) their way back to the Leni Lenape. ____future____ tense

7. In the following sentence, replace the blank with the singular present tense form of the
(5) underlined verb: All sodas <u>fizz</u>, but this one ____fizzes____ too much.

8. Circle the eight helping verbs from this list:
(6)

his   an   far   what   where   bee   (being)   (been)   day   night   rust   fan
(could)   (should)   wood   (has)   (have)   dad   dew   (does)   (did)   shell   well

In the space to the right, diagram the simple subject and simple predicate of sentences 9 and 10.

9. A search party will follow the boys into Indian country.   party | will follow
(1, 3)

10. Hide the canoe under the brush.   (you) | Hide
(1, 3)

11. In the blank, write whether the following expression is a sentence fragment, run-on sentence, or
(2) complete sentence: Just before daylight when Half Arrow woke him. ____sentence fragment____

12. Add a period and capital letter to correct the following run-on sentence: Cuyloga, True Son's
(2) Indian father, stands strong and impassive. His eyes reveal a deep welcome.

13. Circle each abstract noun from this sentence: By staying home from the movie to study, Nelly
(4) demonstrated (maturity) and (self-control).

14. Circle the collective noun in this sentence: The (audience) appreciates the dazzling performance of
(4) *Joseph and the Coat of Many Colors*.

15. Circle each letter than should be capitalized in this sentence: (C)onrad (R)ichter, author of (T)he (L)ight in
(9) *the* (F)orest, was born in (P)ennsylvania and later moved to (N)ew (M)exico.

16. Write the plural form of the noun *quiz*. _____quizzes_____
(7)

17. Unscramble these words to make an interrogative sentence.
(1)

you   what   about   do   know   Solomon

What do you know about Solomon?

For 18–25, circle the correct word to complete each sentence.

18. Will a glass of milk (advert, (appease,) avert) Loren's growling stomach?
(6)

19. The (antebellum, (inhospitable,) mutual) hermit chased all trespassers away.
(9)

20. (Common, Bicameral, (Mutual)) means "reciprocal."
(8)

21. ((Common,) Bicameral, Mutual) means "shared."
(8)

22. The noun *misery* is (concrete, (abstract)).
(4)

23. The noun *manatee* is ((concrete,) abstract).
(4)

24. A ((quorum,) hospice, caucus) is a number of persons needed in a meeting for business to take
(10) place.

25. The Latin word *hospes* means (ill, pilgrim, (guest)).
(9)

Circle the correct word to complete sentences 1–10.

1. Since I feel (ambiguous, bellicose, (ambivalent)) about both candidates, I can't decide who will
(3, 11) make the better President.

2. The (ambiguous, (amiable), bellicose) flight attendant greeted each passenger with a bright smile.
(11, 12)

3. David asked, "Nelly, ((may), can) I borrow your newest music CD?"
(14)

4. *Johnny Tremain* and *The Light in the Forest* (has, (have)) courageous heroes.
(12)

5. ((Do), Does) Indians and colonists really scalp one another in *The Light in the Forest*?
(12)

6. The Latin word (*hospes, vorare, (amare)*) means "to love."
(12)

7. A ((census), lobby, caucus) is an official count of people in any given place.
(13)

8. (Ambiguous, (Contemptible), Ambivalent) means deserving scorn; despicable.
(15)

9. (Amicable, (Contemptuous), Contemptible) means showing scorn; scornful.
(15)

10. We ((shall), will) drive to Niagra Falls this afternoon.
(8)

For sentences 11–13, circle the entire verb phrase and name its tense "past," "present," or "future" perfect.

11. Through the tiny keyhole in the old oak door, Mrs. Curtis (has spied) a masked bandit!
(15) _____present_____ perfect

12. High Bank and Niskitoon (had accompanied) Thitpan on his mission of revenge for Little Crane's
(15) death. _____past_____ perfect

13. By the end of the week, we (shall have completed) our persuasive essays. _____future_____
(15) perfect

14. Underline each noun is the following sentence, and circle the one that is collective: The hungry
(4) black <u>bear</u> spotted a (school) of <u>fish</u> swimming down the <u>river</u>.

15. Circle each abstract noun from this list: ((affectation)) warrior ((rage)) ((forgiveness)) ((affection))
(4)

16. Circle each possessive noun from this list: tribes ((tribe's)) ((tribes')) forests ((forest's)) ((forests'))
(7)

For 17–19, write the plural of each noun.

17. birch _____birches_____
(10, 11)

18. proxy _____proxies_____
(10, 11)

19. monkey ___monkeys___
(10, 11)

Circle each preposition in sentences 20 and 21.

20. The mothers (in) the tribe wish their sons would remain (at) home (because of) their youth.
(14)

21. (According to) the narrator, one son goes (into) the forest (along with) his friend.
(14)

22. Circle each letter that should be capitalized in the sentence below.
(9)

(m)rs. (c)urtis yelled, "(s)top that masked bandit before he or she steals my (d)ictionary (of) (word) (o)rigins!"

Diagram the simple subject and simple predicate of sentences 23 and 24.

23. Does Thitpan choose Disbeliever as a guide for the war party?
(2, 3)

Thitpan	Does choose

24. Why has Thitpan rejected Cuyloga as a guide?
(2, 3)

Thitpan	has rejected

25. Circle the complete sentence from the word groups below.
(2)

Conrad Richter lived in the Southwest there he devoted himself to fiction.

When the boat comes close to the bank of the river.

(True Son expresses his disapproval of harming children.)

Give after Lesson 25

Circle the correct word(s) to complete sentences 1–11.

1. (Incrimination, Recrimination, (Approbation)) is praise or commendation.
(16, 19)

2. In the end, True Son (have, (has)) finally learned the truth.
(12)

3. In 1818, Dr. Thomas Bowdler ((censored), censured, averted), or edited, Shakespeare's plays.
(18)

4. (Do, (Does)) True Son regret warning the white people about the ambush?
(12)

5. The following sentence is (declarative, interrogative, imperative, (exclamatory)): It's an ambush!
(1)

6. The following is a (sentence fragment, run-on sentence, (complete sentence)): True Son didn't
(2) answer.

7. A(n) (ex post facto law, writ of habeas corpus, (pocket veto)) occurs when the President holds a
(7, 20) bill unsigned until Congress adjourns.

8. A(n) ((ex post facto law), writ of habeas corpus, pocket veto) is one that allows punishment for a
(7, 20) crime that was not illegal at the time it was committed.

9. ((Probity), Censure, Recrimination) is integrity, honesty, and uprightness.
(19)

10. The Latin root *prob-* suggests (accusation, (honesty), scorn).
(19)

11. To (appease, lobby, (censure)) is to condemn or blame.
(18)

For 12 and 13, write the plural form of each singular noun.

12. Timothy ____Timothys____
(10, 11)

13. child ____children____
(10, 11)

14. Circle each letter that should be capitalized in the following passage: (i)n (c)onrad (r)ichter's (t)he (l)ight
(4, 9) *in the (f)orest,* (c)uyloga says, '(i) am (c)uyloga. (c)uyloga knows his son. (h)e is like (c)uyloga. (i)f he is
double-tongued and a spy, then (c)uyloga is also."

15. Circle each preposition from this sentence: Cuyloga explains (to) the warriors that he cannot watch
(14) them put his son (to) the fire, (in spite of) True Son's disloyalty.

For sentences 16–19, circle the entire verb phrase. Then complete the name of its tense by adding
"past," "present," or "future."

16. Cuyloga (had adopted) True Son into his family. ____past____ perfect tense
(15)

17. By the end of the story, True Son (will have returned) to the Butler Family. _____future_____
(15) perfect tense

18. (Will) Cuyloga (be mourning) for the rest of his life? _____future_____ progressive tense
(17)

19. Cuyloga (had been planning) on True Son's help in his later years. _____past_____ perfect
(15, 17) progressive tense

20. In the sentence below, underline each concrete noun and circle the two that are abstract.
(4)

True Son suffers (rejection) and (isolation) from his family.

21. Circle the gerund in this sentence: (Leaving) Cuyloga breaks True Son's heart.
(16)

22. Circle the infinitive in this sentence: (To remain) with the Indians would mean certain death.
(19)

For 23 and 24, circle to indicate whether the expression is a phrase or a clause.

23. with a sickening feeling and a sad heart   ((phrase) clause)
(20)

24. as he leaves his beloved family   (phrase, (clause))
(20)

25. In the space below, diagram the simple subject and simple predicate of the following sentence:
(3) True Son had been born into a frontier family.

True Son	had been born

Circle the correct word to complete sentences 1–14.

1. *Paradise Lost* features characters familiar to all, (**e.g.**, i.e., id est); Adam, Eve, God, and Satan.
(21)

2. (Judicial, Jurisdiction, **Judicious**) means having or exercising good judgment.
(22)

3. A (progressive, **perfect**) verb form shows action that has been completed.
(15, 17)

4. The sentence below is (declarative, interrogative, imperative, **exclamatory**):
(1)

You're too late!

5. The following is a (**sentence fragment**, run-on sentence, complete sentence):
(2)

Too proud to consider seeking re-admittance to Heaven through repentence.

6. The most commonly used adjectives, and the shortest, are the (**articles**, pronouns) *a, an,* and *the.*
(23, 24)

7. Examples of (**possessive**, descriptive) adjectives are *his, her, their, your, its, our,* and *my.*
(23, 24)

8. The following word group is a (phrase, **clause**): when the second in command proposed to
(20) subdue men as slaves

9. The following sentence contains a(n) (**action**, linking) verb: Satan felt self-doubt, fear, and envy.
(3, 18)

10. The abbreviation (e.g. **i.e.**, etc.) comes from a Latin term meaning "that is to say."
(21)

11. (**Jurisdiction**, Judicial, Judicious) is the range or extent of authority; power.
(22)

12. The Latin root (*prob-, crim-,* **lev-**) means to lighten or to raise.
(24)

13. When people feel they did not receive fair treatment in a lower court, they appeal to a higher
(23) court, an (appropriate, **appellate**, animated) court.

14. To (incriminate, amend, **apportion**) is to give out parts so that everyone gets his or her fair share.
(23)

For 15 and 16, write the plural form of each singular noun.

15. thief _____thieves_____
(10, 11)

16. liability _____liabilities_____
(10, 11)

Circle each letter than should be capitalized in 17 and 19.

17. **M**y professor said, "**I**n 1642, **j**ohn **m**ilton began to compose the dramatic version of *paradise* *lost*
(9, 25) based on the ancient **g**reek model of tragedy."

18. (dear) (professor) (holt),
(22, 25)
   (j)ohn (milton's) *paradise (l)ost* helps the reader to better understand (c)hristianity and religions of the (west).

                         (s)incerely,
                         (a)ndy

19. Circle each preposition in this sentence: (According to) this epic poem, Satan seduces Eve (by
(14) means of) nightmares and falsehoods.

20. Circle each abstract noun from this list: (repentence) garden beasts Eve (power) Adam
(4)

21. Circle the gerund from this sentence: Satan, also known as Lucifer, enjoys (plotting) the downfall
(16, 21) of mankind.

22. Circle the two infinitives from this sentence: Raphael's mission is (to explain) Satan's dreams and
(19) (to warn) Adam and Eve against further temptation.

23. For a–d, circle the correct irregular verb form.
(12)

   (a) They (has, (have))   (b) I ((am), is, are)   (c) He (do, (does))   (d) It (have, (has))

24. In the following sentence, circle the verb phrase and name its tense: Satan is tempting Adam and
(17) Eve. _____present progressive_____ tense

25. Diagram each word of the following sentence: The first woman heard speaking.
(3, 21)

Give after Lesson 35

Circle the correct word(s) to complete sentences 1–11.

1. The research assistant was (gravity, gravitate, (gravid)) with suggestions for the scientist.
(27)

2. Jane Eyre makes a(n) (illusion, (allusion), delusion) to Rochester's keeping a strange, hermit-like
(26) madwoman on the third floor.

3. The following sentence is (declarative, (imperative), interrogative, exclamatory): Stop the bleeding
(1) by applying pressure.

4. The following word group is a (sentence fragment, (run-on sentence), complete sentence): Mr.
(2) Mason arrives at Thornfield from Jamaica, someone stabs him during the night.

5. The following word group is a (phrase, (clause)): for he quietly left in the morning.
(20)

6. The noun or pronoun following a preposition is called the (subject, (object), modifier) of the
(28) preposition.

7. Vertical lines created the (delusion, (illusion), allusion) that the shape was taller than it really was.
(26)

8. A (hector, (cicerone), filibuster) guides sightseers through a museum or other interesting landmark.
(28)

9. (Cicero, (Hector), Pontius Pilate) was a Trojan warrior whose name now means "to bully,
(28) intimidate, or torment."

10. To (phase, (filibuster), faze) is to obstruct legislative action by long speeches or debate.
(29)

11. To (phase, filibuster, (faze)) is to perturb, disturb, or fluster.
(30)

12. Circle the concrete noun from this list: Cantonese   theory   compassion   (madwoman)   deceit
(4)

13. Circle the gerund from this sentence: The (stabbing) of Rochester's guest reveals the severity of
(16) the madwoman's illness.

14. Write the plural form of the singular noun *cry*. _____cries_____
(10, 11)

15. Circle each letter that should be capitalized in the following passage:
(9, 22)
(d)uring the marriage ceremony of (r)ochester and (j)ane, someone says, "(t)he marriage cannot go on. (i)
declare the existence of an impediment."

16. Circle the three prepositions in the following sentence: (Owing to) news (about) Rochester's
(14) previous marriage, Jane leaves Thornfield (with) a broken heart.

17. Underline each prepositional phrase, circling the object of each preposition in the following sentence:

(28)

Charlotte Brontë, author of _Jane Eyre_, spent much of her life under the influence of the parsonage at Haworth, Yorkshire, in northern England.

18. In the sentence below, circle the verb phrase and name its tense.

(8)

Jane's cousin, St. John Rivers, will ask Jane to marry him. _____future_____ tense

19. Circle the word from this list that is _not_ a helping verb: is, am, are, was, were, be, being, been, has, have, had, do, does, did, shall, will, should, would, sound, can, could, may, might, must

(6)

20. Circle the linking verb in this sentence: St. John seems sincere in his offer to marry Jane.

(18)

21. For a–d, circle the correct irregular verb form.

(12)

   (a) We (was, were)   (b) It (do, does)   (c) You (has, have)   (d) She (has, have)

For sentences 22 and 23, underline the verb and circle the direct object if there is one. Then circle to indicate whether the verb is transitive or intransitive.

22. Jane Eyre senses someone's need for her. (transitive, intransitive)

(21, 26)

23. During the night, Jane dreams about Rochester. (transitive, intransitive)

(21, 26)

24. Circle the indirect object in the following sentence: The dream gives Jane hope of Rochester's need for her.

(30)

25. Fill in the diagram below using each word of this sentence: Rochester tells Jane the unfortunate news of his wife's death.

(24, 30)

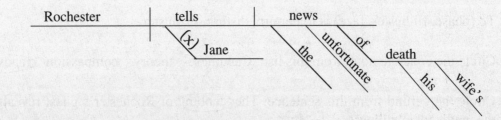

Give after Lesson 40

Circle the correct word to complete sentences 1–12.

1. Atticus Finch, as a (suffrage, hector, (nestor)) among defense lawyers, is appointed to the Tom
(31) Robinson case.

2. Atticus explains to Scout and Jem that his (conscious, (conscience), apportion) mandates his
(32) acceptance of the case.

3. This sentence is (declarative, imperative, (interrogative), exclamatory): Why is *To Kill a*
(1) *Mockingbird* a meaningful title?

4. The word group below is a (sentence fragment, (run-on sentence), complete sentence).
(2)

        F. Scott Fitzgerald wrote novels of human drama *The Great Gatsby* is an example.

5. This word group is a ((phrase), clause): after Nick's return from the Teutonic migration known as
(20) the Great War

6. Coordinating (verbs, (conjunctions), nouns) join parts of a sentence that are equal.
(33)

7. Correlative (nouns, adjectives, (conjunctions)) always come in pairs.
(35)

8. (Democracy, (Hedonism), Jurisdiction) is the theory that pleasure is the highest good.
(31)

9. (Hedonism, Delusion, (Suffrage)) is the right to vote.
(25)

10. A stentorian voice is (soft, melodious, (loud)).
(33)

11. We use the abbreviation ((et al), etc., i.e.), meaning "and others," when we are referring to
(34) additional people.

12. The root *krat-* comes from the Greek word meaning (pleasure, vote, power). ⬭
(35)

13. Write the plural form of the singular noun *banjo*. ___banjos___
(10, 11)

14. Replace the blank with the singular, present tense verb form of the underlined verb in this
(5) sentence: Teachers usually <u>clarify</u> their instructions, but Mr. Green always ___clarifies___ his
instructions.

15. Circle each letter that should be capitalized in this sentence: (t)he setting for (f) (s)cott (f)itzgerald's (t)he
(9, 25) (g)reat (g)atsby is (n)ew (y)ork (c)ity and (l)ong (i)sland in 1922.

16. In the following sentence, underline each prepositional phrase and circle the object of each
(14, 28) preposition: <u>Away from his Midwestern (town)</u>, Nick enjoys the company <u>of the wealthy</u>
(Buchanans).

17. From the following list, circle the word that is *not* a helping verb: is, am, are, was, were, be,
(6) being, been,(here) has, have, had, do, does, did, shall, will, should, would, may, might, must, can,
could

18. Circle each coordinating conjunction from this list:(and)(but)(yet) out,(nor) off,(or)(so) did, was,(for)
(33)

19. Circle the correlative conjunctions in this sentence: During her tour of the White House, Maggie
(35) met(not only)the President(but also)the First Lady.

20. Circle the gerund in this sentence: Jorday Baker, the Buchanan's friend, likes(golfing.)
(16)

21. In the following sentence, circle the verb phrase and name its tense: Gatsby(was staring)toward a
(17) "single green light, minute and far away." _____past progressive_____ tense

22. Circle the linking verb in the following sentence: Nick(becomes)uncomfortable around Tom and
(18) Myrtle, Tom's mistress.

23. Add periods where they are needed in the following sentence: M. B. U. Tifal, R. N. primped in
(31) front of the mirror before beginning her seven a. m. shift at the hospital.

Complete the diagrams of sentences 24 and 25.

24. Does Tom give Myrtle a red nose?
(21, 30)

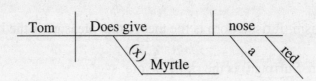

25. Nick reveals not only the careless cruelty of the Buchanans but also the high-reaching dreams of
(28, 29) Gatsby.

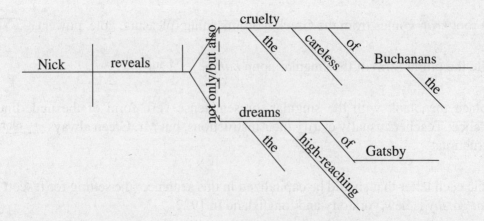

Give after Lesson 45

Circle the correct word(s) to complete sentences 1–10.

1. Doctor Chu said that elderly people and small children might be (perceptible, (susceptible),
(3, 40) bellicose) to the West Nile virus.

2. Phil gave the taxi driver ((explicit), implicit, felicitous) directions to the airport.
(37, 39)

3. The following is a (sentence fragment, run-on sentence, (complete sentence)): Cross the moat, and
(2) enter the courtyard.

4. This word group is a ((phrase), clause): during the reign of King Arthur in the sixth century
(20)

5. Of the many works of Mark Twain, *A Connecticut Yankee in King Arthur's Court* is one of his
(39) (goodest, better, (best)).

6. (Fortuitous, Sybaritic, (Stoic)) means indifferent to pleasure and pain.
(36)

7. (Fortuitous, (Sybaritic), Stoic) means extravagant and sensual.
(36)

8. ((Fortuitous), Sybaritic, Stoic) means lucky.
(37)

9. (Explicit, (Implicit), Susceptible) means implied or suggested but not directly expressed.
(39)

10. The roots *ven-* and *vent-* come from the Latin word *venire* meaning (seize, (come), power).
(38)

11. Circle the abstract noun from this list: England, (reign), King Arthur, mechanic, castle, moat
(4)

Circle each letter than should be capitalized in 12 and 13.

12. (earlier in (march, (i) read the short story "(to (build a (fire.".
(9)

13. (dear (doc (wok,
(25)
       (for our banquet, can you fix a dish representative of the (far (east?

           (warmly,
           (kung (pao

14. Write the plural form of the singular noun *virus*. _____viruses_____
(10, 11)

15. Add periods where they are needed in the following passage: Ms. L. M. Green has not felt well
(31) since two p.m. yesterday. I believe she has the flu.

16. In the following sentence, circle the verb phrase and label its tense:
(17)
     Hank Morgan (will be awaking) in Camelot. _____future progressive_____ tense

17. For sentences a and b, circle the verb phrase and then circle to indicate whether it is an action or
(3, 18) linking verb.

    (a) The bully Hercules (feels) heroic today. (action, (linking))

    (b) (Does) Hank (feel) a lump on his head? ((action), linking)

18. Circle the two possessive adjectives in this sentence: After Hercules whacks (Hank's) head with a
(24) crowbar, Hank wakes up in (King Arthur's) Kingdom.

19. Circle the correlative conjunctions in this sentence: Hank is (not only) captured (but also) sentenced
(35) to death.

20. Circle the predicate nominative in this sentence: A total eclipse of the sun is Hank's (escape)
(36)

For 21–23, write whether the italicized noun is nominative, objective, or possessive case.

21. The braggart magician who had helped Arthur in his rise to the throne was *Merlin*.
(37)   _____nominative_____ case

22. Hank Morgan is a casualty of this feudalistic, barbaric *society*. _____objective_____ case
(37)

23. Does *Hank's* prior knowledge of the eclipse prove beneficial? _____possessive_____ case
(37)

Complete the diagrams of sentences 24 and 25.

24. Hank Morgan supplants Merlin and becomes Arthur's advisor.
(21, 36)

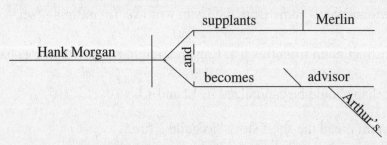

25. Life in the castle proves both difficult and provocative.
(24, 38)

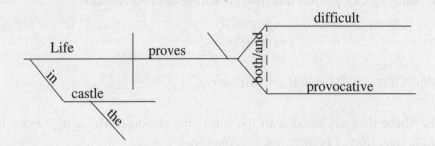

Give after Lesson 50

Circle the correct word(s) to complete sentences 1–11.

1. The grand (finite, conjecture, (finale)) of the fireworks show included bright red, white, and blue
(43) flashes in the sky.

2. Scientists (agitate, finite, (conjecture)) as to the age of the planet Earth.
(45)

3. The past participle of the verb *balance* is ((balanced), balancing).
(13)

4. Of the two stories, Jack London's is the ((more), most) interesting.
(39)

5. The following is a (complete sentence, run-on sentence, (sentence fragment)): Being vulnerable,
(2) liable, and open to influence.

6. (Do, (Does)) *The Maltese Falcon* provide a model for today's detective novel?
(12)

7. You may repair the leaky pipe (anyway, (any way), anyways) you want.
(44)

8. Yesterday Fong was ill, but today he feels (alright, (all right)).
(41)

9. The root (*ag-, fin-,* (*ject-*)) comes from a Latin word meaning "throw" or "hurl."
(45)

10. ((Agitate), Conjecture, Intervene) is a verb meaning "to stir or excite."
(42)

11. A (conjecture, agenda, (trajectory)) is the curved path taken by a projectile such as a missile,
(45) meteor, or bullet.

12. Circle each coordinating conjunction in this sentence: Charles Dickens wrote *A Tale of Two*
(33) *Cities* (and) *A Christmas Carol,* (but) he didn't write *The Christmas Box.*

13. Circle the gerund in this sentence: (Reflecting) on past experiences may affect our future decisions.
(16)

14. Write the plural form of the singular noun *prefix.* _____prefixes_____
(10, 11)

15. Circle the appositive in this sentence: Scrooge's partner, (Jacob Marley), warns Scrooge to change
(42) his ways.

16. Circle each letter that should be capitalized in the following sentence: (c)harles (d)ickens was born
(22, 25) (f)ebruary 7, 1812, in (p)ortsmouth, (e)ngland.

17. Circle the infinitive in the following sentence: Dickens did more (to benefit) the poor in England
(19) than all the statesmen in Parliament.

18. In the following sentence, underline each prepositional phrase, circling the object of each
(14, 28) preposition:

In addition to the (ghost) of (Jacob Marley), three Christmas Spirits appear to (Mr. Scrooge.)

19. In the following sentence, circle the verb phrase and name its tense: Which Christmas traditions
(15) (have come) to the United States from Germany? _____ present perfect _____ tense

20. For sentences a and b, circle the verb phrase and then circle to indicate whether it is transitive or
(26) intransitive.

(a) In his writing, Charles Dickens (shows) compassion for children. ((transitive) intransitive)

(b) (Is) everyone (smiling) at the end of *A Christmas Carol*? (transitive (intransitive))

21. Circle the sentence below that is written correctly. Choose A or B.
(44)

A Charles Dickens writes that kind of a novel.

(B Charles Dickens writes that kind of novel.)

22. Add periods and commas as needed in the following sentence: My favorite aunt, Mrs. May L.
(41, 43) Swing, plays golf on Tuesdays, Thursdays, and Saturdays.

23. In the following sentence, write whether the italicized word is nominative, objective, or
(37) possessive case: Scrooge is a stingy old *man* who hates his fellow humans and Christmas.
_____ nominative _____ case

Complete the diagrams of sentences 24 and 25.

24. Ebenezer Scrooge is the character to watch.
(24, 36)

25. Does Scrooge understand the condemned ghost?
(21, 45)

Circle the correct word(s) to complete sentences 1–10.

1. Eight associate justices plus one chief justice (compose, comprise) the U.S. Supreme Court.
(46)

2. The Latin root *tract-* means (to drag or draw, to come, to throw).
(47)

3. I think that poem by Jane Austen is the (good, better, best) of the two.
(40)

4. The dark-haired princess tap dancing on stage is (her, she).
(50)

5. Ms. Hsu and (we, us) visited the Louvre while in Paris, France.
(50)

6. The humorous birthday card arrived in a large turquoise (envelop, envelope).
(50)

7. Early morning fog may (envelop, envelope) the coast line.
(50)

8. The Latin verb (*venire, capere, ducere*) means "to lead."
(49)

9. A (deduction, retraction, conjecture) is a withdrawal or taking back of something previously said.
(47)

10. (Everyone, Every one) of the candidates will participate in the debate next month.
(24)

11. In the following sentence, underline each prepositional phrase, circling the object of each
(14, 28) preposition:

Some critics believe that the title of Jane Austen's *Mansfield Park* represents her abolitionist views on behalf of the slaves in Antigua.

12. Circle the verb phrase in the sentence below. Then circle to indicate whether the verb is transitive
(26) or intransitive.

In Jane Austen's *Emma*, does Emma Woodhouse respond with surprise to Jane Fairfax and Frank Churchill's engagement? (transitive, intransitive)

13. Write the (a) past tense and (b) past participle of the irregular verb *drink*.
(49)

(a) _____drank_____   (b) _____(has) drunk_____

14. Add periods and commas as needed in the following sentence:
(31, 43)

John F. Kennedy, the thirty-fifth U.S. President, was voted "most likely to succeed" out of his high school class.

15. Circle the coordinating conjunction in this sentence: A close reading of *Emma* discloses a tight
(33) narrative web, a severely restricted setting and a few characters.

16. In the following sentence, circle the pronoun and name its case: Fortunately, (she) gives
(50) tremendous attention to detail. _____nominative_____ case

17. Write the plural form of the singular noun *trilogy*. _____trilogies_____
(10, 11)

18. Circle each third person plural pronoun from this list: he, him, she, her,(they)(them), we, us, you
(48)

19. Circle each nominative case pronoun from this list: me, him,(I)(she), them,(they)(he), her,(we) us
(50)

20. Circle each letter that should be capitalized in the following sentence:(m)rs. (c)urtis said, "(n)o,(i)
(9) don't think(j)ane(a)usten made any money during her lifetime from her novel(m)ansfield(p)ark."

21. In the following sentence, circle the verb phrase and name its tense:(Was)Mr. Huang(teasing) you
(17) about a missing homework assignment? _____past progressive_____ tense

22. Circle each infinitive in this sentence: Cleopatra chose(to die)by snake bite rather than(to live)
(19) without Mark Antony.

23. Circle each possessive noun from this list:(people's) peoples, cross, crosses,(cross's)(crosses')
(7)

24. Write the second person singular or plural personal pronoun. _____you_____
(48)

25. In the space below, diagram the following sentence: Writing and entertaining absorbed this
(29, 34) woman of many interests.

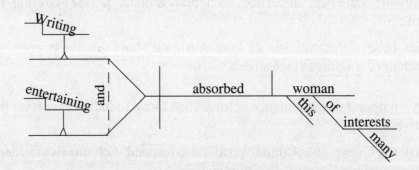

Circle the correct word(s) to complete sentences 1–14.

1. The Latin root *sec-* or *sequ-*, as in *second* and *sequel*, means (to lead, (to follow), to draw).
(51)

2. The ((uninterested), disinterested) scholar refused to listen to Melville Dewey's reasons for a new
(52) library organization system.

3. Tim McGraw considers Willie Stargell the (more, (most)) daunting of all the sluggers.
(40)

4. The following word group is a ((phrase), clause): designed to spread his philosophies
(20)

5. A predicate (adjective, (nominative), preposition) follows a linking verb and renames the subject.
(36)

6. In October, that elm tree will lose (it's, (its)) leaves.
(53)

7. I gave my email address to Elle, Allison, and (he, (him)) so that they can contact me.
(51)

8. The italicized words in the following sentence are ((participles), gerunds): The *chirping* fire
(45) detector indicated a *dying* battery.

9. Calvin Coolidge is the only U. S. President to be (sweared, (sworn)) into office by his father.
(49)

10. ((Apollo), Bacchus, Mercury) is a Romanized Greek god associated with calm rationality.
(53)

11. (Apollonian, (Bacchanalian), Delphic) means frenzied, riotous, wanton, and debauched.
(53)

12. ((Delphic), Bacchanalian, Dionysian) means unclear, ambiguous, or obscure.
(55)

13. (Delphic, (Biennial), Consequential) means every two years.
(54)

14. A disinterested person is (frenzied, (neutral), ambivalent).
(52)

15. Write the plural form of the singular noun *canary*. _____canaries_____
(10, 11)

16. In the following sentence, circle the entire verb phrase and name its tense: Curious about Jesus'
(17) crucifixion, the historian (had been discovering) differences in the crucifixions of Dismas, Gestas,
and Jesus. __past perfect progressive__ tense

17. Add periods and commas as needed in the passage below. Then circle each letter that should be
(31, 43) capitalized.

(m)r. (m)andee, (i)'ve never heard the names (d)ismas and (g)estas. (w)ere they the thieves crucified with
(j)esus?

18. Circle the appositive in this sentence: John L. Jones, ("Casey" Jones,) died trying to brake his
(42) Illinois Central Cannonball train.

19. Circle each infinitive in this sentence: (To change) directions while sailing a boat is called ("to
(19) tack.")

20. In the following sentence, underline the dependent clause and circle the subordinating
(54) conjunction: Ms. Biskit served her famous turnip muffins (even though) no one was hungry.

21. Circle each objective case personal pronoun from this list: (me) (him) I , she, (them) they, he, (her)
(51) we, (us)

22. Circle the gerund phrase in the following sentence: (Following the directions) is the best way to
(16, 55) assemble your new bicycle.

23. In the following sentence, underline each prepositional phrase, circling the object of each
(14, 28) preposition:

In addition to this (novel,) I would like to read its sequel on account of all the good (reports) I have
heard about the (author.)

Diagram sentences 24 and 25.

24. Refusing a bath characterized Louis XIV of France.
(29, 56)

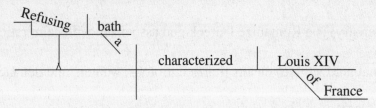

25. Florence Nightingale liked to travel.
(21)

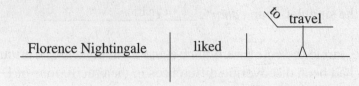

Circle the correct words to complete sentences 1–15.

1. After you file the proper documents with the Department of Motor Vehicles, the car will be
(53) (your's, (yours)).

2. Fong, Salvador, and ((he), him) play baseball on the same team.
(50)

3. The police placed (flairs, (flares)) on the road to warn motorists of a traffic accident ahead.
(56)

4. (Mercurial, (Jovial)) means merry, jolly, and mirthful.
(57)

5. Sometimes politicians ((slander), libel) one another while orally debating controversial topics.
(58)

6. The contentious candidate for mayor distributed flyers filled with (slander, (libel)) about the
(58) incumbent.

7. The Greek root (*ag-*, (*amphi-*), *ject-*) means "on both sides" or "around."
(59)

8. Lauren, an (ambivalent, (ambidextrous), ambient) basketball player, shoots well with both her
(59) right and left hands.

9. The (torturous, (tortuous)) mountain road made driving to the resort hazardous.
(60)

10. The following word group is a (phrase, (clause)): as she leaps onto the black stallion
(20)

11. Of the two research articles, this one is the ((more), most) thorough and precise.
(40)

12. A ((subordinating), coordinating) conjunction introduces a dependent clause.
(54)

13. The italicized words in the following sentence are (participles, (gerunds)): Johanna enjoys *playing*
(16, 55) the saxophone and *pitching* the softball.

14. Had Miss Yu (freeze, froze, (frozen)) the bananas before dipping them in chocolate and rolling
(49) them in nuts?

15. John Chapman, Stanley R. Soog, and Samuel Clemens gave (theirselves, (themselves))
(57) pseudonyms.

16. Write the plural form of the singular noun *handful*. _____ handfuls _____
(10, 11)

17. Replace the blank in this sentence with the correct verb form: Fernando (present perfect tense of
(15, 49) *tear*) _____ has torn _____ a ligament in his left knee.

18. In the sentence below, add periods and commas as needed, and circle each letter that should be
(31, 60) capitalized:

(Y)es, (I) heard (D)r. (S)teinkraus say, "(T)he last name on (N)apoleon's dying lips was (J)osephine—his first wife."

19. Underline the dependent clause and circle the subordinating conjunction in this sentence:
(54) Europeans had only flavored ice (until) Marco Polo introduced ice cream made from milk.

20. Circle each adjective in the following sentence: (The) (innovative) (Chinese) court of Kublai Khan
(23, 24) created (the) (first) (creamy) ice cream.

21. Circle the appositive in the following sentence: Pearl Bailey, (a famous singer) sang "The
(42) Star-Spangled Banner" at the baseball game in 1974, when Hank Aaron hit his seven-hundred-fifteenth home run.

22. Circle each nominative case personal pronoun from this list: me, him, (I) (she) (they) them, (he) her,
(50) (we) us

23. In the following sentence, underline the participial phrase and circle the word it modifies: The
(45, 46) (artist) sculpting bronze statues stepped back to admire his creations.

Diagram sentences 24 and 25.

24. Harry S Truman's parents gave him the *S* without a period.
(29, 30)

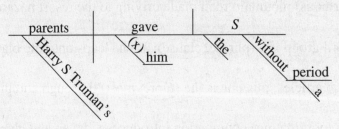

25. John F. Kennedy was the youngest elected President, but Theodore Roosevelt was the youngest
(38, 55) acting President.

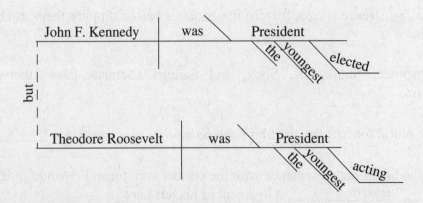

Give after Lesson 70

Circle the correct words to complete sentences 1–15.

1. (Who's, Whose) cell phone is ringing?
(64)

2. Josh says that his sister and (he, him) will surf at the beach this weekend.
(50)

3. (Who, Whom) are you assisting?
(64)

4. Marco responds faster than (me, I).
(63)

5. The Greek prefix *ep-* or *epi-* means (supine, upon, prostrate).
(61)

6. (Ephemeral, Primal, Prone) means fleeting; momentary; "lasting for a day."
(61)

7. The Latin word *primus* gives us the prefix *prim-*, meaning (outer, first, loath).
(62)

8. In Jane Austen's *Mansfield Park* and *Pride and Prejudice*, a tradition of (epidermis,
(62) primogeniture, ambivalence) assures that the eldest son will inherit his father's estate.

9. (Prone, Supine) means lying with the face or front downward; prostrate.
(63)

10. A (flare, epidermis, modus vivendi) is a manner of living; a practical arrangement that is
(64) acceptable to all concerned.

11. Sadly, the two politicians now (loath, loathe, prostrate) one another because of differences in
(65) philosophy on controversial issues.

12. The following word group is a (phrase, clause): a man of such enduring fame
(20)

13. Of the two scientists, Albert Einstein is (more, most) famous.
(40)

14. Euclid's deductive mind, (which, that) led him to write the most influential treatise on logical
(62) geometry, secured his place in history.

15. Euclid wrote *Elements* (hisself, himself).
(57)

16. Write the plural form of the singular noun *flash*. _____flashes_____
(10, 11)

17. In the following sentence, replace the blank with the correct verb form: Isaac (present
(17) progressive tense of *win*) _____is winning_____ the race for dominance in his class.

18. In the following sentence, add periods and commas as needed, and circle each letter that should
(43, 60) be capitalized: risa said, "let's go to the beach and explore the tide pools. i would like to see a
sea anemone, a starfish, and an abalone."

19. In the following sentence, underline the dependent clause and circle the subordinating
(54) conjunction: Since Isaac showed promise in academics, his mother allowed him to give up
farming and return to school.

20. Add quotation marks as needed in the following sentence:
(65, 66)
"A man must resolve either to put out nothing new," said Isaac Newton, "or to become a slave to
defend it."

21. Circle the appositive in the sentence below:
(42)
Isaac Newton's book *Mathematical Principles of Natural Philosophy* presents his three laws of
motion.

22. Circle the gerund phrase in the sentence below:
(16, 55)
Misunderstanding the laws of motion caused Gerald to fail the physics exam.

23. In the following sentence, underline the participial phrase and circle the word it modifies:
(56) Defending his theories, the famous scientist grew caustic and reclusive.

Diagram sentences 24 and 25.

24. Do you know the background of Galileo Galilei?
(21, 29)

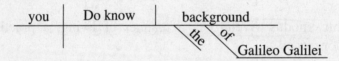

25. William Harvey, Johannes Kepler, and Galileo Galilei provided Isaac Newton the scientific
(30, 45) discoveries to unify his theories.

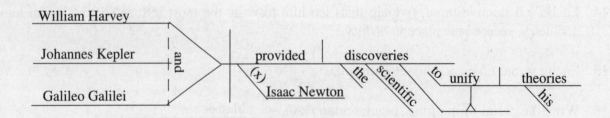

Give after Lesson 75

Circle the correct word(s) to complete sentences 1–15.

1. To (who, (whom)) should the secretary deliver the message?
(64)

2. April consumed a huge potato, but Marco ate more cauliflower than (her, (she)).
(63)

3. Loryn and ((I), me) shall shop at the mall for some fruit-flavored lip gloss.
(50)

4. Because of a storm at sea, ((we), us) surfers experienced turbulent rides on gigantic waves.
(63)

5. The italicized clause in the following sentence is ((essential), nonessential): Please read a book *that*
(62) *is on the classics list.*

6. *The Prince and the Pauper*, ((which), that) can be found in the fiction section, tells about two boys
(62) who trade clothing one day and exchange lives as well.

7. To serve his community, Matthew (builded, (built)) a large pen for lost dogs.
(70)

8. Each of the girls (want, (wants)) (their, (her)) own name spelled correctly.
(68)

9. Neighbors have formed a(n) (bicameral, contemptible, (ad hoc)) patrol to halt recent vandalism.
(66)

10. The (grisly, (grizzly)) bear roamed many parts of California years ago.
(67)

11. Cows and horses eat plants; they are (carnivorous, ephemeral, (herbivorous)).
(68)

12. (Lightening, (Lightning)) often accompanies thunder and rain.
(69)

13. Estée is ((lightening), lightning) her work place by opening curtains and letting in sunshine.
(69)

14. The Latin verb *credere,* as in *credence* and *credulity,* means ((to believe), to shout, to eat).
(70)

15. ((Credulity), Recrimination, Censure) is the willingness to believe, accept, or trust without
(70) sufficient evidence; gullibility.

16. Write the plural form of the singular noun *sentry.* _____ sentries _____
(10, 11)

17. In the sentence below, replace the blank with the correct verb form.
(15, 49)
    Esther, Martha, and Ruth (past perfect tense of *sing*) _____ had sung _____ the doxology
    together every Sunday morning for over sixty-five years.

18. In the sentence below, add periods and commas as needed. Then circle each letter that should be
(31, 41) capitalized.

    (O)n the way to (S)eattle, (W)ashington, (J)ordan and (N)atalie sat on the bus behind (M)rs. (V)an (S)pronsen and
    (D)r. (B)urrill.

19. In the following sentence, underline the dependent clause and circle the subordinating
₍₅₄₎ conjunction: Tristan read H. G. Wells's *The Time Machine* (because) his dad suggested it.

20. Add quotation marks as needed in the following sentence: On a snowy evening in the town
₍₆₆₎ square, some carolers shivered as they sang the fourth verse of "Good King Wenceslas."

21. Underline each word that should be italicized in the following sentence: <u>Poor Richard's</u>
₍₆₉₎ <u>Almanac</u>, published by Ben Franklin, contained aphorisms, or proverbs, in addition to calendar,
weather, and astronomical information.

22. Circle the gerund phrase in the sentence below.
_(28, 55)
Tristan won the grand prize by (remembering Rasputin's identity)

23. In the following sentence, underline the participial phrase and circle the word it modifies:
_(45, 56)
<u>Having set her daughter's hair with fifty-six curlers,</u> (Mrs. Temple) fell into bed exhausted.

Diagram sentences 24 and 25.

24. Neither of the contestants knows the pseudonym for Walker Smith.
₍₂₉₎

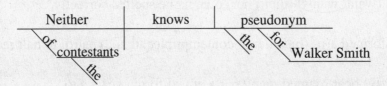

25. Stefan and she brought Mrs. Cameron some homemade tamales.
_(30, 34)

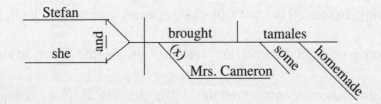

Circle the correct words to complete sentences 1–15.

1. Nelly's (fiduciary, (limp), epidermis) was due to her sprained ankle.
(75)

2. Christine gave a (concurrent, (cursory), ephemeral) look at her notes before the history test.
(74)

3. The basketball finale ran (tortuous, cursory, (concurrent)) with the opening of baseball season.
(74)

4. To "bite the dust" is a(n) (ephemeral, literal, (figurative)) expression.
(72)

5. The Latin word *fides*, forming the base of *affidavit* and *fiduciary*, means (to run, (faith), to eat).
(73)

6. Some (grizzly, limpid, (noisy)) parrots interfered with the outdoor concert.
(71)

7. An inspector identified the (limp, noisy, (noisome)) gas as propane.
(71)

8. Neither of the poodles (obey, (obeys)) his master.
(68)

9. The twins play brass and percussion, but Woolie plays more instruments than ((they), them).
(63)

10. (Her and Grandma, Grandma and her, (Grandma and she)) will assist you and (he, (him)) before the
(50, 51) party.

11. Ms. Villagran, will you please escort (we, (us)) visitors to our seats?
(63)

12. The italicized clause in the following sentence is (essential, (nonessential)): Great Britain's Prime
(62) Minister Winston Churchill, *who led courageously during World War II*, greatly modernized the
navy.

13. George has (lied, lay, (lain)) in the hammock all afternoon.
(71, 72)

14. One of the conductors ((write), writes) ((their), his/her) own music for the orchestra.
(53, 68)

15. Do you know the actor ((who), that, which) played Captain Kangaroo?
(61)

16. Write the plural form of the singular noun *wolf*. _____wolves_____
(10, 11)

17. In the following sentence, replace the blank with the correct verb form: Nelly (present perfect
(17) progressive tense of *limp*) _____has been limping_____ ever since she sprained her
ankle.

18. In the sentence below, add punctuation marks as needed and circle each letter that should be
(9, 69) capitalized.

"(H)ave you read any of (L)ouisa (M)ay (A)lcott's novels?" asked (J)uan, the student sitting to my left.

19. In the following sentence, underline the dependent clause and circle the subordinating
(54) conjunction: (As) you know, we do not use apostrophes to form plurals.

20. Add quotation marks as needed in the sentence below.
(65, 66)

Sara Joshepa wrote a true poem titled "Mary Had a Little Lamb."

21. Underline each word that should be italicized in the sentence below.
(69)

Bonjour and buenos dias are common greetings in the foreign language classes at my school.

22. Circle the two gerund phrases in the sentence below.
(16, 56)

(Purchasing thoughtful, little gifts) is Carla's way of (expressing her appreciation for her friends.)

23. In the following sentence, underline the participial phrase and circle the word it modifies:
(55, 56) Searching his memory, (Jacob) recalled that Beowulf killed the monster Grendel.

Diagram sentences 24 and 25.

24. The annual mystery award is the "Edgar," an award for the year's best mystery.
(36, 42)

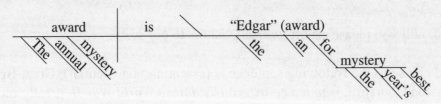

25. The stories of Edgar Allen Poe feature characters recounting their grotesque, grisly deeds.
(21, 56)

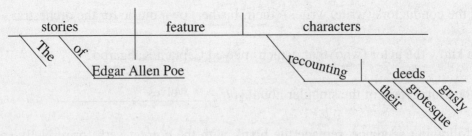

Circle the correct words to complete sentences 1–15.

1. Carla (don't, (doesn't)) have (no, (any)) energy today.
(78)

2. The street vendors sold much, but Nalani and Emiko sold more than ((they), them).
(63)

3. Grandpa thinks that (Me and Risa, Risa and me, (Risa and I)) should stand between the podium
(50, 51) and (he, (him)) for the family photo.

4. ((Us, (We)) music students acknowledge the intense competition in the industry.
(50, 63)

5. The italicized clause in the following sentence is (essential, (nonessential)): The documentary,
(62) *which appeared on TV last Saturday*, shows how citizens have united to fight illiteracy in a local
prison.

6. Stephanie Chang ((drew), drawn) pictures of Alice and the White Rabbit from *Alice in
(70) Wonderland*.

7. (Do, (Does)) one of your state representatives receive visitors at (their, (his/her)) office?
(12. 53)

8. Steven hadn't ((ever), never) (saw, (seen)) a tidepool teeming with marine life.
(78)

9. The Latin verb *flectere* means (after, (bend), before).
(76)

10. Failure to adequately warm up the leg muscles can lead to sore hip ((flexors), ad moninem, modus
(76) operandi).

11. The United States (denotes, (connotes)) freedom to many people in the world.
(77)

12. The Latin prefix *post-* means ((after), bend, before).
(78)

13. Katrina's deceased grandfather received a (postdate, (posthumous), postscript) medal for his
(78) bravery in World War II.

14. Students who (flout, (flaunt), genuflect) their high grades are not popular.
(79)

15. *Pilgrim's Progress* chronicles a man's (Penelope, fiduciary, (odyssey)) through the successes and
(80) failures of life.

16. Write the plural form of the singular noun *quarry*. _____ quarries _____
(10, 11)

17. In the following sentence, replace the blank with the correct verb form: The businessman
(15) (present perfect tense of *shine*) _____ has shined _____ his dress shoes.

For 18 and 19, circle each letter that should be capitalized, and add punctuation marks as needed.

18. (L)auren said, "(i) think (m)arcus is very handsome."
(58, 65)

19. "(O)h, (m)arcus is kind, considerate, and good-natured as well," added (m)ackenzie.
(47, 65)

20. In the following sentence, underline the dependent clause and circle the subordinating
(54) conjunction: (Since) Harriet Beecher Stowe wrote *Uncle Tom's Cabin*, Abraham Lincoln labelled
her "the little lady who made this big war."

21. In the following sentence, underline each word that should be italicized: In Beatrix Potter's novel
(69) Peter Rabbit, we learn the names of Peter's siblings—Flopsy, Mopsy, and Cottontail.

22. Circle the gerund phrase in this sentence: Did (reading *A Farewell to Arms*) depress you?
(56)

23. In the following sentence, underline the participial phrase and circle the word it modifies:
(56) Having read *A Christmas Carol*, (Allison) wanted to read other novels by Charles Dickens.

Diagram sentences 24 and 25.

24. Training a puppy can be a frustrating, time-consuming process.
(21, 56)

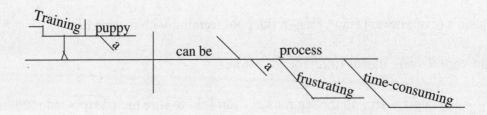

25. Graham enthusiastically admired the 1967 Ford Mustang with chrome rims and a dual
(29, 80) carburetor.

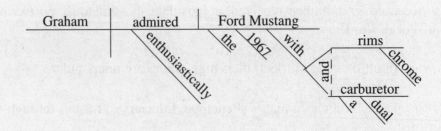

Circle the correct words to complete sentences 1–15.

1. Mackenzie (don't, (doesn't)) give (no, (any)) advice unless you ask for it.
(78)

2. Becca ((isn't), ain't, aren't) as worried as (me, (I)).
(63, 78)

3. (Me and you, You and me, (You and I)) shall rescue Mr. Linh and (he, (him)) from the newspaper
(50, 51) reporters.

4. The word *not* is an (adjective, (adverb), appositive).
(78)

5. Shant plays football (good, (well)). He plays a ((good), well) game of defense.
(81)

6. A parasite, an organism that lives on or in another organism, gets (it's, (its)) nourishment from the
(53) host.

7. David hadn't ((ever), never) (saw, (seen)) an electric guitar like that.
(78)

8. (Lightening, (Gerrymandering), Filibustering) allows politicians to change voting districts to their
(81) favor.

9. Most (Penelopes, (constituents), procrusteans) demand honesty and loyalty from their politicians.
(81)

10. Candice plans to do her homework now and clean her room ((later), latter).
(82)

11. The Federal Government acquires land for roads from private citizens through its Constitutional
(83) right of (gerrymandering, enacting clause, (eminent domain)).

12. The (primogeniture, (enacting clause), fiduciary) of a bill allows for its execution.
(83)

13. Karina watched the ((ascent), assent, flout) of her helium-filled balloon until it disappeared in a
(85) cloud.

14. Did parents (ascent, (assent), flout) to the principal's proposal to ban the sale of candy at school?
(85)

15. The underlined part of the following sentence is (essential, (nonessential)): Norman Rockwell,
(62) who illustrated many magazine covers and calendars, usually painted realistic and humorous
scenes from everyday life.

16. Write the comparative form of the adjective *bad*. _____ worse _____
(40)

17. In the blank, write the correct verb form:
(17)

          Andy and Ian _____ are pitching _____ horseshoes at the carnival.
                    (present progressive tense of *pitch*)

For 18 and 19, add punctuation marks as needed, circle each letter than should be capitalized, and underline each part that should be italicized.

18. "(T)imothy, did you write last month's book report on (J)ohnny (T)remain, (B)eowulf, or (T)he (S)carlet
(65, 73) (L)etter?" asked (P)rofessor (C)ho.

19. "(I)f (I) remember correctly," said (T)imothy, "my (O)ctober book report was on (M)oby (D)ick."
(47, 65)

20. In the following sentence, underline each dependent clause and circle each subordinating
(54) conjunction: Kimberly reminded her classmates (that) they would be excused for lunch (as soon as)
they stopped their talking.

21. Add hyphens where they are needed in the following sentence: VanderLaan's well-executed lay-
(79, 82) up scored the winning basket for the undefeated team.

22. Circle the gerund phrase in the sentence below.
(21, 55)
Andrew enjoys (sketching his friend's profile)

23. In the sentence below, underline the participial phrase and circle the word it modifies.
(77)
Scrambling up the rocky mountainside, (Derek) reached the top before Amanda.

Diagram sentences 24 and 25.

24. The Chatkeonopadols, whom we respect, serve the community by offering free medical
(56, 61) treatment.

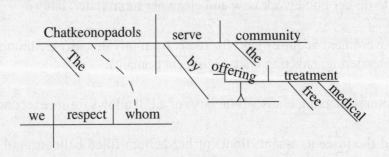

25. A spreading brushfire seriously challenges firefighters.
(56, 80)

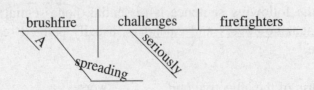

Give after Lesson 95

Circle the correct words to complete sentences 1–15.

1. The word *real* is an (adjective, adverb).
(89)

2. The word *surely* is an (adjective, adverb).
(89)

3. Is Ishmael feeling (well, good) today?.
(81)

4. Can't (nobody, anybody) see the dangers connected with Ahab's challenge?
(78)

5. Ahab lost his leg to the white whale, and the crewmen (was, were) in danger of losing their lives.
(12)

6. The italicized word in the following sentence is an (adjective, adverb): The crewmen drank *early*
(23, 80) to the destruction of the white whale.

7. The italicized word in the following sentence is an (adjective, adverb): With Ahab the crewmen
(23, 80) drank an *early* oath to the destruction of Moby Dick.

8. Ishmael hadn't (ever, never) (saw, seen) the great white whale known as Moby Dick.
(78)

9. Moby Dick, "the *w*icked *w*hite *w*hale," is an example of (assonance, consonance, alliteration).
(90)

10. "The crew's sense of excitement" is an example of (assonance, consonance, alliteration).
(90)

11. "The *o*ld sailor's *o*men *o*pened n*o* one's eyes" is an example of (assonance, consonance,
(90) alliteration).

12. The Sons of Liberty demanded that the British (slander, appeal, repeal) its tax on tea.
(89)

13. The British government refused to recognize the Colonists' (slander, appeal, repeal) for no
(89) taxation without representation.

14. Since the losing party disagrees with the lower court's decision, it will make a(n) (slander,
(89) appeal, repeal) to a higher court.

15. We waited in a long line to purchase our tickets to see the (premier, premiere, Penelope) of the
(88) movie.

16. Write the superlative form of the adverb *skillfully*. ___most (or least) skillfully___
(87)

17. Circle the conjunctive adverb in this sentence: Queequeg became very ill, and I thought he would
(88) die; however, he miraculously recovered.

For 18 and 19, circle each letter that should be capitalized, and add punctuation marks as needed.

18. (h)erman (m)elville wrote (m)oby (d)ick, a novel of amazing depth. (i)t can be read on several levels.
(42, 59)

19. "(t)here she blows!" exclaimed (c)aptain (a)hab. "(i)t is (m)oby (d)ick."
(9, 65)

20. Insert a colon where it is needed in the sentence below.
(90)

After harpooning a whale, the crew must do the following tasks**:** lash the carcass with ropes to the ship, strip off the meat and blubber, and melt down the blubber.

21. Underline each word that should be italicized in the following sentence: Ernest Hemingway
(69) wrote such novels as <u>A Farewell to Arms</u>, <u>For Whom the Bell Tolls</u>, and <u>The Old Man and the Sea</u>.

22. Circle the gerund phrase in the following sentence: The crew feared (the prophesying of Fedallah,)
(55, 56) Captain Ahab's highly regarded servant and seer.

23. In the sentence that follows, underline the participial phrase and circle the word it modifies:
(45, 56) <u>Frightened by a violent storm,</u> the (crew) pleaded to return home.

Diagram sentences 24 and 25.

24. Later, Ahab briefly spotted Moby Dick as the whale dived under their boat.
(54, 85)

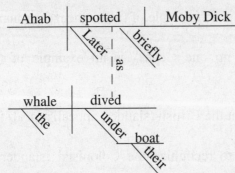

25. Pursuing the whale causes the loss of harpoons, boats, and lives.
(28, 56)

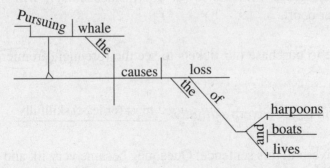

Circle the correct words to complete sentences 1–15.

1. The word (real, really) is an adverb.
(89)

2. Down the pole (come, comes) two fire fighters to the rescue.
(75)

3. In the sentence that follows, the italicized part is (essential, nonessential): My cell phone, *which*
(62) *has now become a major nuisance*, interrupts my conversations with people at the lunch table.

4. In the sentence that follows, the italicized part is a(n) (noun, adjective, adverb) phrase: *During*
(97) *the Presidential election of 2004,* flaws in voting machines surfaced.

5. Only two people on the team, you and (me, I), made more than ten tackles on the opposing
(42) football team.

6. A dependent clause may be connected to an independent clause by a (coordinating,
(54) subordinating) conjunction.

7. The following sentence is (simple, compound): I shall photograph this flower, for the plant
(1, 34) blooms only once a year.

8. I can't find that brand of spaghetti sauce (nowhere, anywhere) in the store.
(78)

9. After a long struggle, the mouse (repeals, appeals, succumbs) to the cat's playfulness.
(89, 94)

10. Prometheus escaped from hell, just (like, as) the ancient prophecy predicted.
(92)

11. The student demonstrated how a (protoplasm, catacomb, catapult) might be employed in
(93, 95) medieval times to protect a castle.

12. The (recumbent, incumbent, protean) cows stood up and sauntered towards the barn.
(84, 94)

13. The diagram shows the cell of a plant, including its (protocol, protoplasm, catacomb).
(93, 95)

14. (Catacombs, Protoplasms, Prototypes) made an eerie setting for the novel.
(93, 95)

15. Did you vote for the (prototype, incumbent, catapult) or a new candidate?
(94, 95)

16. Write the comparative form of the adverb *daintily*. ____more (or less) daintily____
(87)

17. Circle the conjunctive adverb in the following sentence: The word *cholesterol* carries a negative
(88) meaning in the minds of most people; however, high density lipoprotein, or HDL cholesterol, is
helpful in the body.

For 18 and 19, circle each letter than should be capitalized, and add punctuation marks as needed.

18. (m)r. (g)reen wrote, "(d)id you know that blood cholesterol levels can usually be controlled through
(43, 65) dietary reform?"

19. "(w)rong answer!" hollered (d)r. (s)terol. "(r)ed meat, not eggs or dairy products, constitutes the largest
(9, 65) food-derived source of cholesterol."

20. Write the proofreading symbol for "Begin a new paragraph." _____
(91)

21. Underline each word that should be italicized in this sentence:
(69)

The French word faux pas refers to a social blunder.

22. Circle the infinitive phrase in the sentence below.
(94)

The courtier refused to bow before that evil king.

23. In the sentence below, underline the participial phrase and circle the word it modifies.
(56)

(Courtiers) attempting to gain prestige and favor will bow before an evil king.

Diagram sentences 24 and 25.

24. The cheetah can accelerate to forty-five mph in two seconds.
(29, 94)

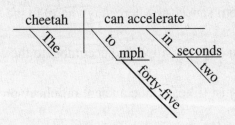

25. An ancient diety who protected doors and gates was January.
(36, 61)

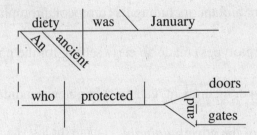

Circle the correct words to complete sentences 1–14.

1. The word (sure, surely) is an adverb.
(89)

2. Lavinia likes football, so Chris and (her, she) watched every game of the season.
(50, 52)

3. The italicized part of the following sentence is a(n) (essential, nonessential) part: The teacher's
(42, 62) assistant, *Breanna*, sorted and graded all the dictation tests.

4. The sentence below is (simple, compound, complex, compound-complex).
(59, 99)

        Because of Johny's quick response, a terrible accident was avoided.

5. The italicized part of the following sentence is a(n) (noun, adjective, adverb) clause: My friend
(97) Sam won't do any task *that might reveal his intelligence or creativity*.

6. The following sentence is (active, passive) voice: The team is coached by Mr. Sousa.
(27)

7. There is complete agreement (between, among) the six volleyball players about Kristi being
(93) captain.

8. Mr. Gevrikyan hasn't (ever, never) visited Washington, D.C.
(78)

9. An (ade, aid, aide) is an assistant or helper.
(96)

10. Thomas will (rectify, eulogize, succumb) the record books if there are any inaccuracies.
(97)

11. On graduation day, Isabel's (aide, euphoria, eulogy) spread to her classmates, and they all
(98) celebrated together.

12. The Greek prefix (dys-, eu-, proto-) means bad or difficult.
(99)

13. (Bona fide, Caveat emptor, Carpe diem) means "in good faith," or genuine.
(100)

14. The Greek prefix (dys-, eu-, proto-) means well or good.
(98)

15. In the following sentence, underline the dependent clause and circle the subordinating
(54) conjunction:

    When Parker scored the winning run, his baseball team sprinted out onto the field.

16. Write the superlative form of the adverb *superficially*. <u>most (or least) superficially</u>
(87)

17. Circle the conjunctive adverb in the following sentence: All book reports are due next week;
(88) however, Annalie may have an extra week to complete hers.

18. In the following sentence, add punctuation marks as needed: No, I haven't seen Sean's three-ring
(89) binder. Have you asked Berlyn?

19. Circle each letter that should be capitalized in the following sentence: mr. ramirez said, "learning
(4, 9) latin and greek words and roots has increased my english vocabulary."

20. Write the possessive form of the plural noun *tulips*. _____tulips'_____
(95)

21. Circle the infinitive phrase in the following sentence:
(94)

I would like more time to practice for the talent show.

22. Write the proofreading symbol that means "begin a new paragraph." _____
(91)

23. Circle the sentence below that has parallel structure:
(100)

The engineers developed the prototype, patented their invention, and test its efficiency.

The engineers developed the prototype, patented their invention, and tested its efficiency.

The engineers develop the prototype, patented their invention, and test its efficiency.

Diagram sentences 24 and 25.

24. Did eating too much dessert give Clotilda dyspepsia?
(30, 55)

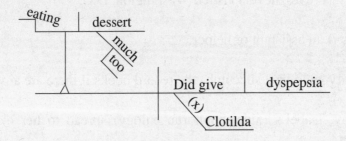

25. Julianne's plan is to go to college after she finishes high school.
(36, 94)

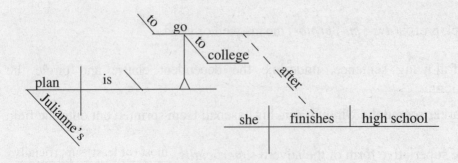

Circle the correct words to complete sentences 1–14.

1. Jan's mother makes beautiful cakes, so Jan and (her, (she)) will provide dessert for the reception.
(50, 62)

2. The following sentence is ((simple), compound, complex, compound-complex): Because of a
(59, 99) conspiracy to murder Prospero, Ariel drives Stephano, Trinculo, and Caliban through filthy ditches, swamps, and brier patches.

3. Ima Snoozer hadn't ((ever), never) heard such a boring lecture.
(78)

4. Arguments flared (between, (among)) the five castaways.
(14, 93)

5. The italicized part of the following sentence is a(n) (noun, (adjective), adverb) clause: Prospero
(97, 98) mildly rebukes those *that plot evil against him.*

6. The italicized part of the following sentence is a(n) (essential, (nonessential)) part: The rightful
(42, 62) duke, *Prospero,* grants his full, sovereign forgiveness to all.

7. The Latin verb (*currere,* (*rogare,*) *flectere*) means "to ask" or "to propose."
(101)

8. To (flare, repeal, (interrogate)) is to examine by questioning.
(101)

9. In the dictionary, abbreviations such as *n. adj., v.t.,* and *v.i.* indicate a word's (definition,
(105) pronunciation, (part of speech)).

10. The term (*son-,* (*quis,*) *cub-*) means "to seek" or "to obtain."
(102)

11. The *ple-* found in words such as complete, complement, deplete, and replete means ((to) fill, to
(103) ask, to obtain).

12. The root *err-,* from the Latin word *errare,* means (to sound, (to wander), to obtain).
(105)

13. The Latin root *son-,* as in *sonata,* means (stray, (sound), difficult).
(104)

14. Dissonant means harsh, clashing, or unpleasant in (color, temperament, (sound)).
(104)

15. Use proofreading symbols to indicate four corrections in the sentence below.
(32, 91)

One of the kittens left it's paw prints across Mildreds half eaten sand wich.

16. Underline the dependent clause and circle the subordinating conjunction in the sentence below.
(54)

Will an upright person be rewarded (if) he or she does the right thing?

17. Write the superlative form of the adverb *penitently.* __most penitently____
(87)

18. Circle the conjunctive adverb in the following sentence: Prospero sails back to Milan to reign
(88) once more; (however,) he gives up sorcery for the rest of his life.

19. Write the possessive form of each of these plural nouns:
(95)

monkeys ___monkeys'___   teachers ___teachers'___

women ___women's___   mice ___mice's___

20. Write the four principal parts of the verb *shake*.
(72)

present tense ___shake___ ;   present participle ___(is) shaking___ ;

past tense ___shook___ ;   past participle ___(has) shaken___

21. On the line below, rewrite this sentence using active voice: Gonzalo was rewarded by Prospero
(27) for his saintly behavior.

Prospero rewarded Gonzalo for his saintly behavior.
_____

22. In the sentences below, circle each letter than should be capitalized and add punctuation marks as
(2, 41) needed.

(s)hakespeare's *The Tempest* combines music, conspiracy, romance, comedy, and pathos (.) (s)hakespeare
wrote this play late in his career.

23. Of the two sentences below, which is clearer? Circle the clearer sentence.
(101, 102)

High in the tree, Ed spotted a bald eagle looking through his binoculars.

(Looking through his binoculars, Ed spotted a bald eagle high in the tree.)

Diagram sentences 24 and 25.

24. Having studied the vocabulary gave me more confidence for our last test.
(55, 56)

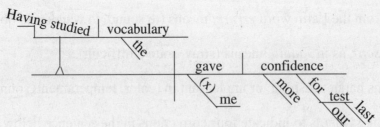

20. Now is the time to do your homework.
(56, 85)

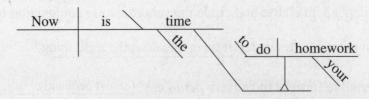

Circle the correct words to complete sentences 1–14.

1. The word (sure, (surely)) is an adverb.
(87, 89)

2. Our neighbors will (recieve, (receive)) parking violations if they park in front of their houses on
(111) Tuesdays.

3. Since Ms. Snoozer had car trouble, Carey and ((she), her) missed the bridal procession.
(50)

4. The Latin root *loqu-*, as in colloquy, means ((speak), backward, foot).
(111)

5. The Latin prefix *retro-*, as in retrospect, means ((backward), word, grieve).
(110)

6. The italicized part of the following sentence is a(n) ((essential), nonessential) part: Our dog
(62) *Boomer* jumped onto the diving board to watch us swim in the pool.

7. The italicized part of the following sentence is a(n) ((noun), adjective, adverb) clause: The doctor
(97, 98) insists *that Phil rest after surgery*.

8. If I (was, (were)) Phil, I would take a long vacation.
(106)

9. We haven't had (no, (any)) snow here in several years.
(78)

10. The sentence below is (simple, compound, complex, (compound-complex)).
(59, 99)

Because she worked so hard in the laboratory, Christina made a major breakthrough in her cancer research, but she was exhausted.

11. The Latin root *verbum-*, as in verbiage, means (grieve, backward, (word)).
(107)

12. The Latin root *ped-*, as in pedometer, means (speak, (foot), word).
(108)

13. The Latin root *dole-*, as in dolorous, means ((grieve), word, foot).
(109)

14. In ((retrospect), verbatum, condolence), the young woman rejoiced that she had completed her
(110) college degree.

15. Underline the dependent clause and circle the subordinating conjunction in the sentence below.
(54)

Doctors recommend increased fluid intake and bed rest (when) one has flu symptoms.

16. Write the comparative form of the adverb *badly*. _____ worse _____
(87)

17. Circle the conjunctive adverb in the following sentence: Dr. Droner delivered a verbose history
(88) of his personal achievements; (moreover) he innundated the audience with trivial details that made some people yawn.

18. On the line below, rewrite the following sentence to make it more concise: Margaret made the
(101) essay more clearer owing to the fact that she deleted the extra, unnecessary words.

Margaret made the essay clearer by deleting unnecessary words. (Answers may vary slightly.)

19. Use proofreading symbols to make four corrections in the sentences below.
(32, 91)

Mutt didn't want me to leave. He gave me a doleful look as i steped out the door.

20. On the line below, rewrite the following sentence using active voice: Scot and Deb are excited
(27) about next month's Florida trip.

Next month's Florida trip excites Scot and Deb.

21. Combine the following word and suffix to make a new word. *chap* + *ed* = __chapped__
(109, 110)

22. Write the possessive form of each noun or noun pair.
(95)

James ___James's___; geologists ___geologists'___;

Jan and Van (their cat) ___Jan and Van's___; Mr. Fox ___Mr. Fox's___

23. Circle the clearer sentence below.
(101, 102)

The motorist encountered a landslide driving along a canyon road.

Driving along a canyon road, the motorist encountered a landslide.

24. Circle each silent letter in these words: watch   yolk   succumb   wrist
(107, 108)

25. Diagram this sentence in the space below: While the loquacious professor talks about his many
(56, 99) honors, Ida Mae plans on avoiding his next lecture.

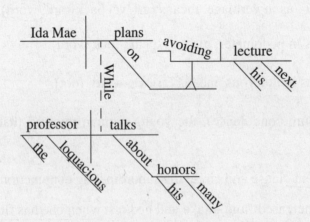

More Practice Lesson 1

Circle the simple subject and underline the simple predicate in each sentence. If the subject is understood, write "(you)" after the sentence.

1. Is (exercise) beneficial?

2. <u>Join</u> me at the park for some exercise. (you)

3. (Chase Blakely) <u>runs</u> four miles each day.

4. His (beagle) <u>goes</u> with him.

5. (They) <u>circle</u> the park twice at six-minutes per mile pace.

6. <u>Have</u> (you) <u>seen</u> them?

7. Yesterday, Chase's (beagle) <u>disappeared</u>.

8. Perhaps the (dog) <u>is</u> lost!

9. <u>Keep</u> your eyes open for him. (you)

10. <u>Is</u> Chase's (dog) <u>swimming</u> in the lake?

11. <u>Has</u> (he) <u>wandered</u> into the city streets?

12. (Chase) <u>has been searching</u> for him all morning.

13. <u>Will</u> (you) <u>help</u> Chase and me?

14. Today, there <u>are</u> no (dogs) in sight.

15. A (jogger) in a baseball cap <u>saw</u> a beagle near the highway.

16. The (beagle) near the highway <u>was barking</u> at the jogger.

17. <u>Can</u> (you) <u>imagine</u> Chase's anguish over his lost dog?

18. <u>Will</u> Chase's (dog) <u>find</u> his way home?

19. <u>Has</u> (he) <u>been stolen</u> by a dognapper?

20. Here <u>comes</u> Chase's (beagle)!

Circle each letter that should be capitalized in these sentences.

1. The eastern hemisphere has four continents: Europe, Asia, Africa, and Australia.

2. The western hemisphere has two continents, North America and South America.

3. The seventh continent, Antarctica, is at the southern tip of both hemispheres.

4. Did Mr. Andrew Angles cross the Atlantic Ocean on a ship called Queen Mary?

5. My friend Miss Farris teaches English and Spanish at Arroyo High School in El Monte, California.

6. Many years ago, Grandpa Curtis hiked Mount Whitney.

7. On Wednesday, Uncle Bill will go fishing in Peck Park Lake.

8. Next October the Sanchez family will cruise the St. Lawrence River.

9. Did a shot at Fort Sumter start the Civil War?

10. The first major man-made canal in the United States was the Erie Canal, which connected Lake Erie with the Hudson River.

11. From the top of Mount Wilson, I could see Catalina Island off the coast of California.

12. On Tuesday, Mr. Yu flew from Los Angeles International Airport to his home in Newark, New Jersey.

13. From the plane he saw the Mojave Desert, the Sierra Nevada Mountains, the Mississippi River, and the Statue of Liberty.

14. Sir Cumference, a member of the British Parliament, wanted to sail around the world but made it only as far as Iceland.

Underline the entire verb phrase in each sentence.

1. Mark Twain <u>was born</u> in the town of Florida, Missouri, on November 30, 1835.

2. His family <u>had moved</u> there from Tennessee.

3. Twain <u>must have had</u> a happy childhood in Hannibal, Missouri.

4. He <u>may have watched</u> the steamboats on the Mississippi River.

5. <u>Did</u> he <u>explore</u> the great forests as a child?

6. <u>Had</u> his father <u>been</u> a successful lawyer?

7. His mother <u>might have encouraged</u> his sense of humor.

8. For four years, Mark Twain <u>was piloting</u> riverboats on the Mississippi.

9. He <u>must have become</u> familiar with all the towns along the river.

10. <u>Shall</u> we <u>read</u> his first short story, "The Celebrated Jumping Frog of Calaveras County"?

11. <u>Can</u> you <u>imagine</u> life on the Mississippi in those days?

12. <u>Would</u> you <u>have befriended</u> Huck Finn?

13. <u>Does</u> Tom Sawyer's life <u>appeal</u> to you?

14. <u>Could</u> you <u>have lived</u> with the Widow Douglas and her sister, Miss Watson?

15. Judge Thatcher <u>had invested</u> money for Huck.

16. Dressed as a girl, Huck <u>will visit</u> Mrs. Loftus.

17. Peter Wilks <u>has</u> recently <u>died</u>.

18. Dr. Robinson and Levi Bell <u>have recognized</u> the guise of the duke and the king.

Circle each letter that should be capitalized in these sentences.

1. We remember Sir Thomas More for his literary work *Utopia* which describes an imaginary ideal society.

2. Abraham Lincoln said, "Truth is generally the best vindication against slander."

3. Have you read the poem "Paul Revere's Ride" by Henry Wadsworth Longfellow?

4. Ralph Waldo Emerson wrote, "It is better to suffer injustice than to do it."

5. Geoffrey Chaucer's *The Canterbury Tales* shows the life of fourteenth century English society.

6. Henry Ward Beecher once said, "It is not work that kills men; it is worry."

7. In *The Book of Martyrs*, John Foxe wrote about martyrs of the Christian church.

8. Robert Leighton said, "God's choice acquaintances are humble [people]."

9. In the late 1500s, Edmund Spenser wrote his masterpiece, *The Faerie Queen*, an allegorical, epic romance.

10. Curious, Benito asked, "Why did Delilah cut Samson's hair?"

11. President Dwight D. Eisenhower said, "The spirit of man is more important than mere physical strength, and the spiritual fiber of a nation than its wealth."

12. A Puritan named John Trapp once said, "Conscience is God's spy and man's overseer."

13. Like Spenser's *Faerie Queen*, John Bunyan's *Pilgrim's Progress* is an allegory, a narrative in which the characters and places are symbols.

14. i. Electric energy   ii. radiant energy
    a. Charge   a. Light
    b. Circuits   b. Colors

15. In the book of *Hebrews*, God promises, "I will never leave you, nor forsake you."

More Practice Lesson 22

Circle each letter that should be capitalized in these sentences.

1. **d**oes **b**ea **h**elty sneak green beans into her peach pies?

2. **l**ast spring, **i** took **p**rofessor **q**uilty's social studies class.

3. **d**id **m**iss **b**lom teach **s**panish at **s**tanford **u**niversity?

4. **d**o **g**randma and **g**randpa **o**tto speak **g**erman?

5. **o**n **s**unday, **f**ather **o**'**r**ourke will officiate in **l**atin at **h**oly **a**ngels **c**atholic **c**hurch in **l**oveland, **c**olorado.

6. **w**ill **d**ad meet **a**unt **m**argaret for lunch?

7. **a**t the hospital, **r**abbi **f**eingold read to several patients from the **t**orah.

8. **u**nder his arm, **w**assim carried a well-used copy of the **k**oran, **i**slam's holy book.

9. **y**es, **i** believe **d**r. **d**inwitty works at **h**untington **m**emorial **h**ospital.

10. **h**as **c**aptain **r**ice returned from the **u**.**s**. **a**ir **f**orce?

11. **a**fter a twelve-month tour of duty, **s**ergeant **l**opez will return from **s**audi **a**rabia.

12. **h**e has written frequently to his father in **t**exas.

13. **i**n her distress, **s**aryati called upon **a**llah, the **a**rabic term for **g**od.

14. **i**n **a**ugust, **u**ncle **j**asper flew from **n**ewark, **n**ew **j**ersey, to **h**onolulu, **h**awaii.

15. **y**esterday, **m**ieko reminisced about her years in a **j**apanese internment camp in **c**alifornia during **w**orld **w**ar **i**i

16. **c**an you tell the difference between a beagle and a **r**ussian wolfhound?

Underline each adjective in these sentences.

1. <u>Three</u> <u>main</u> <u>climate</u> zones include <u>the</u> <u>frigid</u> zone, <u>the</u> <u>temperate</u> zone, and <u>the</u> <u>torrid</u> zone.

2. <u>The</u> <u>polar</u> climate of <u>the</u> <u>frigid</u> zone causes <u>a</u> <u>frozen</u> <u>ice</u> cap throughout <u>the</u> <u>entire</u> year.

3. In <u>the</u> <u>tundra</u> climate of <u>this</u> <u>frigid</u> zone, <u>some</u> plants will grow, but <u>no</u> trees will grow.

4. <u>The</u> <u>taiga</u> climate of <u>the</u> <u>temperate</u> zone allows for <u>vast</u> forests of <u>conifer</u> trees.

5. <u>The</u> <u>marine</u> climate has <u>moderate</u> temperatures and <u>much</u> rain and is found on <u>west</u> coasts of <u>some</u> continents.

6. <u>The</u> <u>continental</u> steppe is <u>a</u> <u>treeless</u> plain with <u>cold</u> winters, <u>hot</u> summers, and <u>little</u> rainfall.

7. In <u>the</u> interiors of <u>some</u> continents, we find <u>the</u> <u>humid</u> <u>continental</u> climate with <u>hot</u> summers, <u>cold</u> winters, and <u>much</u> rainfall.

8. <u>The</u> <u>humid</u> <u>subtropic</u> climate has <u>hot</u>, <u>moist</u> summers, <u>mild</u> winters, <u>thick</u> forests, and <u>dense</u> populations.

9. <u>This</u> climate is found on <u>east</u> coasts of continents.

10. <u>The</u> <u>subtropical</u> desert, on <u>the</u> <u>other</u> hand, produces <u>hot</u>, <u>dry</u> summers and <u>cold</u>, <u>dry</u> winters.

11. <u>The</u> <u>Mediterranean</u> climate has <u>a</u> <u>mild</u>, <u>rainy</u> winter and <u>a</u> <u>hot</u>, <u>dry</u> summer.

12. <u>Luscious</u> <u>citrus</u> fruits, <u>olive</u> trees, and <u>cedar</u> trees grow in <u>this</u> type of <u>temperate</u> zone.

13. <u>The</u> <u>tropical</u> rain forest in <u>the</u> <u>torrid</u> zone is known for <u>its</u> <u>scorching</u> heat, <u>humid</u> atmosphere, <u>tall</u> trees, and <u>heavy</u> vines.

14. <u>Many</u> <u>interesting</u> animals live in <u>the</u> savanna where <u>tall</u>, <u>tough</u> grasses and <u>some</u> trees grow.

15. <u>Mr. Haroon's</u> safari took him to <u>remote</u> places.

16. <u>Few</u> people have visited <u>these</u> regions.

17. <u>His</u> jeep lost <u>its</u> brakes as it thundered down <u>a</u> <u>steep</u>, <u>bumpy</u> road.

18. <u>Several</u> <u>swift</u> gnus with <u>curved</u> horns came to <u>the</u> rescue.

Circle each letter that should be capitalized in these sentences.

1. If I'm not mistaken, lieutenant peabody is now stationed in the northwest.

2. mr. and mrs. chen attend bethlehem lutheran church on halifax street.

3. next saturday, miss campos will read "the cat in the hat" to children at the alhambra public library.

4. baptists, methodists, and catholics worship jesus christ as god's son.

5. onping yu, a buddhist monk, often travels to the far east.

6. people came to america to worship in their own way.

7. how did moses and the hebrew people cross the red sea?

8. james studied the natural history of a southwest area called death valley.

9. dr. martin luther king, jr. challenged people from all over the country, but especially from the south.

10. as world war ii was ending, ruth gruber helped thousands of jewish refugees to escape nazi terror and make their homes in our country.

11. dear ms. werk,

   i could not attend english class yesterday because i was sick.

      regretfully,
      tony

12. dear tony,

   you are excused from class. i hope you feel better.

      sincerely,
      ms. werk

13. dear ms. werk,

   dr. bandage says i must remain at home until friday.

      regretfully,
      tony

Circle every capital letter that does not belong in these sentences.

1. In his Physical Education class, Michael played Water Polo and Football.

2. At the Zoo, I saw an African Rhinoceros and a Hippopotamus.

3. In addition to English Walnuts, Colonel Mustard grows Pecans and Washington Apples.

4. His wife has planted Pansies, Marigolds, and African Violets.

5. Would you like French Vanilla or Dutch Chocolate Ice Cream?

6. Until she caught the German measles, Lana was enrolled in Geometry, Biology, and Astronomy.

7. Beth likes Tamales and Enchiladas, but Freddy prefers Chinese Food.

8. Next Spring, we will plant Cucumbers, Green Beans, and Italian Squash.

9. Our Apricots, Peaches, and Plums ripen in early Summer.

10. In the Fall, our Friends, the Lopezes, will move to the South.

11. During the Winter, the Black Squirrels burrow under the snow.

12. I believe Mr. Zee is recovering from a bad case of Conjunctivitis that he caught from his Gnu.

13. Last Summer, he suffered from Gastroenteritis after eating too much New York Cheese Cake.

14. He has been playing Hide-And-Seek and Ping Pong for entertainment.

15. My Mom made Swiss Cheese sandwiches for lunch and Chocolate Eclairs for dessert.

16. Elspeth found a Japanese Beetle in her Chicken Casserole.

Use the standard proofreading symbols to correct the errors in each writing sample.

1. Dear Mr. Groovey,

    thank you for taking care of My chickens while I was in japan on Tuesday, Wednesday, and Thursday. I'm sorry they pecked wholes in your car cover. Wasn't that funny?

    your neighbor,
    Sam

2. Dear Sam,

    i did not find it humorous that your chickens ripped holes in the cover for my new car. Worse yet, they nearly drowned in my swimming pool as they tried to drink the the water. Nevertheless, i shall take the blame for these mishaps since I Had forgotten to give the chickens food or water that day.

    sincerely,
    Harold Groovey

3. mr. Hake will eat green beans, lima beans, and pinto beans; but he he prefers jelly beans.

4. Have you ever misplaced something important to you? One morning, Christie could not find her iron for Pressing her clothes.

5. Later, she found it beside a Carton of milk when she opened the refrigerator!

6. While in the hospital, Uncle lionel had a brain scan. Just as I thought, Dr. Dimwitty could not find any thing.

7. Uncle Lionel sold all his appliances when he Moved to to kansas. Unfortunately, he'd left his false teeth in the the dishwasher!

More Practice Lesson 34

Diagram each sentence.

1. Wilbur and Orville created wonderful kites and mechanical toys.

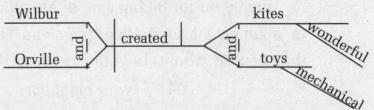

2. The brothers rented, sold, and built bicycles.

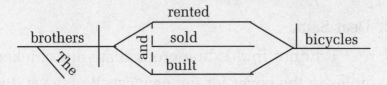

3. They continued to dream and to experiment.

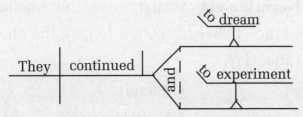

4. Bird-watching gave Orville and Wilbur new ideas.

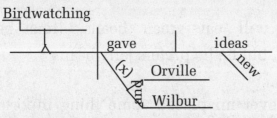

5. The Wright Brothers, tireless and determined, patented an airplane.

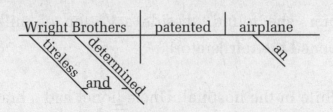

Place commas where they are needed in these sentences.

1. By 1775, a huge rift had developed between the American colonies and England.

2. John Hancock was elected president of the Second Continental Congress on May 10, 1775, the day Fort Ticonderoga fell.

3. On June 17, 1775, the British engaged the Patriots at the Battle of Bunker Hill.

4. On July 6, 1775, the Second Continental Congress adopted a *Declaration of the Causes and Necessity of Taking Up Arms.*

5. George III issued a *Proclamation of Rebellion* on August 23, 1775, declaring that Americans were in open rebellion.

6. Paul Revere, William Dawes, and Dr. Samuel Prescott worked together to warn the colonists that the British soldiers were coming to Lexington, Massachusetts.

7. By March of 1776, the Americans had taken the city of Boston, Massachusetts.

8. On July 4, 1776, the Continental Congress unanimously adopted the *Declaration of Independence.*

9. The *Declaration of Independence* affirms the rights of all people to life, liberty, and the pursuit of happiness.

10. In Philadelphia, Pennsylvania, you can see Independence Hall as well as the Liberty Bell.

For 11–14, place commas where they are needed in these addresses.

11. 11147 Bunbury Street, Saint Louis, Missouri

12. 270 Alta Vista Drive, Tallahassee, Florida

13. 4921 Cedar Avenue, Topeka, Kansas

14. 30 Pine Street, Denver, Colorado

Place commas where they are needed in these sentences.

1. Harvey, please pass the mashed potatoes.

2. Maristela, Ilbea's sister, coaches cross country at the high school.

3. Penny, Kurt's lively beagle, leaps six-foot fences.

4. Did you feed the dog, Molly?

5. I hope, Mauricio, that you locked your python's cage.

6. Allison Curtis, R.N., treated hundreds of patients in Mexico last month.

7. Has Dolores Dolorfino, M.D., diagnosed your ailment yet?

8. May we paint your apartment for you, Mr. Rivas?

9. Richard M. Curtis, D.D.S., will straighten those crooked teeth.

10. I think Miss Vong, Treasurer, conducted the meeting in October.

11. Salvador Placencia, pastor of Yardly Friends Church, opened the meeting with prayer.

12. Did Sergio Cabrera, Ph.D., speak at your graduation ceremony?

13. The famous Pac Couch, District Attorney, won another case in court today.

14. We will eat lunch at the Peacock Cafe, my favorite restaurant.

15. Our school's vice principal, Mrs. Margie Kierstein, suggested that we plant seven new evergreen trees.

16. I hope, dear friend, that you recover quickly.

17. Jumana Musulli, a noteable theologian, discussed the Dead Sea Scrolls.

18. The youngest city council candidate, Isael Hermosillo, has an excellent chance of winning.

Place commas where they are needed.

1. Dear Trevor,
   Please walk the dog.
       Love,
       Jared

2. My dear brother,
   I couldn't find Rex.
       Sorry,
       Trevor

3. Dear Cousin,
   I'll see you at the train station next Saturday!
       Yours truly,
       Justin

4. The index listed "Washington, George" on page 447.

5. She wrote "Hake, Danielle" since the application requested last name first.

6. Jonathan Edwards and George Whitefield, both dynamic preachers, sparked the Great Awakening in Colonial America.

7. In fact, this religious movement encouraged the creation of new institutions of higher learning.

8. Princeton University, for example, grew out of the early revivalist William Tennent's Log College.

9. In addition, the Anglican King's College became Columbia University.

10. The Baptists, I understand, established what is now Brown University.

11. Furthermore, the Congregationalists established Dartmouth College in 1769.

12. On numerous trips to the colonies, George Whitefield preached about the need for each individual to experience a "new birth."

13. Renowned for his "fire and brimstone" sermons, Jonathan Edwards warned sinners about the fate of those who would not repent.

14. "New Lights," supporters of the revival, split from the "Old Lights," those who opposed the revival.

15. At the same time, the Great Awakening minimized differences between Protestant denominations.

16. Moreover, church membership increased greatly along with the creation of new churches.

More Practice Lesson 54

Underline the dependent clause in each sentence, and circle the subordinating conjunction.

1. We remember (that) General Thomas Gage served as the military Governor of Massachusetts.

2. (As) General Thomas Gage fortified Boston in the fall of 1774, the colonists prepared small militias called Minute Men.

3. (Although) the groups of Minute Men were small, they were armed and ready for quick action.

4. (If) the British army approached, William Dawes and Paul Revere would ride out to alert the local townspeople and farmers.

5. The British continued on to Concord (after) they left Lexington.

6. The British won the Battle of Bunker Hill (even though) they lost a thousand men.

7. Ethan Allen led the Green Mountain Boys of Vermont to capture Fort Ticonderoga (while) Boston was being besieged.

8. The Second Continental Congress met in Philadelphia (as) fighting raged.

9. (Even though) the colonists were already fighting against British, the Second Continental Congress adopted the Olive Branch Petition, professing loyalty to the Crown.

10. (While) the colonists were battling for their rights, they desired peace with the British.

11. The Continental Congress assumed governmental responsibilities (when) the British refused to cooperate.

12. (When) the troops around Boston were declared a Continental Army, George Washington was named its commander.

13. The Continental Congress created a navy and sought allies in Europe (since) George III had rejected the Olive Branch Petition.

14. Parliament closed the colonies to all trade (as soon as) George III rejected the Olive Branch Petition.

For 1–6, underline each participial phrase and circle the word it modifies.

1. The (pilgrim) strengthened by adversity, kept the faith.

2. Having stated her objections, (Isabel) stood firm.

3. That (miner) leading the mule is my uncle.

4. Jogging along the levee, (Ms. Rivas) saw some hedgehogs.

5. Having lost his keys, (Nigel) could not start his car.

6. The little (girl) building sand castles is my niece.

For 7–10, complete the diagram of each sentence.

7. Your worrying will accomplish nothing.

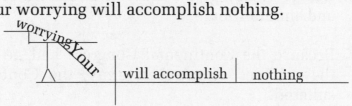

8. Julita enjoys trimming her trees.

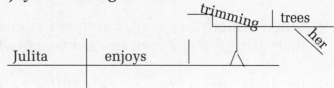

9. Supporting the British, Loyalists fought the Patriots.

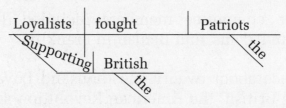

10. Having painted the entire house, Jenny relaxed.

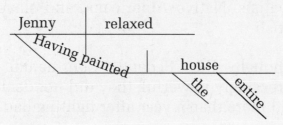

Place commas where they are needed in these sentences.

1. British troops were well armed, supplied, and trained.

2. Although the British had a professional army, communication with commanders across the ocean sometimes broke down.

3. As the cost of war rose, taxes rose also in Great Britain.

4. Since Britain had the largest navy in the world, the Patriots faced a formidable foe.

5. Though George Washington had limited military experience, he managed to lead the poorly trained, undisciplined militia.

6. George Washington's army often lacked food, medicine, and ammunition.

7. Because the Continental Congress had no power to tax the colonies or raise an army, the Continental Army suffered.

8. Though the British troops had many advantages, they were not fighting on their own soil.

9. When Americans read Thomas Paine's *Common Sense,* their attitudes changed toward George III.

10. In June of 1776, a committee appointed by the Continental Congress began drafting a declaration of independence.

11. The committee members included Thomas Jefferson, John Adams, and Benjamin Franklin.

12. Since about twenty-one thousand Loyalists fought with the British, the American Revolution seemed like a civil war.

13. Loyalists, Native Americans, and slaves sided with the British.

14. Although the Second Continental Congress grew increasingly powerful, they did not declare independence until more than a year after fighting had begun.

More Practice Lesson 60

Place commas where they are needed in these sentences.

1. The undisciplined Patriots had to mature, or they would lose the war.

2. George Washington would not surrender, nor would he abandon the cause.

3. Determination strengthens resolve, but vacillation can bring disaster.

4. The Continental Army survived their harsh winter encampments at Valley Forge, for they had faith.

5. The Patriots needed support from other nations, so they looked to France.

6. The Patriots were defeated on Long Island and Manhattan, yet they were victorious at Trenton and Princeton.

7. The war was over, for Cornwallis had laid down his arms.

8. Benjamin Franklin said, "Content makes poor men rich; discontent makes rich men poor."

9. In *Othello*, William Shakespeare wrote, "Poor and content is rich and rich enough."

10. "The noblest mind the best contentment has," wrote Edmund Spencer in *The Faerie Queen*.

11. "To know what is right and not do it is the worst cowardice," said Confucius.

12. An old French proverb says, "Justifying a fault doubles it."

13. Woodrow Wilson said, "I believe in democracy because it releases the energies of every human being."

14. On December 14, 1799, George Washington spoke his last words, "Doctor, I die hard, but I am not afraid to go."

15. On his deathbed in 1848, John Quincy Adams said, "This is the last of earth! I am content."

16. Referring to the American flag, Charles Sumner said, "White is for purity, red for valor, blue for justice."

Place quotation marks where they are needed in these sentences.

1. Oliver Wendell Holmes said, "Fame usually comes to those who are thinking about something else."

2. "They are able because they think they are able," said Virgil in *Aeneid*.

3. A Hindu proverb warns, "Even nectar is poison if taken in excess."

4. "It is better to be the enemy of a wise man," said the Hindu sage, "than the friend of a fool."

5. "A wise man will make haste to forgive," said Samuel Johnson, "because he knows the true value of time, and will not suffer it to pass away in unnecessary pain."

6. A Danish proverb says, "There is no need to hang a bell on a fool."

7. "Dig a well before you are thirsty," advised the Chinese scholar.

8. "Life has taught me to forgive," said Otto von Bismarck, "but to seek forgiveness still more."

9. "Free countries are those in which the rights of man are respected," said Robespierre, "and the laws, in consequence, are just."

10. "Those who deny freedom to others deserve it not for themselves," said Lincoln, "and, under a just God, cannot long retain it."

11. Rudyard Kipling said, "All we have of freedom—all we use or know—This our fathers bought for us, long and long ago."

12. "Freedom exists," said Woodrow Wilson, "only where people take care of the government."

13. Leonardo da Vinci advised, "Reprove a friend in secret, but praise him before others."

14. "A friend should bear his friend's infirmities," wrote Shakespeare.

For 1-16, place quotation marks where they are needed in the dialogs.

We read this dialogue in *The Scarlet Letter* by Nathaniel Hawthorne:

1. "Child, what art thou?" cried the mother.

2. "Oh, I am your little Pearl!" answered the child.

3. "Art thou my child, in very truth?" asked Hester.

4. "Yes; I am little Pearl!" repeated the child, continuing her antics.

We find this dialogue in *Kim* by Rudyard Kipling:

5. "What is this?" said the boy, standing before him. "Hast thou been robbed?"

6. "It is my new *chela* (my disciple) that is gone away from me, and I know not where he is."

7. "And what like of man was thy disciple?"

8. "It was a boy who came to me in place of him who died, on account of the merit which I had gained when I bowed before the Law within there."

We read the following dialog in *Perelandra* by C. S. Lewis:

9. "But do I see you as you really are?" he asked.

10. "Only Maledil sees any creature as it really is," said Mars.

11. "How do you see one another?" asked Ransom.

12. "There are no holding places in your mind for an answer to that."

This dialog comes from Madeleine L'Engle's *A Wrinkle in Time*:

13. The smallest beast, the one holding Meg, said, "And perhaps they aren't used to visitors from other planets."

14. "Used to it!" Calvin exclaimed, "We've never had any, as far as I know."

15. "Why?"

    "I don't know."

16. The middle beast, a tremor of trepidation in his words, said, "You aren't from a dark planet, are you?" *(More practice for his lesson on next page.)*

For 17-29, enclose titles of short literary works in quotation marks.

17. Oliver Wendell Holmes's poem, "Old Ironsides," talks about a warship used in the War of 1812.

18. In his sermon entitled "Selfishness," Charles Finney discusses this disease and gives a cure for it.

19. The class laughed heartily at Artemus Ward's two humorous essays, "My Life Story" and "A Business Letter."

20. In Nathaniel Hawthorne's short story, "The Great Carbuncle," eight people with varying motives all seek the precious jewel, but it is a risky business.

21. In the computer magazine, Robert read an interesting article, "How to Create Your Own Website."

22. Today, the *Mud Valley News* published an editorial titled "Educational Experimentation using Guinea Pigs."

23. Edgar Allen Poe's poem titled "Alone" describes how the author differs from other people.

24. Mr. Hake, a mathematician, gave a lecture entitled "The Pythagorean Theorem for Dummies."

25. Washington Irving's article, "A Republic of Prairie Dogs," attributes human qualities and characteristics to these little animals.

26. For his science class, Andrew wrote an essay called "The Undefinable Black Hole."

27. Benito's short story, "Life on the Princeton Levee," gained notoriety on the East Coast.

28. William Shakespeare wrote many longer plays, but he also wrote some short poems such as "Under the Greenwood Tree."

29. Francis Bacon (1561-1626), an English philosopher, scientist, and writer, wrote an essay called "On Revenge."

Underline all words that should be italicized in print.

1. Shall we watch the movie <u>Gone with the Wind</u>, or would you rather see <u>Mary Poppins</u>?

2. "The Dance of the Sugar Plum Fairies" is a song from <u>The Nutcracker</u>.

3. The Zamora Family enjoyed the <u>Phantom of the Opera</u>.

4. Kurt plays and replays his CD entitled <u>Veggie Tunes II</u>.

5. Have you read that enchanting novel, <u>The Hobbit</u>, by J.R.R. Tolkien?

6. The aircraft carrier <u>Enterprise</u> entered the Persian Gulf.

7. We cruised Glacier Bay in Alaska on a ship called <u>The Scandinavian Princess</u>.

8. They saw <u>Mona Lisa</u>, Leonardo da Vinci's famous painting, when they visited the Louvre in Paris.

9. Leonardo da Vinci also painted <u>Lady with an Ermine</u>, which can be seen at the Czartoryski Museum in Cracow, Poland.

10. Years ago, we rode the train, <u>Super Chief</u>, from Los Angeles to Chicago.

11. The university owns a reproduction of Rodin's famous statue, <u>The Thinker</u>.

12. The <u>Statue of Liberty</u> welcomes immigrants to a land of opportunity.

13. In Melville's novel, <u>Moby Dick</u>, the evil Captain Ahab believes that he alone <u>can conquer</u> the white whale.

14. Aunt Isabel reads the <u>Los Angeles Times</u> newspaper every morning.

15. Uncle Gerardo subscribes to a magazine called <u>Country Living</u>.

Complete this irregular verb chart by writing the past and past participle forms of each verb.

	VERB	PAST	PAST PARTICIPLE
1.	beat	beat	(has) beaten
2.	bite	bit	(has) bitten
3.	bring	brought	(has) brought
4.	build	built	(has) built
5.	burst	burst	(has) burst
6.	buy	bought	(has) bought
7.	catch	caught	(has) caught
8.	come	came	(has) come
9.	cost	cost	(has) cost
10.	dive	dove	(has) dived
11.	drag	dragged	(has) dragged
12.	draw	drew	(has) drawn
13.	drown	drowned	(has) drowned
14.	drive	drove	(has) driven
15.	eat	ate	(has) eaten
16.	fall	fell	(has) fallen
17.	feel	felt	(has) felt
18.	fight	fought	(has) fought
19.	flee	fled	(has) fled
20.	flow	flowed	(has) flowed
21.	fly	flew	(has) flown
22.	forsake	forsook	(has) forsaken

Underline the correct verb form for each sentence.

1. Last night, Scot (beated, <u>beat</u>) Debby in chess.

2. Scot has (beat, <u>beaten</u>) Debby in every game this week.

3. Lydia (brang, <u>brought</u>) us some avocados from her tree.

4. She has (brung, <u>brought</u>) us avocados every year.

5. Last summer, Ed (builded, <u>built</u>) a new garage.

6. He has also (builded, <u>built</u>) a house for his dog.

7. Jim (buyed, <u>bought</u>) Nancy lunch.

8. He has (buyed, <u>bought</u>) her lunch several times this week.

9. During the first inning, Gaby (catched, <u>caught</u>) a high, fly ball in right field.

10. By the fourth inning, she had (catched, <u>caught</u>) seven fly balls.

11. Kim (comed, <u>came</u>) into the restaurant.

12. She said she had (came, <u>come</u>) to meet a friend.

13. Last Monday, bananas (costed, <u>cost</u>) 43¢ a pound.

14. They have (<u>cost</u>, costed) even more in the past.

15. Madeline (<u>dove</u>, <u>dived</u>) with perfect form! either is correct

16. She has never (dove, <u>dived</u>) with perfect form before.

17. Fernando (drawed, <u>drew</u>) the numbers from a hat.

18. He has not yet (drew, <u>drawn</u>) my number.

19. Yin (drived, <u>drove</u>) her parrot to the veterinarian.

20. The noisy parrot has nearly (drove, <u>driven</u>) Yin crazy.

21. Two feet of snow (falled, <u>fell</u>) yesterday.

22. How much snow has (falled, fell, <u>fallen</u>) this winter?

23. The crows and parrots (fighted, <u>fought</u>) over the walnuts.

24. They have (fighted, <u>fought</u>) over these nuts for years.

25. The helicopter (<u>flew</u>, flied) into a cloud.

26. Have you ever (flew, <u>flown</u>) in a helicopter?

Complete this irregular verb chart by writing the past and past participle forms of each verb.

	VERB	PAST	PAST PARTICIPLE
1.	give	gave	(has) given
2.	go	went	(has) gone
3.	hang (execute)	hanged	(has) hanged
4.	hang (dangle)	hung	(has) hung
5.	hide	hid	(has) hidden
6.	hold	held	(has) held
7.	lay	laid	(has) laid
8.	lead	led	(has) led
9.	lend	lent	(has) lent
10.	lie (recline)	lay	(has) lain
11.	lie (deceive)	lied	(has) lied
12.	lose	lost	(has) lost
13.	make	made	(has) made
14.	mistake	mistook	(has) mistaken
15.	put	put	(has) put
16.	raise	raised	(has) raised
17.	ride	rode	(has) ridden
18.	rise	rose	(has) risen
19.	run	ran	(has) run
20.	see	saw	(has) seen
21.	sell	sold	(has) sold

Underline the correct verb form for each sentence.

1. Trini (given, <u>gave</u>) Juan her word.

2. She has (<u>given</u>, gave) him no reason to doubt her.

3. Effie (gone, <u>went</u>) to Greece last summer.

4. Has she (<u>gone</u>, went) every summer?

5. We (hanged, <u>hung</u>) a picture of George Washington in the library.

6. We have (hanged, <u>hung</u>) six pictures in all.

7. Edgar (hided, <u>hid</u>) his brother's birthday gift.

8. Perhaps he has (hid, <u>hidden</u>) it too well.

9. Fong gently (holded, <u>held</u>) the injured sparrow.

10. He has (<u>held</u>, holded) the sparrow all morning.

11. Olga (layed, <u>laid</u>) her recipe too close to the stove.

12. She should not have (<u>laid</u>, lain) the recipe there!

13. After lunch, exhausted construction workers (laid, <u>lay</u>) in the shade.

14. They have (laid, <u>lain</u>) there every day after lunch.

15. Unfortunately, Christie (losed, <u>lost</u>) her keys again.

16. Have you (losed, <u>lost</u>) yours also?

17. Adelina (maked, <u>made</u>) two hundred tamales.

18. She thought she had (maked, <u>made</u>) too many.

19. Last year, I (<u>put</u>, putted) my earnings in the bank.

20. I have (<u>put</u>, putted) four hundred dollars in the bank.

21. People (rised, <u>rose</u>) from their seats as the bride entered.

22. Mia had always (rose, <u>risen</u>) before dawn.

23. We (<u>saw</u>, seen) each other yesterday.

24. We have (saw, <u>seen</u>) each other every day.

25. Sheung (selled, <u>sold</u>) me his old bicycle.

Complete this irregular verb chart by writing the past and past participle forms of each verb.

	VERB	PAST	PAST PARTICIPLE
1.	set	set	(has) set
2.	shake	shook	(has) shaken
3.	shine (light)	shone	(has) shined
4.	shine (polish)	shined	(has) shined
5.	shut	shut	(has) shut
6.	sit	sat	(has) sat
7.	slay	slew	(has) slain
8.	sleep	slept	(has) slept
9.	spring	sprang, sprung	(has) sprung
10.	stand	stood	(has) stood
11.	strive	strove	(has) striven
12.	swim	swam	(has) swum
13.	swing	swung	(has) swung
14.	take	took	(has) taken
15.	teach	taught	(has) taught
16.	tell	told	(has) told
17.	think	thought	(has) thought
18.	wake	woke, waked	(has) waked
19.	weave	wove	(has) woven
20.	wring	wrung	(has) wrung
21.	write	wrote	(has) written

Underline the correct verb form for each sentence.

1. Yesterday, I (setted, <u>set</u>) my keys on this shelf.

2. I have always (setted, <u>set</u>) them there.

3. Baby Ben gurgled and (<u>shook</u>, shaked, shaken) his rattle.

4. He had never (shook, shaked, <u>shaken</u>) a rattle before.

5. Venus (shined, <u>shone</u>) brightly last night.

6. Sometimes, it has (<u>shined</u>, shone) even brighter.

7. Ms. Floosie (<u>shined</u>, shone) her black shoes before work.

8. She had (<u>shined</u>, shone) her shoes every Monday.

9. Effie (shutted, <u>shut</u>) her gate to keep the dog in the yard.

10. Have you (shutted, <u>shut</u>) your gate?

11. Rex the Gecko (sitten, <u>sat</u>) under the heat lamp.

12. Has he (sitted, <u>sat</u>) there for long?

13. Gloria (<u>slept</u>, sleeped) through the noisy commotion.

14. She must have (<u>slept</u>, sleeped) for twelve hours!

15. We (standed, <u>stood</u>) in line to buy tickets.

16. Have you ever (standed, <u>stood</u>) in that line?

17. Yesterday, James (<u>swam</u>, swum) for exercise.

18. He must have (swam, <u>swum</u>) two miles.

19. Has Debby (took, <u>taken</u>) Pantaloons to the dog groomer?

20. Yes, she (<u>took</u>, taken) Pantaloons to the groomer earlier.

21. Alba (teached, <u>taught</u>) me some Spanish vocabulary.

22. She had already (teached, <u>taught</u>) me the basics.

23. Has Ilbea (telled, <u>told</u>) you her funny story?

24. Yes, she (telled, <u>told</u>) us last night.

25. Have you (thinked, <u>thought</u>) about learning to cook?

26. Yes, I (thinked, <u>thought</u>) I would ask you to help me.

Underline each adverb in these sentences.

1. <u>Later</u>, I <u>clearly</u> understood what had happened <u>earlier</u>.

2. Geese were honking <u>very</u> <u>loudly</u>, so I went <u>out</u> to shoo them <u>away</u>.

3. I had <u>not</u> <u>quite</u> succeeded <u>when</u> my neighbor Jean walked <u>by</u>.

4. <u>Rather</u> <u>sourly</u>, Jean scowled and told me that the geese should <u>not</u> leave.

5. "The geese were <u>here</u> <u>first</u>," she said <u>defensively</u>.

6. <u>Completely</u> annoyed, I shooed <u>more</u> <u>vehemently</u> and hollered <u>stridently</u>.

7. I jumped <u>up</u> and <u>down</u> and <u>resolutely</u> ignored my <u>extremely</u> rude neighbor.

8. I picked <u>up</u> acorns and tossed them <u>everywhere</u>, but the geese <u>hardly</u> noticed.

9. <u>Soon</u>, another gaggle of geese flew <u>over</u> and <u>then</u> landed <u>nearby</u>.

10. They stood <u>still</u> and studied me <u>carefully</u> as I continued to <u>frantically</u> jump and holler.

11. <u>Entirely</u> surrounded by honking geese, I <u>barely</u> noticed that Jean was throwing things <u>too</u>.

12. I would<u>n't</u> allow the geese to stay <u>there</u>.

13. I was <u>too</u> angry.

14. <u>Meanwhile</u>, Jean was <u>casually</u> tossing bread crumbs <u>around</u>.

15. More geese came <u>even</u> <u>closer</u>, and <u>soon</u> I couldn't move.

16. Bread crumbs sailed <u>above</u>, and the geese knocked me <u>down</u>.

17. Unable to stand <u>up</u>, I whimpered <u>helplessly</u>.

18. Geese honked <u>above</u>; I lay <u>beneath</u>; they had <u>decidedly</u> won.

Replace commas with semicolons where they are needed in these sentences.

1. U. S. cities with Spanish names include Los Angeles, California; Santa Fe, New Mexico; Pueblo, Colorado; and Amarillo, Texas.

2. Which interstate highway passes through Albuquerque, New Mexico; Amarillo, Texas; and Memphis, Tennessee?

3. Cecilia plays the bass guitar; Nedra plays the xylophone, drums, and cymbals.

4. Asparagus and turnips are vegetables; mangos, guavas, and tangelos are fruits.

5. Cecil washed his father's car today; moreover, he will wax it tomorrow.

6. Jenny ran five miles, biked ten miles, and swam two miles; consequently, she didn't want to play tennis with me.

7. I have painted houses, garages, and fences; however, I've never painted a car.

8. In October, a pound of apples cost 39¢; in November, 49¢; in December, 59¢; and in January, 99¢.

9. We painted all day; therefore, we finished before our guests arrived.

10. Monty and Allison will be here; also, Jenny will come if she can.

11. Ida creates beautiful sculptures; for example, she made an elephant and a giraffe last week.

12. Rob cleaned up the science lab; furthermore, he organized all the specimens and chemicals in the closet.

13. It was raining; nevertheless, I walked around the park for fresh air and exercise.

14. I forgot my umbrella; as a result, my clothes were soaking wet.

15. Would you rather explore Boston, Massachusetts; Cairo, Egypt; Madrid, Spain; or Copenhagen, Denmark?

More Practice Lesson 91

Use proofreading symbols to indicate corrections in the following writing samples.

1. We the People of the united States, in order to form a More perfect union, establish justice, insure domestic tranquility, provide for the common defense, promote the (tr) welfare general, and secure the blessings of liberty to ourselves and our posterity, do ordain and establish this Constitution for the United States of America.

2. Ms. Tseng asked her class to write the U. S. Presidents in order. Sybil's list began like this: George Washington, Chester A. Arthur, John Adams, Thomas Jefferson, James Madison, James Monroe....

"That's incorrect," said Ms. Tseng. "What's wrong with it?" asked Sybil. "Chester A. Arthur is the twenty-first President, not the second," replied Ms. Tseng.

3. Congressional chaplains, the the official clergymen of Congress, oppen daily sessions of the House and Senate with prayer. This practice began with the Continental Congress in 1774, and has continued ever since. In 1789, the Senate elected Samuel Provoost, and the House elected the Reverend William Lynn as their first chaplains.

4. Article 2, Section 1 of the Constitution created the electoral college, the formal body that elects the President of the United States. Each state has as many electors in the electoral college as it has senators and representatives in Congress. On a date fixed by Congress, the people in each state vote for members of the electoral college. When citizens vote for a President, they are actually voting for electors pledged to vote for their candidate. After the popular voting, the winning electors meet in their there respective state capitals to cast one ballots for President and one ballot for Vice President.

Insert apostrophes where they are needed in these sentences.

1. He couldn't remember where he'd spent the Christmas of '93.

2. I don't recall his phone number, but I'm sure it has several *4*s in it.

3. They're making Valentines and drawing *x*'s and *o*'s to represent kisses and hugs.

4. "I've been standin' in this line for an hour," he complained.

5. "I'm sorry," said the cashier, "but we've been working as fast as we can."

6. Aren't you curious about the meaning of her delphic comments?

7. Wasn't she born in '52?

8. You shouldn't say such bad things about the mayor; that's slander.

9. He's ambivalent; he can't decide.

10. It won't last long, for it's ephemeral.

11. Tomorrow, she'll explain her primal objectives.

12. I'd appreciate it if you'd explain the meaning of the word *supine.*

13. The detective couldn't figure out the modus operandi of the thief.

14. In the past, they've engaged in heated, ad hominem debates.

15. We've photographed some herbivorous animals, but we haven't seen any carnivorous animals yet.

16. There's lightning lightening the sky, but there isn't any rain.

17. If you've driven that tortuous road, then you're aware of the twists and turns.

18. "What's that honkin' noise?" asked Milly.

19. "Jill's practicin' the trumpet," replied Bill.

20. I don't think it's primal, but I'm sure it's important.

For 1–4, complete each sentence diagram.

1. Ancient Greeks admired physical fitness; citizens exercised at the public gymnasium.

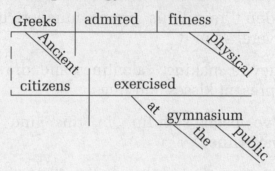

2. Asclepius, who usually carried a snake coiled around his staff, was the Greek god of healing.

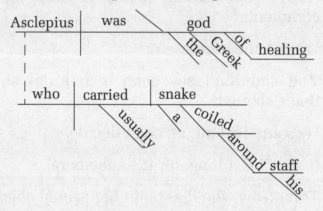

3. Hippocrates carefully observed patients' symptoms before he made a diagnosis.

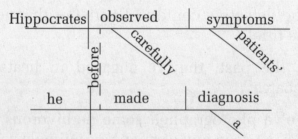

4. Having sworn the Hippocratic oath, Dr. Ngo gave his patients his best effort.

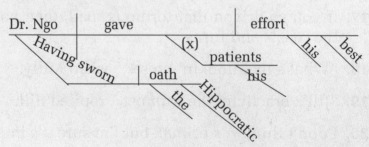

For 5–8, diagram each sentence in the space provided.

5. Developing more successful methods of healing was Hippocrates' goal.

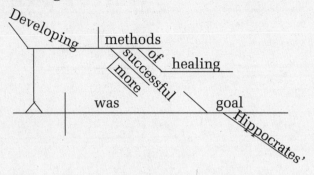

6. Hippocrates, the founder of scientific medicine, practiced and taught on the island of Cos.

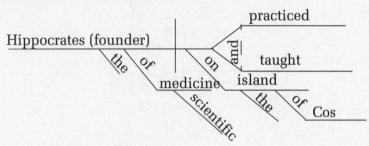

7. After we study the whole system, we can understand the various parts of the body.

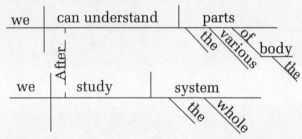

8. The great Pericles died in a plague since the ancient world had no protection against epidemic diseases.

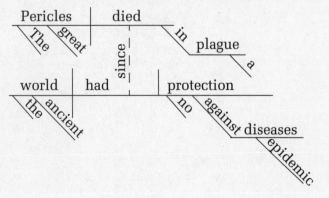

For 1–4, write whether the sentence is declarative, interrogative, exclamatory, or imperative.

1. I'm reading *Johnny Tremain* by Esther Forbes. _____
(1)

2. Have you read any other Newbery Honor books? _____
(1)

3. Memorize the Preamble of the Constitution of the United States of America. _____
(1)

4. You did it! _____
(1)

5. Circle each letter that should be capitalized in the following sentence: On monday, u.s. citizens
(4) will celebrate independence day.

In the space to the right, diagram the simple subject and simple predicate of sentences 6 and 7.

6. Have you heard of the Sons of Liberty?
(1, 3)

7. Johnny burned his hand.
(1, 3)

For 8–15, circle the best word to complete each sentence.

8. The United States has a(n) (indirect, direct, belligerent) democracy.
(1, 3)

9. A pitbull with a(n) (antebellum, indirect, bellicose) disposition frightened Shant's German
(1, 3) shepherd.

10. The thief's (impeachment, affection, affectation) of innocence didn't fool me.
(4, 5)

11. (Advert, Avert, Appease) means "to turn away" or "to prevent."
(2)

12. A (bicameral, bellicose, direct) legislature has two branches.
(4)

13. (Affectation, Affection, Belligerence) is tender feeling, or fondness.
(5)

14. To "refer to" is to (advert, avert, appease).
(2)

15. To (advert, avert, impeach) is to bring formal charges against a public official.
(4)

For 16–18, write whether the word group is a sentence fragment, run-on sentence, or complete sentence.

16. Indians kidnap a four-year-old boy he acts like an Indian after eleven years. _____
(2)

17. The stairway terrifies John Butler. _____
(2)

18. Feeling a dreaded sickness coming on. _____
(2)

Make complete sentences from fragments 19 and 20. Answers will vary.

19. The pain in his forehead. _____
(2)

20. Floating down the river. _____
(2)

21. Add a period and capital letter to correct the following run-on sentence: True Son had stayed in
(2) the insidious company of white people too long their milkwarm water had gotten into his blood.

22. Circle each action verb in the following sentence: White men shot and scalped Little Crane, True
(3) Son's friend.

For 23 and 24, replace the blank with the singular present tense form of the italicized verb.

23. Most students usually *remember* their assignments, but Andrew always _____ his
(5) assignments.

24. Justin and Trevor *study* their vocabulary. Jared _____ his vocabulary.
(5)

25. Circle the correct verb form for this sentence: My dog dug a hole and (buries, buried) his bone.
(5)

1. In the sentence below, circle each noun and label it *S* for singular or *P* for plural.
(7)

The skillful players dribbled and tossed basketballs up and down the court.

2. In the sentence below, circle each noun and label it *F* for feminine, *M* for masculine, *I* for
(7) indefinite, or *N* for neuter.

In his new family, True Son has sisters with dark eyes.

3. Circle the compound noun in the following sentence: The boys remained hidden during the
(7) daytime.

4. Circle the possessive noun in the following sentence: Uncle Wilse's scalp will always bear the
(7) marks of the boys' tomahawks.

5. Circle the correct verb form for the following sentence: The boys discussed their mission and
(5) then (steal, stole) a canoe.

6. In the sentence below, circle the verb phrase and label it past, present, or future.
(5, 8)

True Son and Half Arrow will find their way back to the Leni Lenape. _____ tense

7. In the following sentence, replace the blank with the singular present tense form of the
(5) underlined verb: All sodas <u>fizz</u>, but this one _____ too much.

8. Circle the eight helping verbs from this list:
(6)

his   an   far   what   where   bee   being   been   day   night   rust   fan
could   should   wood   has   have   dad   dew   does   did   shell   well

In the space to the right, diagram the simple subject and simple predicate of sentences 9 and 10.

9. A search party will follow the boys into Indian country.
(1, 3)

10. Hide the canoe under the brush.
(1, 3)

11. In the blank, write whether the following expression is a sentence fragment, run-on sentence, or
(2) complete sentence: Just before daylight when Half Arrow woke him. _____

12. Add a period and capital letter to correct the following run-on sentence: Cuyloga, True Son's
(2) Indian father, stands strong and impassive his eyes reveal a deep welcome.

13. Circle each abstract noun from this sentence: By staying home from the movie to study, Nelly
(4) demonstrated maturity and self-control.

14. Circle the collective noun in this sentence: The audience appreciates the dazzling performance of
(4) *Joseph and the Coat of Many Colors*.

15. Circle each letter than should be capitalized in this sentence: conrad richter, author of *the light in*
(9) *the forest*, was born in pennsylvania and later moved to new mexico.

16. Write the plural form of the noun *quiz*. _____
(7)

17. Unscramble these words to make an interrogative sentence.
(1)

you what about do know Solomon

_____

For 18–25, circle the correct word to complete each sentence.

18. Will a glass of milk (advert, appease, avert) Loren's growling stomach?
(6)

19. The (antebellum, inhospitable, mutual) hermit chased all trespassers away.
(9)

20. (Common, Bicameral, Mutual) means "reciprocal."
(8)

21. (Common, Bicameral, Mutual) means "shared."
(8)

22. The noun *misery* is (concrete, abstract).
(4)

23. The noun *manatee* is (concrete, abstract).
(4)

24. A (quorum, hospice, caucus) is a number of persons needed in a meeting for business to take
(10) place.

25. The Latin word *hospes* means (ill, pilgrim, guest).
(9)

Circle the correct word to complete sentences 1–10.

1. Since I feel (ambiguous, bellicose, ambivalent) about both candidates, I can't decide who will
(3, 11) make the better President.

2. The (ambiguous, amiable, bellicose) flight attendant greeted each passenger with a bright smile.
(11, 12)

3. David asked, "Nelly, (may, can) I borrow your newest music CD?"
(14)

4. *Johnny Tremain* and *The Light in the Forest* (has, have) courageous heroes.
(12)

5. (Do, Does) Indians and colonists really scalp one another in *The Light in the Forest*?
(12)

6. The Latin word (*hospes, vorare, amare*) means "to love."
(12)

7. A (census, lobby, caucus) is an official count of people in any given place.
(13)

8. (Ambiguous, Contemptible, Ambivalent) means deserving scorn; despicable.
(15)

9. (Amicable, Contemptuous, Contemptible) means showing scorn; scornful.
(15)

10. We (shall, will) drive to Niagra Falls this afternoon.
(8)

For sentences 11–13, circle the entire verb phrase and name its tense "past," "present," or "future"
perfect.

11. Through the tiny keyhole in the old oak door, Mrs. Curtis has spied a masked bandit!
(15) _____ perfect

12. High Bank and Niskitoon had accompanied Thitpan on his mission of revenge for Little Crane's
(15) death. _____ perfect

13. By the end of the week, we shall have completed our persuasive essays. _____
(15) perfect

14. Underline each noun is the following sentence, and circle the one that is collective: The hungry
(4) black bear spotted a school of fish swimming down the river.

15. Circle each abstract noun from this list: affectation warrior rage forgiveness affection
(4)

16. Circle each possessive noun from this list: tribes tribe's tribes' forests forest's forests'
(7)

For 17–19, write the plural of each noun.

17. birch _____
(10, 11)

18. proxy _____
(10, 11)

19. monkey _____
(10, 11)

Circle each preposition in sentences 20 and 21.

20. The mothers in the tribe wish their sons would remain at home because of their youth.
(14)

21. According to the narrator, one son goes into the forest along with his friend.
(14)

22. Circle each letter that should be capitalized in the sentence below.
(9)

      mrs. curtis yelled, "stop that masked bandit before he or she steals my *dictionary of word origins*!"

Diagram the simple subject and simple predicate of sentences 23 and 24.

23. Does Thitpan choose Disbeliever as a guide for the war party?
(2, 3)

24. Why has Thitpan rejected Cuyloga as a guide?
(2, 3)

25. Circle the complete sentence from the word groups below.
(2)

      Conrad Richter lived in the Southwest there he devoted himself to fiction.

      When the boat comes close to the bank of the river.

      True Son expresses his disapproval of harming children.

Give after Lesson 25

Circle the correct word(s) to complete sentences 1–11.

1. (Incrimination, Recrimination, Approbation) is praise or commendation.
(16, 19)

2. In the end, True Son (have, has) finally learned the truth.
(12)

3. In 1818, Dr. Thomas Bowdler (censored, censured, averted), or edited, Shakespeare's plays.
(18)

4. (Do, Does) True Son regret warning the white people about the ambush?
(12)

5. The following sentence is (declarative, interrogative, imperative, exclamatory): It's an ambush!
(1)

6. The following is a (sentence fragment, run-on sentence, complete sentence): True Son didn't
(2) answer.

7. A(n) (ex post facto law, writ of habeas corpus, pocket veto) occurs when the President holds a
(7, 20) bill unsigned until Congress adjourns.

8. A(n) (ex post facto law, writ of habeas corpus, pocket veto) is one that allows punishment for a
(7, 20) crime that was not illegal at the time it was committed.

9. (Probity, Censure, Recrimination) is integrity, honesty, and uprightness.
(19)

10. The Latin root *prob-* suggests (accusation, honesty, scorn).
(19)

11. To (appease, lobby, censure) is to condemn or blame.
(18)

For 12 and 13, write the plural form of each singular noun.

12. Timothy _____
(10, 11)

13. child _____
(10, 11)

14. Circle each letter that should be capitalized in the following passage: in conrad richter's *the light*
(4, 9) *in the forest*, cuyloga says, "i am cuyloga. cuyloga knows his son. he is like cuyloga. if he is
double-tongued and a spy, then cuyloga is also."

15. Circle each preposition from this sentence: Cuyloga explains to the warriors that he cannot watch
(14) them put his son to the fire, in spite of True Son's disloyalty.

For sentences 16–19, circle the entire verb phrase. Then complete the name of its tense by adding
"past," "present," or "future."

16. Cuyloga had adopted True Son into his family. _____ perfect tense
(15)

17. By the end of the story, True Son will have returned to the Butler Family. _____
_(15)_ perfect tense

18. Will Cuyloga be mourning for the rest of his life? _____ progressive tense
_(17)_

19. Cuyloga had been planning on True Son's help in his later years. _____ perfect
_(15, 17)_ progressive tense

20. In the sentence below, underline each concrete noun and circle the two that are abstract.
_(4)_
True Son suffers rejection and isolation from his family.

21. Circle the gerund in this sentence: Leaving Cuyloga breaks True Son's heart.
_(16)_

22. Circle the infinitive in this sentence: To remain with the Indians would mean certain death.
_(19)_

For 23 and 24, circle to indicate whether the expression is a phrase or a clause.

23. with a sickening feeling and a sad heart   (phrase, clause)
_(20)_

24. as he leaves his beloved family   (phrase, clause)
_(20)_

25. In the space below, diagram the simple subject and simple predicate of the following sentence:
_(3)_ True Son had been born into a frontier family.

Give after Lesson 30

Circle the correct word to complete sentences 1–14.

1. *Paradise Lost* features characters familiar to all, (e.g., i.e., id est); Adam, Eve, God, and Satan.
(21)

2. (Judicial, Jurisdiction, Judicious) means having or exercising good judgment.
(22)

3. A (progressive, perfect) verb form shows action that has been completed.
(15, 17)

4. The sentence below is (declarative, interrogative, imperative, exclamatory):
(1)

You're too late!

5. The following is a (sentence fragment, run-on sentence, complete sentence):
(2)

Too proud to consider seeking re-admittance to Heaven through repentence.

6. The most commonly used adjectives, and the shortest, are the (articles, pronouns) *a, an,* and *the.*
(23, 24)

7. Examples of (possessive, descriptive) adjectives are *his, her, their, your, its, our,* and *my.*
(23, 24)

8. The following word group is a (phrase, clause): when the second in command proposed to
(20) subdue men as slaves

9. The following sentence contains a(n) (action, linking) verb: Satan felt self-doubt, fear, and envy.
(3, 18)

10. The abbreviation (e.g., i.e., etc.) comes from a Latin term meaning "that is to say."
(21)

11. (Jurisdiction, Judicial, Judicious) is the range or extent of authority; power.
(22)

12. The Latin root (*prob-, crim-, lev-*) means to lighten or to raise.
(24)

13. When people feel they did not receive fair treatment in a lower court, they appeal to a higher
(23) court, an (appropriate, appellate, animated) court.

14. To (incriminate, amend, apportion) is to give out parts so that everyone gets his or her fair share.
(23)

For 15 and 16, write the plural form of each singular noun.

15. thief _____
(10, 11)

16. liability _____
(10, 11)

Circle each letter than should be capitalized in 17 and 19.

17. my professor said, "in 1642, john milton began to compose the dramatic version of *paradise lost*
(9, 25) based on the ancient greek model of tragedy."

18. dear professor tholt,
(22, 25)

  john milton's *paradise lost* helps the reader to better understand christianity and religions of the west.

  sincerely,
  andy

19. Circle each preposition in this sentence: According to this epic poem, Satan seduces Eve by
(14) means of nightmares and falsehoods.

20. Circle each abstract noun from this list: repentence   garden   beasts   Eve   power   Adam
(4)

21. Circle the gerund from this sentence: Satan, also known as Lucifer, enjoys plotting the downfall
(16, 21) of mankind.

22. Circle the two infinitives from this sentence: Raphael's mission is to explain Satan's dreams and
(19) to warn Adam and Eve against further temptation.

23. For a–d, circle the correct irregular verb form.
(12)

  (a) They (has, have)   (b) I (am, is, are)   (c) He (do, does)   (d) It (have, has)

24. In the following sentence, circle the verb phrase and name its tense: Satan is tempting Adam and
(17) Eve. _____ tense

25. Diagram each word of the following sentence: The first woman heard speaking.
(3, 21)

Circle the correct word(s) to complete sentences 1–11.

1. The research assistant was (gravity, gravitate, gravid) with suggestions for the scientist.
(27)

2. Jane Eyre makes a(n) (illusion, allusion, delusion) to Rochester's keeping a strange, hermit-like
(26) madwoman on the third floor.

3. The following sentence is (declarative, imperative, interrogative, exclamatory): Stop the bleeding
(1) by applying pressure.

4. The following word group is a (sentence fragment, run-on sentence, complete sentence): Mr.
(2) Mason arrives at Thornfield from Jamaica, someone stabs him during the night.

5. The following word group is a (phrase, clause): for he quietly left in the morning.
(20)

6. The noun or pronoun following a preposition is called the (subject, object, modifier) of the
(28) preposition.

7. Vertical lines created the (delusion, illusion, allusion) that the shape was taller than it really was.
(26)

8. A (hector, cicerone, filibuster) guides sightseers through a museum or other interesting landmark.
(28)

9. (Cicero, Hector, Pontius Pilate) was a Trojan warrior whose name now means "to bully,
(28) intimidate, or torment."

10. To (phase, filibuster, faze) is to obstruct legislative action by long speeches or debate.
(29)

11. To (phase, filibuster, faze) is to perturb, disturb, or fluster.
(30)

12. Circle the concrete noun from this list: Cantonese   theory   compassion   madwoman   deceit
(4)

13. Circle the gerund from this sentence: The stabbing of Rochester's guest reveals the severity of
(16) the madwoman's illness.

14. Write the plural form of the singular noun *cry*. _____
(10, 11)

15. Circle each letter that should be capitalized in the following passage:
(9, 22)
during the marriage ceremony of rochester and jane, someone says, "the marriage cannot go on. i
declare the existence of an impediment."

16. Circle the three prepositions in the following sentence: Owing to news about Rochester's
(14) previous marriage, Jane leaves Thornfield with a broken heart.

17. Underline each prepositional phrase, circling the object of each preposition in the following
(28) sentence:

Charlotte Brontë, author of *Jane Eyre*, spent much of her life under the influence of the
parsonage at Haworth, Yorkshire, in northern England.

18. In the sentence below, circle the verb phrase and name its tense.
(8)

Jane's cousin, St. John Rivers, will ask Jane to marry him. _____ tense

19. Circle the word from this list that is *not* a helping verb: is, am, are, was, were, be, being, been,
(6) has, have, had, do, does, did, shall, will, should, would, sound, can, could, may, might, must

20. Circle the linking verb in this sentence: St. John seems sincere in his offer to marry Jane.
(18)

21. For a–d, circle the correct irregular verb form.
(12)

   (a) We (was, were)   (b) It (do, does)   (c) You (has, have)   (d) She (has, have)

For sentences 22 and 23, underline the verb and circle the direct object if there is one. Then circle to
indicate whether the verb is transitive or intransitive.

22. Jane Eyre senses someone's need for her. (transitive, intransitive)
(21, 26)

23. During the night, Jane dreams about Rochester. (transitive, intransitive)
(21, 26)

24. Circle the indirect object in the following sentence: The dream gives Jane hope of Rochester's
(30) need for her.

25. Fill in the diagram below using each word of this sentence: Rochester tells Jane the unfortunate
(24, 30) news of his wife's death.

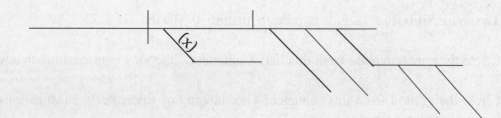

Circle the correct word to complete sentences 1–12.

1. Atticus Finch, as a (suffrage, hector, nestor) among defense lawyers, is appointed to the Tom
(31) Robinson case.

2. Atticus explains to Scout and Jem that his (conscious, conscience, apportion) mandates his
(32) acceptance of the case.

3. This sentence is (declarative, imperative, interrogative, exclamatory): Why is *To Kill a*
(1) *Mockingbird* a meaningful title?

4. The word group below is a (sentence fragment, run-on sentence, complete sentence).
(2)

         F. Scott Fitzgerald wrote novels of human drama *The Great Gatsby* is an example.

5. This word group is a (phrase, clause): after Nick's return from the Teutonic migration known as
(20) the Great War

6. Coordinating (verbs, conjunctions, nouns) join parts of a sentence that are equal.
(33)

7. Correlative (nouns, adjectives, conjunctions) always come in pairs.
(35)

8. (Democracy, Hedonism, Jurisdiction) is the theory that pleasure is the highest good.
(31)

9. (Hedonism, Delusion, Suffrage) is the right to vote.
(25)

10. A stentorian voice is (soft, melodious, loud).
(33)

11. We use the abbreviation (*et al., etc., i.e.*), meaning "and others," when we are referring to
(34) additional people.

12. The root *krat-* comes from the Greek word meaning (pleasure, vote, power).
(35)

13. Write the plural form of the singular noun *banjo*. _____
(10, 11)

14. Replace the blank with the singular, present tense verb form of the underlined verb in this
(5) sentence: Teachers usually <u>clarify</u> their instructions, but Mr. Green always _____ his
instructions.

15. Circle each letter that should be capitalized in this sentence: the setting for f. scott fitzgerald's *the*
(9, 25) *great gatsby* is new york city and long island in 1922.

16. In the following sentence, underline each prepositional phrase and circle the object of each
(14, 28) preposition: Away from his Midwestern town, Nick enjoys the company of the wealthy
Buchanans.

17. From the following list, circle the word that is *not* a helping verb: is, am, are, was, were, be,
(6) being, been, here, has, have, had, do, does, did, shall, will, should, would, may, might, must, can,
could

18. Circle each coordinating conjunction from this list: and, but, yet, out, nor, off, or, so, did, was, for
(33)

19. Circle the correlative conjunctions in this sentence: During her tour of the White House, Maggie
(35) met not only the President but also the First Lady.

20. Circle the gerund in this sentence: Jorday Baker, the Buchanan's friend, likes golfing.
(16)

21. In the following sentence, circle the verb phrase and name its tense: Gatsby was staring toward a
(17) "single green light, minute and far away." _____ tense

22. Circle the linking verb in the following sentence: Nick becomes uncomfortable around Tom and
(18) Myrtle, Tom's mistress.

23. Add periods where they are needed in the following sentence: Ms B U Tifal, RN, primped in
(31) front of the mirror before beginning her seven a m shift at the hospital.

Complete the diagrams of sentences 24 and 25.

24. Does Tom give Myrtle a red nose?
(21, 30)

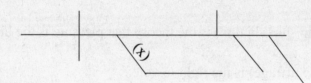

25. Nick reveals not only the careless cruelty of the Buchanans but also the high-reaching dreams of
(28, 29) Gatsby.

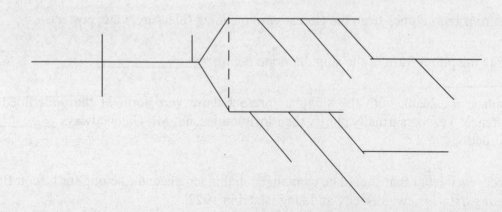

Circle the correct word(s) to complete sentences 1–10.

1. Doctor Chu said that elderly people and small children might be (perceptible, susceptible,
(3, 40) bellicose) to the West Nile virus.

2. Phil gave the taxi driver (explicit, implicit, felicitous) directions to the airport.
(37, 39)

3. The following is a (sentence fragment, run-on sentence, complete sentence): Cross the moat, and
(2) enter the courtyard.

4. This word group is a (phrase, clause): during the reign of King Arthur in the sixth century
(20)

5. Of the many works of Mark Twain, *A Connecticut Yankee in King Arthur's Court* is one of his
(39) (goodest, better, best).

6. (Fortuitous, Sybaritic, Stoic) means indifferent to pleasure and pain.
(36)

7. (Fortuitous, Sybaritic, Stoic) means extravagant and sensual.
(36)

8. (Fortuitous, Sybaritic, Stoic) means lucky.
(37)

9. (Explicit, Implicit, Susceptible) means implied or suggested but not directly expressed.
(39)

10. The roots *ven-* and *vent-* come from the Latin word *venire* meaning (seize, come, power).
(38)

11. Circle the abstract noun from this list: England, reign, King Arthur, mechanic, castle, moat
(4)

Circle each letter than should be capitalized in 12 and 13.

12. earlier in march, i read the short story "to build a fire.".
(9)

13. dear doc wok,
(25)
       for our banquet, can you fix a dish representative of the far east?

                warmly,
                kung pao

14. Write the plural form of the singular noun *virus*. _____
(10, 11)

15. Add periods where they are needed in the following passage: Ms I M Green has not felt well
(31) since two p m yesterday I believe she has the flu

16. In the following sentence, circle the verb phrase and label its tense:
(17)
    Hank Morgan will be awaking in Camelot. _____ tense

17. For sentences a and b, circle the verb phrase and then circle to indicate whether it is an action or
(3, 18) linking verb.

    (a) The bully Hercules feels heroic today. (action, linking)

    (b) Does Hank feel a lump on his head? (action, linking)

18. Circle the two possessive adjectives in this sentence: After Hercules whacks Hank's head with a
(24) crowbar, Hank wakes up in King Arthur's Kingdom.

19. Circle the correlative conjunctions in this sentence: Hank is not only captured but also sentenced
(35) to death.

20. Circle the predicate nominative in this sentence: A total eclipse of the sun is Hank's escape.
(36)

For 21–23, write whether the italicized noun is nominative, objective, or possessive case.

21. The braggart magician who had helped Arthur in his rise to the throne was *Merlin*.
(37) _____ case

22. Hank Morgan is a casualty of this feudalistic, barbaric *society*. _____ case
(37)

23. Does *Hank's* prior knowledge of the eclipse prove beneficial? _____ case
(37)

Complete the diagrams of sentences 24 and 25.

24. Hank Morgan supplants Merlin and becomes Arthur's advisor.
(21, 36)

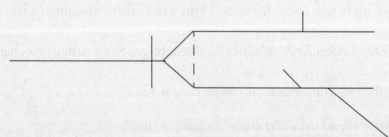

25. Life in the castle proves both difficult and provocative.
(24, 38)

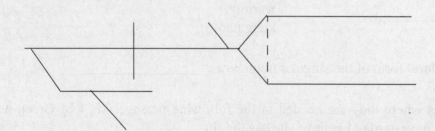

Give after Lesson 50

Circle the correct word(s) to complete sentences 1–11.

1.
(43) The grand (finite, conjecture, finale) of the fireworks show included bright red, white, and blue flashes in the sky.

2.
(45) Scientists (agitate, finite, conjecture) as to the age of the planet Earth.

3.
(13) The past participle of the verb *balance* is (balanced, balancing).

4.
(39) Of the two stories, Jack London's is the (more, most) interesting.

5.
(2) The following is a (complete sentence, run-on sentence, sentence fragment): Being vulnerable, liable, and open to influence.

6.
(12) (Do, Does) *The Maltese Falcon* provide a model for today's detective novel?

7.
(44) You may repair the leaky pipe (anyway, any way, anyways) you want.

8.
(41) Yesterday Fong was ill, but today he feels (alright, all right).

9.
(45) The root (*ag-*, *fin-*, *ject-*) comes from a Latin word meaning "throw" or "hurl."

10.
(42) (Agitate, Conjecture, Intervene) is a verb meaning "to stir or excite."

11.
(45) A (conjecture, agenda, trajectory) is the curved path taken by a projectile such as a missile, meteor, or bullet.

12.
(33) Circle each coordinating conjunction in this sentence: Charles Dickens wrote *A Tale of Two Cities* and *A Christmas Carol*, but he didn't write *The Christmas Box*.

13.
(16) Circle the gerund in this sentence: Reflecting on past experiences may affect our future decisions.

14.
(10, 11) Write the plural form of the singular noun *prefix*. _____

15.
(42) Circle the appositive in this sentence: Scrooge's partner, Jacob Marley, warns Scrooge to change his ways.

16.
(22, 25) Circle each letter that should be capitalized in the following sentence: charles dickens was born february 7, 1812, in portsmouth, england.

17.
(19) Circle the infinitive in the following sentence: Dickens did more to benefit the poor in England than all the statesmen in Parliament.

18. In the following sentence, underline each prepositional phrase, circling the object of each
(14, 28) preposition:

In addition to the ghost of Jacob Marley, three Christmas Spirits appear to Mr. Scrooge.

19. In the following sentence, circle the verb phrase and name its tense: Which Christmas traditions
(15) have come to the United States from Germany? _____ tense

20. For sentences a and b, circle the verb phrase and then circle to indicate whether it is transitive or
(26) intransitive.

(a) In his writing, Charles Dickens shows compassion for children. (transitive, intransitive)

(b) Is everyone smiling at the end of *A Christmas Carol*? (transitive, intransitive)

21. Circle the sentence below that is written correctly. Choose A or B.
(44)

A Charles Dickens writes that kind of a novel.

B Charles Dickens writes that kind of novel.

22. Add periods and commas as needed in the following sentence: My favorite aunt Mrs May I
(41, 43) Swing plays golf on Tuesdays Thursdays and Saturdays

23. In the following sentence, write whether the italicized word is nominative, objective, or
(31, 41) possessive case: Scrooge is a stingy old *man* who hates his fellow humans and Christmas.
_____ case

Complete the diagrams of sentences 24 and 25.

24. Ebenezer Scrooge is the character to watch.
(24, 36)

25. Does Scrooge understand the condemned ghost?
(21, 45)

Circle the correct word(s) to complete sentences 1–10.

1. Eight associate justices plus one chief justice (compose, comprise) the U.S. Supreme Court.
(46)

2. The Latin root *tract-* means (to drag or draw, to come, to throw).
(47)

3. I think that poem by Jane Austen is the (good, better, best) of the two.
(40)

4. The dark-haired princess tap dancing on stage is (her, she).
(50)

5. Ms. Hsu and (we, us) visited the Louvre while in Paris, France.
(50)

6. The humorous birthday card arrived in a large turquoise (envelop, envelope).
(50)

7. Early morning fog may (envelop, envelope) the coast line.
(50)

8. The Latin verb (*venire, capere, ducere*) means "to lead."
(49)

9. A (deduction, retraction, conjecture) is a withdrawal or taking back of something previously said.
(47)

10. (Everyone, Every one) of the candidates will participate in the debate next month.
(24)

11. In the following sentence, underline each prepositional phrase, circling the object of each
(14, 28) preposition:

Some critics believe that the title of Jane Austen's *Mansfield Park* represents her abolitionist views on behalf of the slaves in Antigua.

12. Circle the verb phrase in the sentence below. Then circle to indicate whether the verb is transitive
(26) or intransitive.

In Jane Austen's *Emma*, does Emma Woodhouse respond with surprise to Jane Fairfax and Frank Churchill's engagement? (transitive, intransitive)

13. Write the (a) past tense and (b) past participle of the irregular verb *drink*.
(49)

(a) _____   (b) _____

14. Add periods and commas as needed in the following sentence:
(31, 43)

John F Kennedy the thirty-fifth US President was voted "most likely to succeed" out of his high school class

15. Circle the coordinating conjunction in this sentence: A close reading of *Emma* discloses a tight
(33) narrative web, a severely restricted setting, and a few characters.

16. In the following sentence, circle the pronoun and name its case: Fortunately, she gives
(50) tremendous attention to detail. _____ case

17. Write the plural form of the singular noun *trilogy*. _____
(10, 11)

18. Circle each third person plural pronoun from this list: he, him, she, her, they, them, we, us, you
(48)

19. Circle each nominative case pronoun from this list: me, him, I, she, them, they, he, her, we, us
(50)

20. Circle each letter that should be capitalized in the following sentence: mrs. curtis said, "no, i
(9) don't think jane austen made any money during her lifetime from her novel *mansfield park.*"

21. In the following sentence, circle the verb phrase and name its tense: Was Mr. Huang teasing you
(17) about a missing homework assignment? _____ tense

22. Circle each infinitive in this sentence: Cleopatra chose to die by snake bite rather than to live
(19) without Mark Antony.

23. Circle each possessive noun from this list: people's, peoples, cross, crosses, cross's, crosses'
(7)

24. Write the second person singular or plural personal pronoun. _____
(48)

25. In the space below, diagram the following sentence: Writing and entertaining absorbed this
(29, 34) woman of many interests.

Circle the correct word(s) to complete sentences 1–14.

1. The Latin root *sec-* or *sequ-,* as in *second* and *sequel,* means (to lead, to follow, to draw).
(51)

2. The (uninterested, disinterested) scholar refused to listen to Melville Dewey's reasons for a new
(52) library organization system.

3. Tim McGraw considers Willie Stargell the (more, most) daunting of all the sluggers.
(40)

4. The following word group is a (phrase, clause): designed to spread his philosophies
(20)

5. A predicate (adjective, nominative, preposition) follows a linking verb and renames the subject.
(36)

6. In October, that elm tree will lose (it's, its) leaves.
(53)

7. I gave my email address to Elle, Allison, and (he, him) so that they can contact me.
(51)

8. The italicized words in the following sentence are (participles, gerunds): The *chirping* fire
(45) detector indicated a *dying* battery.

9. Calvin Coolidge is the only U. S. President to be (sweared, sworn) into office by his father.
(49)

10. (Apollo, Bacchus, Mercury) is a Romanized Greek god associated with calm rationality.
(53)

11. (Apollonian, Bacchanalian, Delphic) means frenzied, riotous, wanton, and debauched.
(53)

12. (Delphic, Bacchanalian, Dionysian) means unclear, ambiguous, or obscure.
(55)

13. (Delphic, Biennial, Consequential) means every two years.
(54)

14. A disinterested person is (frenzied, neutral, ambivalent).
(52)

15. Write the plural form of the singular noun *canary*. _____
(10, 11)

16. In the following sentence, circle the entire verb phrase and name its tense: Curious about Jesus'
(17) crucifixion, the historian had been discovering differences in the crucifixions of Dismas, Gestas,
and Jesus. _____ tense

17. Add periods and commas as needed in the passage below. Then circle each letter that should be
(31, 43) capitalized.

mr mandee i've never heard the names dismas and gestas were they the thieves crucified with
jesus?

18. Circle the appositive in this sentence: John L. Jones, "Casey" Jones, died trying to brake his
(42) Illinois Central Cannonball train.

19. Circle each infinitive in this sentence: To change directions while sailing a boat is called "to
(19) tack."

20. In the following sentence, underline the dependent clause and circle the subordinating
(54) conjunction: Ms. Biskit served her famous turnip muffins even though no one was hungry.

21. Circle each objective case personal pronoun from this list: me, him, I , she, them, they, he, her,
(51) we, us

22. Circle the gerund phrase in the following sentence: Following the directions is the best way to
(16, 55) assemble your new bicycle.

23. In the following sentence, underline each prepositional phrase, circling the object of each
(14, 28) preposition:

In addition to this novel, I would like to read its sequel on account of all the good reports I have
heard about the author.

Diagram sentences 24 and 25.

24. Refusing a bath characterized Louis XIV of France.
(29, 56)

25. Florence Nightingale liked to travel.
(21)

Circle the correct words to complete sentences 1–15.

1. After you file the proper documents with the Department of Motor Vehicles, the car will be
(53) (your's, yours).

2. Fong, Salvador, and (he, him) play baseball on the same team.
(50)

3. The police placed (flairs, flares) on the road to warn motorists of a traffic accident ahead.
(56)

4. (Mercurial, Jovial) means merry, jolly, and mirthful.
(57)

5. Sometimes politicians (slander, libel) one another while orally debating controversial topics.
(58)

6. The contentious candidate for mayor distributed flyers filled with (slander, libel) about the
(58) incumbent.

7. The Greek root (*ag-, amphi-, ject-*) means "on both sides" or "around."
(59)

8. Lauren, an (ambivalent, ambidextrous, ambient) basketball player, shoots well with both her
(59) right and left hands.

9. The (torturous, tortuous) mountain road made driving to the resort hazardous.
(60)

10. The following word group is a (phrase, clause): as she leaps onto the black stallion
(20)

11. Of the two research articles, this one is the (more, most) thorough and precise.
(40)

12. A (subordinating, coordinating) conjunction introduces a dependent clause.
(54)

13. The italicized words in the following sentence are (participles, gerunds): Johanna enjoys *playing*
(16, 55) the saxophone and *pitching* the softball.

14. Had Miss Yu (freeze, froze, frozen) the bananas before dipping them in chocolate and rolling
(49) them in nuts?

15. John Chapman, Stanley R. Soog, and Samuel Clemens gave (theirselves, themselves)
(57) pseudonyms.

16. Write the plural form of the singular noun *handful*. _____
(10, 11)

17. Replace the blank in this sentence with the correct verb form: Fernando (present perfect tense of
(15, 49) *tear*) _____ a ligament in his left knee.

18. In the sentence below, add periods and commas as needed, and circle each letter that should be
(31, 60) capitalized:

yes i heard dr steinkraus say "the last name on napoleon's dying lips was josephine—his first
wife."

19. Underline the dependent clause and circle the subordinating conjunction in this sentence:
(54) Europeans had only flavored ice until Marco Polo introduced ice cream made from milk.

20. Circle each adjective in the following sentence: The innovative Chinese court of Kublai Khan
(23, 24) created the first creamy ice cream.

21. Circle the appositive in the following sentence: Pearl Bailey, a famous singer, sang "The
(42) Star-Spangled Banner" at the baseball game in 1974, when Hank Aaron hit his
seven-hundred-fifteenth home run.

22. Circle each nominative case personal pronoun from this list: me, him, I, she, they, them, he, her,
(50) we, us

23. In the following sentence, underline the participial phrase and circle the word it modifies: The
45, 46 artist sculpting bronze statues stepped back to admire his creations.

Diagram sentences 24 and 25.

24. Harry S Truman's parents gave him the *S* without a period.
(29, 30)

25. John F. Kennedy was the youngest elected President, but Theodore Roosevelt was the youngest
(38, 55) acting President.

Circle the correct words to complete sentences 1–15.

1. (Who's, Whose) cell phone is ringing?
(64)

2. Josh says that his sister and (he, him) will surf at the beach this weekend.
(50)

3. (Who, Whom) are you assisting?
(64)

4. Marco responds faster than (me, I).
(63)

5. The Greek prefix *ep-* or *epi-* means (supine, upon, prostrate).
(61)

6. (Ephemeral, Primal, Prone) means fleeting; momentary; "lasting for a day."
(61)

7. The Latin word *primus* gives us the prefix *prim-,* meaning (outer, first, loath).
(62)

8. In Jane Austen's *Mansfield Park* and *Pride and Prejudice*, a tradition of (epidermis,
(62) primogeniture, ambivalence) assures that the eldest son will inherit his father's estate.

9. (Prone, Supine) means lying with the face or front downward; prostrate.
(63)

10. A (flare, epidermis, modus vivendi) is a manner of living; a practical arrangement that is
(64) acceptable to all concerned.

11. Sadly, the two politicians now (loath, loathe, prostrate) one another because of differences in
(65) philosophy on controversial issues.

12. The following word group is a (phrase, clause): a man of such enduring fame
(20)

13. Of the two scientists, Albert Einstein is (more, most) famous.
(40)

14. Euclid's deductive mind, (which, that) led him to write the most influential treatise on logical
(62) geometry, secured his place in history.

15. Euclid wrote *Elements* (hisself, himself).
(57)

16. Write the plural form of the singular noun *flash.* _____
(10, 11)

17. In the following sentence, replace the blank with the correct verb form: Isaac (present
(17) progressive tense of *win*) _____ the race for dominance in his class.

18. In the following sentence, add periods and commas as needed, and circle each letter that should
(43, 60) be capitalized: risa said "let's go to the beach and explore the tide pools i would like to see a sea
anemone a starfish and an abalone"

19. In the following sentence, underline the dependent clause and circle the subordinating
(54) conjunction: Since Isaac showed promise in academics, his mother allowed him to give up
farming and return to school.

20. Add quotation marks as needed in the following sentence:
(65, 66)

A man must resolve either to put out nothing new, said Isaac Newton, or to become a slave to
defend it.

21. Circle the appositive in the sentence below:
(42)

Isaac Newton's book *Mathematical Principles of Natural Philosophy* presents his three laws of
motion.

22. Circle the gerund phrase in the sentence below:
(16, 55)

Misunderstanding the laws of motion caused Gerald to fail the physics exam.

23. In the following sentence, underline the participial phrase and circle the word it modifies:
(56) Defending his theories, the famous scientist grew caustic and reclusive.

Diagram sentences 24 and 25.

24. Do you know the background of Galileo Galilei?
(21, 29)

25. William Harvey, Johannes Kepler, and Galileo Galilei provided Isaac Newton the scientific
(30, 45) discoveries to unify his theories.

Circle the correct word(s) to complete sentences 1–15.

1. To (who, whom) should the secretary deliver the message?
(64)

2. April consumed a huge potato, but Marco ate more cauliflower than (her, she).
(63)

3. Loryn and (I, me) shall shop at the mall for some fruit-flavored lip gloss.
(50)

4. Because of a storm at sea, (we, us) surfers experienced turbulent rides on gigantic waves.
(63)

5. The italicized clause in the following sentence is (essential, nonessential): Please read a book *that*
(62) *is on the classics list*.

6. *The Prince and the Pauper*, (which, that) can be found in the fiction section, tells about two boys
(62) who trade clothing one day and exchange lives as well.

7. To serve his community, Matthew (builded, built) a large pen for lost dogs.
(70)

8. Each of the girls (want, wants) (their, her) own name spelled correctly.
(68)

9. Neighbors have formed a(n) (bicameral, contemptible, ad hoc) patrol to halt recent vandalism.
(66)

10. The (grisly, grizzly) bear roamed many parts of California years ago.
(67)

11. Cows and horses eat plants; they are (carnivorous, ephemeral, herbivorous).
(68)

12. (Lightening, Lightning) often accompanies thunder and rain.
(69)

13. Estée is (lightening, lightning) her work place by opening curtains and letting in sunshine.
(69)

14. The Latin verb *credere,* as in *credence* and *credulity*, means (to believe, to shout, to eat).
(70)

15. (Credulity, Recrimination, Censure) is the willingness to believe, accept, or trust without
(70) sufficient evidence; gullibility.

16. Write the plural form of the singular noun *sentry*. _____
(10, 11)

17. In the sentence below, replace the blank with the correct verb form.
(15, 49)
Esther, Martha, and Ruth (past perfect tense of *sing*) _____ the doxology
together every Sunday morning for over sixty-five years.

18. In the sentence below, add periods and commas as needed. Then circle each letter that should be
(31, 41) capitalized.

on the way to seattle washington jordan and natalie sat on the bus behind mrs van spronsen and
dr r u ill

19. In the following sentence, underline the dependent clause and circle the subordinating
(54) conjunction: Tristan read H. G. Wells's *The Time Machine* because his dad suggested it.

20. Add quotation marks as needed in the following sentence: On a snowy evening in the town
(66) square, some carolers shivered as they sang the fourth verse of Good King Wenceslas.

21. Underline each word that should be italicized in the following sentence: Poor Richard's
(69) Almanac, published by Ben Franklin, contained aphorisms, or proverbs, in addition to calendar,
weather, and astronomical information.

22. Circle the gerund phrase in the sentence below.
(28, 55)

Tristan won the grand prize by remembering Rasputin's identity.

23. In the following sentence, underline the participial phrase and circle the word it modifies:
(45, 56)

Having set her daughter's hair with fifty-six curlers, Mrs. Temple fell into bed exhausted.

Diagram sentences 24 and 25.

24. Neither of the contestants knows the pseudonym for Walker Smith.
(29)

25. Stefan and she brought Mrs. Cameron some homemade tamales.
(30, 34)

Give after Lesson 80

Circle the correct words to complete sentences 1–15.

1. Nelly's (fiduciary, limp, epidermis) was due to her sprained ankle.
(75)

2. Christine gave a (concurrent, cursory, ephemeral) look at her notes before the history test.
(74)

3. The basketball finale ran (tortuous, cursory, concurrent) with the opening of baseball season.
(74)

4. To "bite the dust" is a(n) (ephemeral, literal, figurative) expression.
(72)

5. The Latin word *fides*, forming the base of *affidavit* and *fiduciary*, means (to run, faith, to eat).
(73)

6. Some (grizzly, limpid, noisy) parrots interfered with the outdoor concert.
(71)

7. An inspector identified the (limp, noisy, noisome) gas as propane.
(71)

8. Neither of the poodles (obey, obeys) his master.
(68)

9. The twins play brass and percussion, but Woolie plays more instruments than (they, them).
(63)

10. (Her and Grandma, Grandma and her, Grandma and she) will assist you and (he, him) before the
(50, 51) party.

11. Ms. Villagran, will you please escort (we, us) visitors to our seats?
(63)

12. The italicized clause in the following sentence is (essential, nonessential): Great Britain's Prime
(62) Minister Winston Churchill, *who led courageously during World War II*, greatly modernized the
navy.

13. George has (lied, lay, lain) in the hammock all afternoon.
(71, 72)

14. One of the conductors (write, writes) (their, his/her) own music for the orchestra.
(53, 68)

15. Do you know the actor (who, that, which) played Captain Kangaroo?
(61)

16. Write the plural form of the singular noun *wolf*. _____
(10, 11)

17. In the following sentence, replace the blank with the correct verb form: Nelly (present perfect
(17) progressive tense of *limp*) _____ ever since she sprained her
ankle.

18. In the sentence below, add punctuation marks as needed and circle each letter that should be capitalized.
(9, 69)

have you read any of louisa may alcott's novels asked juan the student sitting to my left

19. In the following sentence, underline the dependent clause and circle the subordinating
(54) conjunction: As you know, we do not use apostrophes to form plurals.

20. Add quotation marks as needed in the sentence below.
(65, 66)

Sara Joshepa wrote a true poem titled Mary Had a Little Lamb.

21. Underline each word that should be italicized in the sentence below.
(69)

Bonjour and buenos dias are common greetings in the foreign language classes at my school.

22. Circle the two gerund phrases in the sentence below.
(16, 56)

Purchasing thoughtful, little gifts is Carla's way of expressing her appreciation for her friends.

23. In the following sentence, underline the participial phrase and circle the word it modifies:
(55, 56) Searching his memory, Jacob recalled that Beowulf killed the monster Grendel.

Diagram sentences 24 and 25.

24. The annual mystery award is the "Edgar," an award for the year's best mystery.
(36, 42)

25. The stories of Edgar Allen Poe feature characters recounting their grotesque, grisly deeds.
(21, 56)

Circle the correct words to complete sentences 1–15.

1. Carla (don't, doesn't) have (no, any) energy today.
(78)

2. The street vendors sold much, but Nalani and Emiko sold more than (they, them).
(63)

3. Grandpa thinks that (Me and Risa, Risa and me, Risa and I) should stand between the podium
(50, 51) and (he, him) for the family photo.

4. (Us, We) music students acknowledge the intense competition in the industry.
(50, 63)

5. The italicized clause in the following sentence is (essential, nonessential): The documentary,
(62) *which appeared on TV last Saturday*, shows how citizens have united to fight illiteracy in a local prison.

6. Stephanie Chang (drew, drawn) pictures of Alice and the White Rabbit from *Alice in*
(70) *Wonderland.*

7. (Do, Does) one of your state representatives receive visitors at (their, his/her) office?
(12. 53)

8. Steven hadn't (ever, never) (saw, seen) a tidepool teeming with marine life.
(78)

9. The Latin verb *flectere* means (after, bend, before).
(76)

10. Failure to adequately warm up the leg muscles can lead to sore hip (flexors, ad moninem, modus
(76) operandi).

11. The United States (denotes, connotes) freedom to many people in the world.
(77)

12. The Latin prefix *post-* means (after, bend, before).
(78)

13. Katrina's deceased grandfather received a (postdate, posthumous, postscript) medal for his
(78) bravery in World War II.

14. Students who (flout, flaunt, genuflect) their high grades are not popular.
(79)

15. *Pilgrim's Progress* chronicles a man's (Penelope, fiduciary, odyssey) through the successes and
(80) failures of life.

16. Write the plural form of the singular noun *quarry*. _____
(10, 11)

17. In the following sentence, replace the blank with the correct verb form: The businessman
(15) (present perfect tense of *shine*) _____ his dress shoes.

For 18 and 19, circle each letter that should be capitalized, and add punctuation marks as needed.

18. lauren said i think marcus is very handsome
(58, 65)

19. oh marcus is kind considerate and good-natured as well added mackenzie
(47, 65)

20. In the following sentence, underline the dependent clause and circle the subordinating
(54) conjunction: Since Harriet Beecher Stowe wrote *Uncle Tom's Cabin*, Abraham Lincoln labelled her "the little lady who made this big war."

21. In the following sentence, underline each word that should be italicized: In Beatrix Potter's novel
(69) Peter Rabbit, we learn the names of Peter's siblings—Flopsy, Mopsy, and Cottontail.

22. Circle the gerund phrase in this sentence: Did reading *A Farewell to Arms* depress you?
(56)

23. In the following sentence, underline the participial phrase and circle the word it modifies:
(56)

Having read *A Christmas Carol*, Allison wanted to read other novels by Charles Dickens.

Diagram sentences 24 and 25.

24. Training a puppy can be a frustrating, time-consuming process.
(21, 56)

25. Graham enthusiastically admired the 1967 Ford Mustang with chrome rims and a dual
(29, 80) carburetor.

Give after Lesson 90

Circle the correct words to complete sentences 1–15.

1. Mackenzie (don't, doesn't) give (no, any) advice unless you ask for it.
(78)

2. Becca (isn't, ain't, aren't) as worried as (me, I).
(63, 78)

3. (Me and you, You and me, You and I) shall rescue Mr. Linh and (he, him) from the newspaper
(50, 51) reporters.

4. The word *not* is an (adjective, adverb, appositive).
(78)

5. Shant plays football (good, well). He plays a (good, well) game of defense.
(81)

6. A parasite, an organism that lives on or in another organism, gets (it's, its) nourishment from the
(53) host.

7. David hadn't (ever, never) (saw, seen) an electric guitar like that.
(78)

8. (Lightening, Gerrymandering, Filibustering) allows politicians to change voting districts to their
(81) favor.

9. Most (Penelopes, constituents, procrusteans) demand honesty and loyalty from their politicians.
(81)

10. Candice plans to do her homework now and clean her room (later, latter).
(82)

11. The Federal Government acquires land for roads from private citizens through its Constitutional
(83) right of (gerrymandering, enacting clause, eminent domain).

12. The (primogeniture, enacting clause, fiduciary) of a bill allows for its execution.
(83)

13. Karina watched the (ascent, assent, flout) of her helium-filled balloon until it disappeared in a
(85) cloud.

14. Did parents (ascent, assent, flout) to the principal's proposal to ban the sale of candy at school?
(85)

15. The underlined part of the following sentence is (essential, nonessential): Norman Rockwell,
(62) <u>who illustrated many magazine covers and calendars</u>, usually painted realistic and humorous
scenes from everyday life.

16. Write the comparative form of the adjective *bad*. _____
(40)

17. In the blank, write the correct verb form:
(17)

        Andy and Ian _____ horseshoes at the carnival.
           (present progressive tense of *pitch*)

For 18 and 19, add punctuation marks as needed, circle each letter than should be capitalized, and underline each part that should be italicized.

18. timothy did you write last months book report on johnny tremain beowulf or the scarlet letter
(65, 73) asked professor cho

19. if i remember correctly said timothy my october book report was on moby dick.
(47, 65)

20. In the following sentence, underline each dependent clause and circle each subordinating
(54) conjunction: Kimberly reminded her classmates that they would be excused for lunch as soon as they stopped their talking.

21. Add hyphens where they are needed in the following sentence: VanderLaan's well executed lay
(79, 82) up scored the winning basket for the undefeated team.

22. Circle the gerund phrase in the sentence below.
(21, 55)

Andrew enjoys sketching his friend's profile.

23. In the sentence below, underline the participial phrase and circle the word it modifies.
(77)

Scrambling up the rocky mountainside, Derek reached the top before Amanda.

Diagram sentences 24 and 25.

24. The Chatkeonopadols, whom we respect, serve the community by offering free medical
(56, 61) treatment.

25. A spreading brushfire seriously challenges firefighters.
(56, 80)

Circle the correct words to complete sentences 1–15.

1. The word *real* is an (adjective, adverb).
(89)

2. The word *surely* is an (adjective, adverb).
(89)

3. Is Ishmael feeling (well, good) today?.
(81)

4. Can't (nobody, anybody) see the dangers connected with Ahab's challenge?
(78)

5. Ahab lost his leg to the white whale, and the crewmen (was, were) in danger of losing their lives.
(12)

6. The italicized word in the following sentence is an (adjective, adverb): The crewmen drank *early*
(23, 80) to the destruction of the white whale.

7. The italicized word in the following sentence is an (adjective, adverb): With Ahab the crewmen
(23, 80) drank an *early* oath to the destruction of Moby Dick.

8. Ishmael hadn't (ever, never) (saw, seen) the great white whale known as Moby Dick.
(78)

9. Moby Dick, "the *w*icked *w*hite *w*hale," is an example of (assonance, consonance, alliteration).
(90)

10. "The crew'*s* sen*s*e of ex*c*itement" is an example of (assonance, consonance, alliteration).
(90)

11. "The *o*ld sailor's *o*men *o*pened n*o* one's eyes" is an example of (assonance, consonance,
(90) alliteration).

12. The Sons of Liberty demanded that the British (slander, appeal, repeal) its tax on tea.
(89)

13. The British government refused to recognize the Colonists' (slander, appeal, repeal) for no
(89) taxation without representation.

14. Since the losing party disagrees with the lower court's decision, it will make a(n) (slander,
(89) appeal, repeal) to a higher court.

15. We waited in a long line to purchase our tickets to see the (premier, premiere, Penelope) of the
(88) movie.

16. Write the superlative form of the adverb *skillfully*. _____
(87)

17. Circle the conjunctive adverb in this sentence: Queequeg became very ill, and I thought he would
(88) die; however, he miraculously recovered.

For 18 and 19, circle each letter than should be capitalized, and add punctuation marks as needed.

18. herman melville wrote *moby dick* a novel of amazing depth it can be read on several levels
(42, 59)

19. there she blows exclaimed captain ahab it is moby dick
(9, 65)

20. Insert a colon where it is needed in the sentence below.
(90)

After harpooning a whale, the crew must do the following tasks lash the carcass with ropes to the ship, strip off the meat and blubber, and melt down the blubber.

21. Underline each word that should be italicized in the following sentence: Ernest Hemingway wrote such novels as A Farewell to Arms, For Whom the Bell Tolls, and The Old Man and the Sea.
69)

22. Circle the gerund phrase in the following sentence: The crew feared the prophesying of Fedallah, Captain Ahab's highly regarded servant and seer.
(55, 56)

23. In the sentence that follows, underline the participial phrase and circle the word it modifies: Frightened by a violent storm, the crew pleaded to return home.
(45, 56)

Diagram sentences 24 and 25.

24. Later, Ahab briefly spotted Moby Dick as the whale dived under their boat.
(54, 85)

25. Pursuing the whale causes the loss of harpoons, boats, and lives.
(28, 56)

Circle the correct words to complete sentences 1–15.

1. The word (real, really) is an adverb.
(89)

2. Down the pole (come, comes) two fire fighters to the rescue.
(75)

3. In the sentence that follows, the italicized part is (essential, nonessential): My cell phone, *which*
(62) *has now become a major nuisance*, interrupts my conversations with people at the lunch table.

4. In the sentence that follows, the italicized part is a(n) (noun, adjective, adverb) phrase: *During*
(97) *the Presidential election of 2004,* flaws in voting machines surfaced.

5. Only two people on the team, you and (me, I), made more than ten tackles on the opposing
(42) football team.

6. A dependent clause may be connected to an independent clause by a (coordinating,
(54) subordinating) conjunction.

7. The following sentence is (simple, compound): I shall photograph this flower, for the plant
(1, 34) blooms only once a year.

8. I can't find that brand of spaghetti sauce (nowhere, anywhere) in the store.
(78)

9. After a long struggle, the mouse (repeals, appeals, succumbs) to the cat's playfulness.
(89, 94)

10. Prometheus escaped from hell, just (like, as) the ancient prophecy predicted.
(92)

11. The student demonstrated how a (protoplasm, catacomb, catapult) might be employed in
(93, 95) medieval times to protect a castle.

12. The (recumbent, incumbent, protean) cows stood up and sauntered towards the barn.
(84, 94)

13. The diagram shows the cell of a plant, including its (protocol, protoplasm, catacomb).
(93, 95)

14. (Catacombs, Protoplasms, Prototypes) made an eerie setting for the novel.
(93, 95)

15. Did you vote for the (prototype, incumbent, catapult) or a new candidate?
(94, 95)

16. Write the comparative form of the adverb *daintily*. _____
(87)

17. Circle the conjunctive adverb in the following sentence: The word *cholesterol* carries a negative
(88) meaning in the minds of most people; however, high density lipoprotein, or HDL cholesterol, is
helpful in the body.

For 18 and 19, circle each letter that should be capitalized, and add punctuation marks as needed.

18. mr green wrote did you know that blood cholesterol levels can usually be controlled through
(43, 65) dietary reform

19. wrong answer hollered dr sterol red meat not eggs or dairy products constitutes the largest
(9, 65) food-derived source of cholesterol

20. Write the proofreading symbol for "Begin a new paragraph." _____
(91)

21. Underline each word that should be italicized in this sentence:
(69)

The French word faux pas refers to a social blunder.

22. Circle the infinitive phrase in the sentence below.
(94)

The courtier refused to bow before that evil king.

23. In the sentence below, underline the participial phrase and circle the word it modifies.
(56)

Courtiers attempting to gain prestige and favor will bow before an evil king.

Diagram sentences 24 and 25.

24. The cheetah can accelerate to forty-five mph in two seconds.
(29, 94)

25. An ancient diety who protected doors and gates was January.
(36, 61)

Circle the correct words to complete sentences 1–14.

1. The word (sure, surely) is an adverb.
(89)

2. Lavinia likes football, so Chris and (her, she) watched every game of the season.
(50, 52)

3. The italicized part of the following sentence is a(n) (essential, nonessential) part: The teacher's
(42, 62) assistant, *Breanna*, sorted and graded all the dictation tests.

4. The sentence below is (simple, compound, complex, compound-complex).
(59, 99)

Because of Johny's quick response, a terrible accident was avoided.

5. The italicized part of the following sentence is a(n) (noun, adjective, adverb) clause: My friend
(97) Sam won't do any task *that might reveal his intelligence or creativity*.

6. The following sentence is (active, passive) voice: The team is coached by Mr. Sousa.
(27)

7. There is complete agreement (between, among) the six volleyball players about Kristi being
(93) captain.

8. Mr. Gevrikyan hasn't (ever, never) visited Washington, D.C.
(78)

9. An (ade, aid, aide) is an assistant or helper.
(96)

10. Thomas will (rectify, eulogize, succumb) the record books if there are any inaccuracies.
(97)

11. On graduation day, Isabel's (aide, euphoria, eulogy) spread to her classmates, and they all
(98) celebrated together.

12. The Greek prefix (*dys-, eu-, proto-*) means bad or difficult.
(99)

13. (Bona fide, Caveat emptor, Carpe diem) means "in good faith," or genuine.
(100)

14. The Greek prefix (*dys-, eu-, proto-*) means well or good.
(98)

15. In the following sentence, underline the dependent clause and circle the subordinating
(54) conjunction:

When Parker scored the winning run, his baseball team sprinted out onto the field.

16. Write the superlative form of the adverb *superficially*. _____
(87)

17. Circle the conjunctive adverb in the following sentence: All book reports are due next week;
(88) however, Annalie may have an extra week to complete hers.

18. In the following sentence, add punctuation marks as needed: No I havent seen Seans three ring
(89) binder Have you asked Berlyn

19. Circle each letter that should be capitalized in the following sentence: mr. ramirez said, "learning
(4, 9) latin and greek words and roots has increased my english vocabulary."

20. Write the possessive form of the plural noun *tulips*. _____
(95)

21. Circle the infinitive phrase in the following sentence:
(94)

> I would like more time to practice for the talent show.

22. Write the proofreading symbol that means "begin a new paragraph." _____
(91)

23. Circle the sentence below that has parallel structure:
(100)

> The engineers developed the prototype, patented their invention, and test its efficiency.

> The engineers developed the prototype, patented their invention, and tested its efficiency.

> The engineers develop the prototype, patented their invention, and test its efficiency.

Diagram sentences 24 and 25.

24. Did eating too much dessert give Clotilda dyspepsia?
(30, 55)

25. Julianne's plan is to go to college after she finishes high school.
(36, 94)

Circle the correct words to complete sentences 1–14.

1. Jan's mother makes beautiful cakes, so Jan and (her, she) will provide dessert for the reception.
(50, 62)

2. The following sentence is (simple, compound, complex, compound-complex): Because of a
(59, 99) conspiracy to murder Prospero, Ariel drives Stephano, Trinculo, and Caliban through filthy ditches, swamps, and brier patches.

3. Ima Snoozer hadn't (ever, never) heard such a boring lecture.
(78)

4. Arguments flared (between, among) the five castaways.
(14, 93)

5. The italicized part of the following sentence is a(n) (noun, adjective, adverb) clause: Prospero
(97, 98) mildly rebukes those *that plot evil against him*.

6. The italicized part of the following sentence is a(n) (essential, nonessential) part: The rightful
(42, 62) duke, *Prospero*, grants his full, sovereign forgiveness to all.

7. The Latin verb (*currere, rogare, flectere*) means "to ask" or "to propose."
(101)

8. To (flare, repeal, interrogate) is to examine by questioning.
(101)

9. In the dictionary, abbreviations such as *n. adj., v.t.,* and *v.i.* indicate a word's (definition,
(105) pronunciation, part of speech).

10. The term (*son-, quis, cub-*) means "to seek" or "to obtain."
(102)

11. The *ple-* found in words such as complete, complement, deplete, and replete means (to fill, to
(103) ask, to obtain).

12. The root *err-,* from the Latin word *errare,* means (to sound, to wander, to obtain).
(105)

13. The Latin root *son-,* as in *sonata,* means (stray, sound, difficult).
(104)

14. Dissonant means harsh, clashing, or unpleasant in (color, temperament, sound).
(104)

15. Use proofreading symbols to indicate four corrections in the sentence below.
(32, 91)

    One of the kittens left it's paw prints across Mildreds half eaten sand wich.

16. Underline the dependent clause and circle the subordinating conjunction in the sentence below.
(54)

    Will an upright person be rewarded if he or she does the right thing?

17. Write the superlative form of the adverb *penitently*. _____
(87)

18. Circle the conjunctive adverb in the following sentence: Prospero sails back to Milan to reign
₍₈₈₎ once more; however, he gives up sorcery for the rest of his life.

19. Write the possessive form of each of these plural nouns:
₍₉₅₎

      monkeys _____   teachers _____

      women _____   mice _____

20. Write the four principal parts of the verb *shake*.
₍₇₂₎

      present tense _____;   present participle _____;

      past tense _____;   past participle _____

21. On the line below, rewrite this sentence using active voice: Gonzalo was rewarded by Prospero
₍₂₇₎ for his saintly behavior.

_____

22. In the sentences below, circle each letter than should be capitalized and add punctuation marks as
_(2, 41) needed.

shakespeares *The Tempest* combines music conspiracy romance comedy and pathos shakespeare
wrote this play late in his career.

23. Of the two sentences below, which is clearer? Circle the clearer sentence.
_(101, 102)

      High in the tree, Ed spotted a bald eagle looking through his binoculars.

      Looking through his binoculars, Ed spotted a bald eagle high in the tree.

Diagram sentences 24 and 25.

24. Having studied the vocabulary gave me more confidence for our last test.
_(55, 56)

20. Now is the time to do your homework.
_(56, 85)

Circle the correct words to complete sentences 1–14.

1. The word (sure, surely) is an adverb.
(87, 89)

2. Our neighbors will (recieve, receive) parking violations if they park in front of their houses on
(111) Tuesdays.

3. Since Ms. Snoozer had car trouble, Carey and (she, her) missed the bridal procession.
(50)

4. The Latin root *loqu-*, as in colloquy, means (speak, backward, foot).
(111)

5. The Latin prefix *retro-*, as in retrospect, means (backward, word, grieve).
(110)

6. The italicized part of the following sentence is a(n) (essential, nonessential) part: Our dog
(62) *Boomer* jumped onto the diving board to watch us swim in the pool.

7. The italicized part of the following sentence is a(n) (noun, adjective, adverb) clause: The doctor
(97, 98) insists *that Phil rest after surgery*.

8. If I (was, were) Phil, I would take a long vacation.
(106)

9. We haven't had (no, any) snow here in several years.
(78)

10. The sentence below is (simple, compound, complex, compound-complex).
(59, 99)

Because she worked so hard in the laboratory, Christina made a major breakthrough in her cancer research, but she was exhausted.

11. The Latin root *verbum,* as in verbiage, means (grieve, backward, word).
(107)

12. The Latin root *ped-*, as in pedometer, means (speak, foot, word).
(108)

13. The Latin root *dole-*, as in dolorous, means (grieve, word, foot).
(109)

14. In (retrospect, verbatum, condolence), the young woman rejoiced that she had completed her
(110) college degree.

15. Underline the dependent clause and circle the subordinating conjunction in the sentence below.
(54)

Doctors recommend increased fluid intake and bed rest when one has flu symptoms.

16. Write the comparative form of the adverb *badly*. _____
(87)

17. Circle the conjunctive adverb in the following sentence: Dr. Droner delivered a verbose history
(88) of his personal achievements; moreover, he innundated the audience with trivial details that made some people yawn.

18. On the line below, rewrite the following sentence to make it more concise: Margaret made the essay more clearer owing to the fact that she deleted the extra, unnecessary words.
(101)

_____

19. Use proofreading symbols to make four corrections in the sentences below.
(32, 91)

Mutt didnt want me to leave. He gave me a dole ful look as i steped out the door.

20. On the line below, rewrite the following sentence using active voice: Scot and Deb are excited about next month's Florida trip.
(27)

_____

21. Combine the following word and suffix to make a new word. _chap_ + _ed_ = _____
(109, 110)

22. Write the possessive form of each noun or noun pair.
(95)

James _____;   geologists _____;

Jan and Van (their cat) _____;   Mr. Fox _____

23. Circle the clearer sentence below.
(101, 102)

The motorist encountered a landslide driving along a canyon road.

Driving along a canyon road, the motorist encountered a landslide.

24. Circle each silent letter in these words: watch   yolk   succumb   wrist
(107, 108)

25. Diagram this sentence in the space below: While the loquacious professor talks about his many honors, Ida Mae plans on avoiding his next lecture.
(56, 99)